The Primary Colours of Story

A storyteller's guide to how stories work

By

David Baboulene Ph.D.

Copyright © David Baboulene 2020

All rights reserved

The right of David Baboulene to be identified as the author of this work has been asserted in accordance with sections 77 and 78 of the Copyright, Designs and Patents Act 1988.

No part of this book may be reproduced by any means, nor transmitted, nor translated into a machine language, without the written permission of the publisher.

Published in 2020 by:
DreamEngine Media Group.
Email: publishing@dreamengine.co.uk
www.dreamengine.co.uk

It is hard to remember 20 items on a tray but when you were told the story of *Little Red Riding Hood* when you were four years old, Bang! In it went and you remembered it forever.

A story is a portable, shareable version of a memory.

Table of Contents

The Primary Colours of Story
How This Book is Organised — 6

Section 1 -   Life and Stories — 8
1.1   How Language Works — 10
1.2   Narrative — 14
1.2.1   Narrative Gaps — 19
1.3   What is a story? — 20

Section 2 -   Knowledge Gaps and Subtext — 23
2.1   What is a knowledge gap? — 27
2.2   Subtext — 28
2.3   Where Should you Focus? — 35
2.4   Framing Gaps — 40
2.4.1   Privilege and Revelation — 41
2.4.2   Knowledge gaps through character plans — 49
2.4.3   Knowledge gaps through key question — 54
2.4.4   Knowledge gaps through promise — 70
2.4.5   Knowledge gaps through subplot — 73
2.4.6   Knowledge gaps through narrator — 77
2.4.7   Knowledge gaps through the story world — 82
2.4.8   Knowledge gaps through backstory — 85
2.4.9   Knowledge gaps through harmatia — 88
2.4.10   Knowledge gaps through conflict — 89
2.4.11   Practical Application — 89
2.5   Character Gaps — 90
2.5.1   Plot and character – one and the same — 91
2.5.2   Protagonist and antagonist — 94
2.5.3   Multiple protagonists — 96
2.5.4   Antagonism — 96
2.5.5   The five components of character — 97

2.5.6	Knowledge gaps through action & dialogue	120
2.5.7	Knowledge gaps through subterfuge	129
2.5.8	Knowledge gaps through questions	131
2.5.9	Knowledge gaps through suggestion	132
2.5.10	Knowledge Gaps through suspense	135
2.5.11	Knowledge Gaps through anagnorisis	137
2.6	Storification Gaps	137
2.6.1	True lies and fictional truth	140
2.6.2	Using the Storification	144
2.6.3	Knowledge gaps through character growth	150
2.6.4	Knowledge gaps through vicarious learning	160
2.6.5	Knowledge gaps through surpassing aim	163
2.6.6	Knowledge gaps through moral argument	165
2.6.7	Knowledge gaps through metaphor and allegory	166
2.6.8	Knowledge gaps through recognition	169
2.6.9	Knowledge gaps through peripeteia	174
Section 3 -	**Common Story Dynamics**	**175**
4.1	Conflict in Stories	177
3.1.1	Where can conflict be found?	182
3.1.2	Meaningful conflict	188
3.2	The Hollywood Formula	193
3.2.1	Turning Points	199
3.2.2	Note on turning points	204
3.2.3	The Hollywood formula — major turning points	205
3.3	Aristotle's Principles	211
3.4	Story and the Moral Argument	219
3.4.1	What is morality?	221
3.4.2	Story theme	225
3.5	A Story Theory Exercise	233
3.5.1	Exercise answers	234
3.6	Knowledge Gaps Through Comedy	237
3.7	Unconventional Story Dynamics	243

Section 4 -	Story Development	247
4.1	Begin at the Beginning	249
4.2	The Seed Sprouts...	262
4.3	The End is the New Beginning	263
4.3.1	Storification Example	266
4.4	Combs and Tangles	268
4.5	Scene Design and the Step Outline	270
4.6	The Mystical Art of Crafting Characters	285
4.7	The Mystical Art of Crafting Sequences	289
Section 5 -	In a Nutshell	292
Section 6 -	Glossary of Terms	299
Section 7 -	Bibliography and Further Reading	302
Section 8 -	About the Author	307

How This Book is Organised

This book is divided into four main sections.

Section 1: Life and Stories
The opening chapter provides a little background theory. We investigate the relationship between language, memory and narrative to understand what stories are, why stories exist and how they get their power to grip, engage and influence a human mind.

Section 2: Knowledge Gaps and Subtext
Knowledge gaps are the substance of story. The secret triggers that link instinctive mental reflexes to the power of narrative. A writer works with knowledge gaps in order that a receiver can work with subtext.

The finest authors are the ones best able to use knowledge gaps to create the conditions for subtext. In many ways, this is what the book is all about.

Section 3: Story Dynamics
In section three, we begin to apply what we have learned. Tools and methods are developed for the analysis and evaluation of any and every story.

Traditional story principles are explained. The Hollywood formula, Aristotle's principles, a moral argument, and the central components of orthodox story theory such as conflict, turning points and character arcs. We also lay down the basics of **framing** (the role of the author), **character actions** (the role of the character) and the crowning glory: **storification** (the role of the receiver) — the amorphous, mystical power of story that makes it forever a magical art.

Section 4: The Story Development Process
Everything starts with the story creator and their inspiration. This section looks at a story development process that naturally works with the mechanisms of mind.

Section 5 - 8
The final sections pull it all together such that you leave this work with a complete understanding of what stories are, how stories work, how to find the strengths and weaknesses in a story, isolate and understand a story's potential and — most importantly — how to make the most of your own story ideas.

There is also a glossary of terms, a bibliography and recommendations for further reading.

Incidentally, it would be helpful for your understanding of this book if you watch *Back to the Future* (Zemekis, 1985) and the first episode of *Breaking Bad* (Gilligan, 2008). I use many stories throughout the book as reference pieces, however I go into these two in depth to exemplify story dynamics.

Ok. Let's go! And like all good stories, let's begin at the beginning:

Section 1 - Life and Stories

...around 250,000 years ago, a simple and apparently innocent change took place in the throat architecture of the early *homo sapiens*. You have a small bone in your throat called the hyoid bone. It is the only bone in your body that is not connected to any other bones. As hominids became more upright over time, gravity got to work on this floating bone. Its position in the upper front of the throat articulated relative to a descending larynx...

...and the planet was changed forever.

Whereas it is known that our earlier human ancestors made a range of sounds comparable to other hominids (such as a chimpanzee), this small change in throat architecture enabled suitably endowed *homo sapiens* to produce complex sounds — a similar range to our current capability. More sophisticated communication led naturally to more sophisticated cooperation and suddenly — really very suddenly in evolutionary terms — ten hominids working together became the most powerful creature on Earth (cf., Whipps, 2008).

Leaping forwards a little and cutting a long story very short, if you take sophisticated cooperation to its logical extreme you get civilisation. Everything we have today that we call civilisation is down to language and it all goes back to that tiny floating bone in our throats.

I find it interesting to consider that, today, other primates have a hyoid bone. Chimpanzees, for example, are only a centimetre or so away from being able to make the same range of sounds we make. Life might become interesting if they evolve along the same path as us and start joining in the conversation. There may be one or two things over which they might like to take issue with us, given the chance.[i]

Yeah, yeah. All very interesting. But is language really so important to civilisation?
I'm pleased you asked me that. In creatures without language, the only way to learn something new is to be there and experience it directly. An organism comes into this world armed with its instincts. After that, learning is exclusively a matter of imitation and hands-on, real-time experience. However, with language, ideas and concepts can be communicated without being present at the live, real-time event. We are doing it now. I am communicating complex mental maps to your mind without our even meeting and I can do that because of the power of language. If you think about it, much of the knowledge we gain in the modern world is learned through linguistic exchange, for example in the classroom or through media.[ii]

Isn't there a snag with that?
Well spotted. There is one snag with learning through language. The animal at the root of us did not have complex linguistics. The impact of language is relatively new in evolutionary terms, so working with it is not always as natural or easy as we might hope. For example, while hands-on experience is highly effective, teaching through language can be *boring*. It can be difficult to retain communicated linguistic information. We have all fallen asleep in a lecture or suffered the desperate tedium of revising facts for an examination. As we shall see, the problem is that these analytical, emotion-free methods of communicating do not work well with our processes of mind. That matters because this is where story comes in. Language allows us to communicate ideas, information, argument, exposition, discourse, methods, feelings, concepts — but also **experiences**. When we communicate a cause-effect chain of events, we can automatically trigger natural mental reflexes that are used to make memories.

> **In linguistic exchange, only stories deliver teaching and learning in a way that replicates the way the brain remembers things when we learn from direct experience.**

A well-crafted story can trigger the mental reflexes that lay down memories *as if the recipient has experienced those events for themselves*. Now, that is amazing. Lectures do not do this. Nor do bullet lists of facts. Droning out information at people does not work the mind as nature intended. However, stories *do* trigger these natural mental processes, and this is not just important to humanity... it is bigger than that. It is important to writers. When you, as a writer, use these dynamics expertly you can open the mind of your audience and persuade them to take on ideas, feelings, thoughts they can barely resist and, yes, memories they did not invite in and which they now own. Stories can be mind-altering. You like that idea, right?! And you are right to notice the creepy possibilities that come along with this because, as we shall see, a well-crafted story can be designed to impact the mindset and opinions of a receiver for insidious as well as innocent reasons.

The key words there are 'well-crafted'. In this book you are going to understand how a story can be crafted to stimulate the instinctive, unconscious reflexes of the mind, and how these elements also characterise the most compelling and satisfying stories. And of course, it all begins with language.

1.1 How Language Works

In his ground-breaking *Course in General Linguistics* (1916), Ferdinand de Saussure separated the labels given to objects — what he called the **signifier** — from the meanings they generate in mind — the **signified** — and called the two taken together a **linguistic sign**.

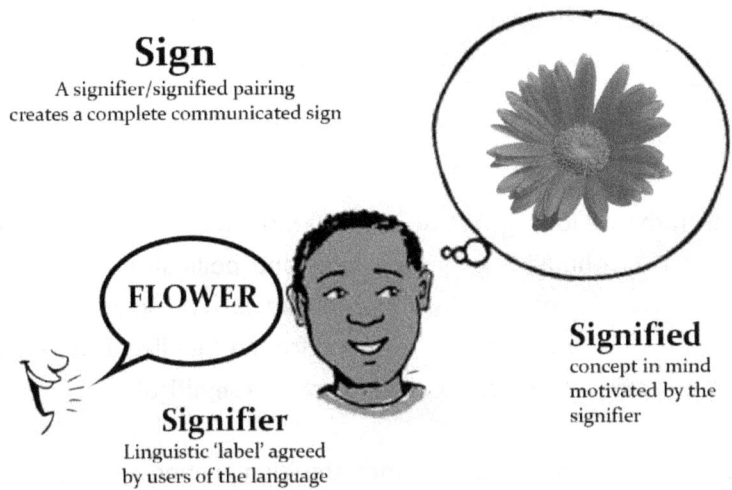

Figure 1 - 'FLOWER' as a sign

The **signifier** is a stimulus to the senses which triggers a mental concept in mind, the **signified**, and the two taken together comprise a complete linguistic sign. The sign is the basic unit of language.

All well and good. CAR. FOOTBALL. LAKE. BEAR. If you know the language, you get the picture in mind from receiving the signifier. However, what we do not get with a sign is **meaning**. For that we need to do some work for ourselves. We have to provide a mental context into which the sign makes sense. When we think of a **flower**, perhaps we think of seeds, petals, stamens, earth, bees, pollination, fields, nature — I am sure you could extend this list easily enough. However, what is much more important to us in the meaning of a sign is how it fits into a human *cultural* context.

Signification
What if the flower is arranged in a bouquet and accompanied by balloons, champagne, wrapped presents and a cake with candles? Now we load up a whole new context in mind to do with celebrating a birthday.

How about if the flower is in a hearse alongside a coffin arriving at a cemetery? Ah. Right. Now we load up a whole new cultural context in mind to do with death, funerals, grief and mourning, a priest and a hole in the ground. Ashes to ashes, dust to dust...

To be honest, I was lucky to have known her at all.

The context we load into mind is not natural to the flower, of course. However, all thoughts of petals, bees and pollination are gone. It takes knowledge of human culture, behaviour and society to create the context for a birthday or a funeral from a sign like a flower. This cultural overlay we place on a sign is called a **signification**.

The important point here is that the signification — the human cultural meaning that overwhelms the sign — must be learned. However, once it is learned, the basic natural context disappears. It is emptied out and a new and powerful signification is instantly and automatically evident to us.

Here is another example of the sign: 'flower'.

Figure 2 - Signification

What comes to mind now? Botany? Earth? Pollination? A death?! A birthday?! Not at all. Anyone with appropriate cultural understanding empties out the basic 'level 1' qualities of the sign 'FLOWER' and receives in mind a signification to do with love, romance and courtship.

Notice how we make a direct and automatic association between the sign and the qualities we have been invited to associate with it throughout our lives, to do with love, romance and courtship. Once the signification is learned, it becomes an unavoidable, irresistible, unconscious reflex.

As you will appreciate by the end of this book, that leap of mind that you make from seeing a rose and, instead of thinking about botany, thinking about love and romance is exactly the reflex that is worked by fine storytelling. This is the button you press to work the intellect and feelings of your victim. I mean reader. In this linguistic exchange there is a gap between what we are given and what we make of it in mind. This is a powerful, instinctive reflex which is the basis to everything that stories are.

Advertisers think along these lines all the time. They know that once a signification is in place, it is an automatic and unconscious association that affects a person's mind and becomes implicit to their knowledge base. When you see a deodorant brand and you somehow feel its use will make you irresistible to the opposite sex; when you see an alcoholic drink and you think its consumption will bring you an endearingly mischievous personality; when you see a detergent and you think its use will save your family from 99% of all known germs, you are being trained to empty out the first level context of the sign (an odour/ poison/ chemical cleaner...), and overlay it with something far more helpful to the salesman. Because you unconsciously interpret every single sign you see, a salesman's logo or brand becomes a powerful form of truth in the world, even when you know it is happening and even when you make a conscious effort to resist. Think of the sign 'CAR', and you may get in mind an image and a context of transport, tyres, engines, journeys, policemen and servicing costs. However, think of the sign 'PORSCHE' and your mind fills with other qualities that did not naturally signify from the basic signifier: 'CAR'. The advertisers have worked hard on their brand, so PORSCHE perhaps signifies speed, freedom, wealth and virility. Even the most cynical of receivers — those who deny that they are susceptible to marketing and refuse to accept that the cultural symbolic force of the logo's signification has entered their thoughts — will receive the intended meaning. They must have done, or they would not be in a position to reject it!

This isn't just marketing, this is meaning in language. And it isn't simply coercion (although it is easy to focus on the cynical side). There are thousands of significations we derive from our cultural understanding moment-by-moment throughout our daily lives. Indeed, they underpin and *define* our cultural understanding and allow us to make it through our daily lives in a modern civilisation. All brought into being by a simple little floating bone in your throat.

1.2   Narrative

We need to talk about fishing nets. (You knew you were in for a good time with this book, didn't you?!)

As a basic sign a fishing net is a pile of string on a quay side. You know what it is, however it has no *meaning* until it is placed in a narrative context which reveals what it *does*. Until a person can understand the narrative that begins with a man weaving a net and ends with a delicious meal on the table, the net does not make sense.

What has been missing from our signs and significations is **change over time.** Change over time places any sign into a narrative context and this is absolutely critical to the functions of mind. A fishing net is an object made of string, however the *meaning* of a fishing net requires us to understand its role in the narrative of which it is a part. A narrative is an event of change over time. Our brains only understand what something means in the context of the narrative of which it is a part. Memories are narratives, and stories are portable, shareable memories.

Why are you distinguishing between story and narrative? Aren't they the same thing?
No. they are not the same thing. Narrative occurs all over the cosmos every second of every day. Somewhere, a lion is chasing down an antelope, a moon is circling a planet, a spider is spinning a web, a tree is falling in the forest. All of these are narratives because they are an event of change over time. However, for a narrative to have any meaning — in the human cultural sense we have been discussing — there must be a human being there to witness it and then interpret it into knowledge in mind). This latter process is called **storification**.

Philosophy is the study of the nature of knowledge, and it is a human endeavour. To put it simply, there can be no knowledge and no meaning without a human mind to do the knowing. There is no knowledge 'out there' in the world. There is only ever knowledge in mind, and all knowledge is from a human perspective. You may find yourself questioning this, in which case go haul your slacks up in the academic arena — something I am steadfastly resisting in this book. For our purposes as writers please take it as written; the functions of mind are functions of narrative. 'Information' is out there in the world. It assaults our senses and we interpret into knowledge in mind. Knowledge only exists in mind and for us to give something meaning is to understand it in a narrative context.

In the same way that a sign can become a signification when a human being overlays it with human cultural meaning in mind (a flower connotes love and romance), so a narrative can be overlaid with human cultural meaning in mind (a person taking a fishing net out on a boat connotes dinner).

The thing that is created in mind — a narrative that makes human sense — is called a story.

> **A narrative is an event of change over time in the real world.**
> **A story is an event of change over time held in mind.**

There are no stories 'out there', only narratives. A story is only ever in mind.

It is the overlaying of cultural knowledge provided by the mind of the receiver that elevates a narrative (an event of change over time out there in the world) into story (narrative meaning in mind).

This is why a tame deer will walk up to a hunter and sniff the end of the gun barrel. They do not have the narrative context for what a gun means. They do not have *knowledge*.

Not sure I get that
I don't blame you. Look at it like this. In receiving a narrative that we have not received before, we are not just passively reading signs. For example, 'the cat sat on the mat' is not a story because it is a simplistic matter of reading signs that give us a one-to-one accurate relationship to what is happening. For it to elevate into something more meaningful, the narrative must leave space for us to add our knowledge and experience to render it into something greater than the sum of the parts. So if I say 'The cat sat on the dog's mat', now we are doing some thinking. We are adding *knowledge* from our personal history and experience to the narrative to turn it into something more; something enhanced with our understanding of the world; something called a story. A receiver needs to be capable of doing this work for the narrative to make sense and to become a story.

If you take a two-year-old to the theatre to watch some Shakespeare, you both receive the same **narrative**. However, you do not both get the same **story** in mind. The child is not knowledgeable enough, so is not able to do the receiver's work in making sense of it. The narrative does not 'storify' for the child.

Do not worry if this is a little tricky. There is a lot to get your head around. Let's try an example.

Here - have a memory
In my book *Story Theory* (2014), I give my readers a memory. Here's how it goes. If I give you this:

> A rabbit.
> An approaching car.

Do the rest yourself.

We start with basic signs and significations. You use your knowledge and understanding of cars and rabbits to join them into a narrative. You know what cars and rabbits do, so you bring them together into a best-fit, logical narrative scenario and conclusion and you get an outcome: A squashed rabbit.

However, let's say that when I complete the telling of my story, it doesn't go as you predicted. The car is bearing down on the rabbit. It seems like curtains for the poor Bunny Wunny... until suddenly, at the very last moment, the rabbit whips out a ramp, crouches underneath it as the tyre hits, the ramp catapults the car over the rabbit's head and sends the car headlong into a tree. In one smooth, continuous action, the rabbit neatly packs up his ramp into his pouch as he completes his roll and runs off safely into the bushes leaving a car with a crumpled bonnet stacked into the tree, with steam hissing from the engine.

Your brain is instantly attracted to this. Why? Because it is an entire narrative and it is a new narrative. It represents new learning.

The <u>conscious</u> part of your brain will reject it as nonsensical, but before that happens, the unconscious mind sees a whole narrative with logic, accepts it as a good fit for an entire progression with an outcome. The story will not become a deep and meaningful part of your belief system (because it won't be repeated or reinforced), however you will be surprised just how embedded this narrative now is. You've seen rabbits in the road and you've seen cars stacked into trees with steam hissing from the crumpled front-end, and now, next time you see a car stacked into a tree, you might well recall this narrative memory, quite involuntarily, and laugh at yourself for looking around for the rabbit with a ramp. You can't help it. I gave you a knowledge gap, filled it in an unexpected way that created a complete narrative, and bingo: you have a new 'memory'.

If we meet one day, you will remember this rabbit/ramp scenario. There is plenty in this book that you will not remember, but this bit will stick because it is a narrative, it makes logical sense, has a clear outcome and it is new to you. It had a gap, which I filled in an unexpected way with new knowledge. So you created a memory, and, even though you consciously rejected it as unreliable meaning, it will still have a presence, rather like Santa Claus is not 'true' but has genuine presence and meaning in your life.

How about a real world example?
No problem. I'm way ahead of you. At this point in my seminars, I show my audience a few of the many dozens of real-world examples of a story provably causing a receiver to lay down a memory which they then take forwards to apply in their real lives.

There are children in the world who have experienced the Heimlich manoeuvre as an event in a fictional story such as *SpongeBob SquarePants*, Disney's *A.N.T. Farm* and the feature film *Mrs. Doubtfire*. The children are not attempting to learn anything from the antics of SpongeBob or Madame Doubtfire, but a logical narrative is shown in which the Heimlich manoeuvre is used. A life is saved and because of the way the narrative is delivered a memory is unconsciously created for the viewer. Later in their lives, this memory is triggered in the real world when the child sees someone choking and they use the Heimlich manoeuvre to save a life in the real world.

The children were relaxing, watching cartoons on television. They were not trying to learn anything and yet they made a memory they later used to save a life. Wow. (Links to examples are given in the endnotes.[iii])

It worked in this way because the situation unfolding in the story world was new to the child watching the television. The gap in their knowledge meant they felt anxious and engaged, because they could not see a narrative progression that would take the choking person to a happy outcome. The way the story was crafted meant their minds were open to learning and suggestion.

At some point the characters' problems were fixed. The cause-effect chain of events led to a happy outcome they had not foreseen and now the whole narrative, featuring the Heimlich manoeuvre, made complete sense and had a clear and positive outcome. The new narrative logic was completed in mind and immediately (and automatically) saved into long-term memory and the children 'accidentally' learned the Heimlich manoeuvre. It happened unconsciously and automatically as soon as the entire story was complete and present in working memory.

Note that it is not simply the delivery of a narrative that triggers the mind of the receiver in this extraordinary way. Your 534th commute to work is a narrative but will not trigger your mental reflexes and it will not be memorable because there is no requirement on you to fill any narrative gaps. It is predictable. For a memory to be made we need a narrative that is incomplete and requires the receiver to work on it to complete it. Which means there must be gaps.

1.2.1 Narrative Gaps

The type of mental leap we make when we see a red rose and get meaning in mind to do with love and romance is not only triggered by objects and events, it is triggered by the presence of the **gap** between what something is and what something means. When we sense a gap — a lack of completeness in the narrative we are building in mind — our mental reflex will try to fill it by pattern-matching against the best possible complete narrative our experience and intelligence can piece together from the information we do have. We are making these leaps — filling these gaps — all the time, we do it automatically and unconsciously, and we are really good at it.

Storification occurs when a narrative in mind becomes complete because a gap is filled with *knowledge that is provided by the receiver* drawing on their own personal history and cultural experience. As soon as such a narrative becomes complete and makes sense it is laid down as a memory and becomes part of the mindset of the receiver.

> Storytelling is not something we just happen to do. It is something we virtually have to do if we want to remember anything. The stories we create are the memories we have (Zaltman, 2003).

Narrative has power when the receiver joins in the process of creating the final story for themselves. By filling gaps they become co-producers on the project. This is where the most important power lies for a storyteller.

1.3 What is a story?

One of the things that amazed me when I first became involved in the study of story was that there was no formal definition of the word 'story'; not one that was agreed by all authorities down the millennia. Such a simple word, so intuitively understood by normal people in life, and yet it had escaped satisfactory definition. We will build a more precise definition later, but for the purposes of this part of our journey, it works like this:

Narration is an information stream which assaults the senses of the receiver. The receiver interprets this information into a knowledge representation in mind. **The narrative built in mind is a story**.

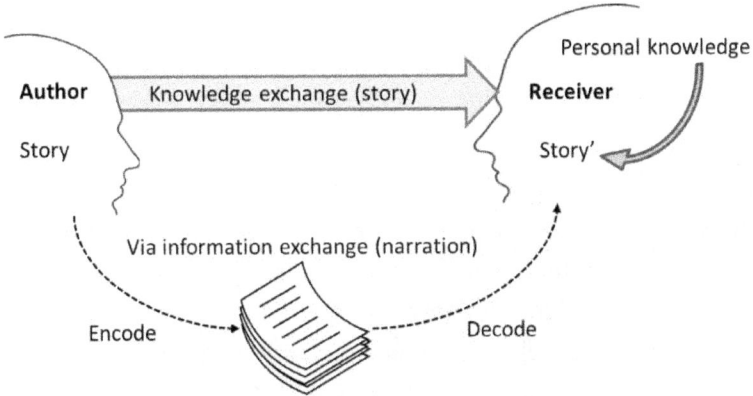

Figure 3: A story is a joint production

How stories work should **not** be thought of as how a reader interprets a text. A story is best seen as a conversation between a writer and a receiver. It is a joint production. The text and media are merely tools which facilitate the conversation, like the wires in a telephone conversation are critical to it happening, but are nothing to do with the content or meaning in the conversation. It is the dynamics of the conversation — the encoding by the author and the decoding by the receiver — that we must understand.

In the illustration above, hopefully you can see the value of a narrative disruption in the text. It is only by leaving gaps that the receiver has the chance to join in. The author encodes by embedding knowledge gaps into the narration. The receiver creates the story in mind by reacting to these knowledge gaps and applying their intelligence to fill those gaps to complete the story in mind for themselves.

The author encodes by crafting knowledge gaps. The receiver decodes by providing the knowledge that goes into the gaps. The knowledge that goes into the gaps is called **subtext**.

That's it, really. Simples. Knowledge gaps are the substance of story. Once you understand knowledge gaps you understand the power source of story. Knowledge gaps are not some clever trick or formula

— this is not some fad that will go away. Stories are *made from* knowledge gaps. Knowledge gaps are fundamental to the power in every story that has ever been told, and will be fundamental to yours.

Knowledge gaps cannot be avoided in your own stories — you use them whether you like it or not — so you might as well learn about them. Like the primary colours in art they are inevitable, they can help you to understand the power in your stories and understanding them will not negatively affect your creativity or inspiration.

The more knowledge gaps there are in a story, the deeper they run and the longer they persist, the more highly rated the story tends to be. I know — because I sat in a university counting them. (I know how to have a good time.)

In the next section we are going to learn everything there is to know about knowledge gaps and the way knowledge gaps can be used to create the conditions for subtext.

Section 2 - Knowledge Gaps and Subtext

> **As we know, there are known knowns; there are things we know we know. We also know there are known unknowns; that is to say we know there are some things we do not know. But there are also unknown unknowns – the ones we don't know we don't know.**
>
> **Donald Rumsfeld, US Defence Secretary (2002)**

Talking of having a good time, let's go back to our fishing net. If you remember, we decided initially that a fishing net is a static object made of string, sitting on the quayside, right?

Wrong.

I would love to think that, by the end of this book, the story expert you will have become will be thinking differently and recognise that a fishing net is not made of string. A fishing net is made of holes. Without the holes, there is no fishing net. Without the holes no fish will be caught. It's the holes that define the net and it is the holes that get you the beneficial outcome when the script runs. Sure, it's the string that you can *see*, but for a writer that is old-school thinking. In our funky new approach to life, the string is only there to show us where the holes are.

A fishing net is an absence of string in all the important places.

As a human being, when you are next a little anxious or excited about something, notice that it is the holes in your knowledge which are the cause of the emotion. Say you are woken at 2.38am by a bump in the night... You sit bolt upright in a cold sweat. What on

Earth was THAT?! you know there is a narrative progression going on somewhere in the house, but it has gaps in it, and it is these gaps that make you anxious and which trigger your brain to fill them in. Your cultural knowledge and experience fill in the gaps and tell you there are nine burglars downstairs and you and your family are all going to be murdered in your beds. This is your unconscious mind pattern-matching against the best-fit narrative — a meaning that fits with the limited information you have. This is an automatic, evolutionary response. It is this mental reflex which writers use to cause grip.

It is this gap-filling which has you creeping down the stairs stark naked and brandishing a nine-iron, only to discover that it was Grandma making a cup of tea. She dropped the tray and that was the noise you heard. You know it was exactly that noise which you heard, because now she sees you naked in the doorway she drops the tray again.

The point is, look what happened in mind. Now you know the source of the crash, you have a complete narrative. There are now no gaps to make you anxious, so your brain can settle and you can go back to sleep. At the same time, your brain automatically lays down a memory because it now has this complete narrative. Next time you hear that crash downstairs, your unconscious mind will offer you up this memory — the Granny-tea narrative — to explain it. You will have an entire script to account for it and because it has no gaps, you will not be anxious or alarmed. You will roll over and go straight back to the sleep of the pure and the innocent.

Turns out it's burglars and you are all murdered in your beds.

Seriously, I hope you get the point. A complete narrative makes us feel confident and assured. We know where life is going. A narrative with gaps in it arouses our emotions. We fire up our intelligence and set to work, projecting into the gaps to complete a sensible narrative from the clues we have. As a writer, when you next go through an event in life, search it for the potential to create holes in it because that is how to make it intriguing and beguiling and turn it into a compelling story, because a story is *made of* gaps in knowledge in just the same way that a fishing net is *made of* holes. A story it is not made of the words in a book or the images on a screen. The information stream — the narration — is not crafted to deliver information. It is crafted to ensure that when the receiver builds the narrative in mind there will be gaps in knowledge in the progression. A narration is a vehicle for knowledge gaps. A story is an absence of knowledge in all the important places.

If I refer to a mutual friend of ours, and I angrily shout: "Oh, my God, she is SUCH a —!"

I left a knowledge gap and it is the bit that's missing that is important. What goes into the gap is precisely the bit that makes the story complete. And guess what: you provided the missing information from your own knowledge and experience. Your mind sensed the gap and your mind desperately needed to fill that gap and your mind stepped up and — unconsciously and automatically — filled the gap.

That, right there, is the power of story from the viewpoint of the receiver and the key to the craft of story from the viewpoint of the writer. Story is a joint production between an author and a receiver. As the author of the above dialogue, I encoded using a knowledge gap and you decoded using your own knowledge and experience. I left a knowledge gap and in doing so I engaged your brain in the story in such a way that you began producing the story for yourself. Do not forget, the truth is not important. You may or may not be right about how that sentence ends (all will be revealed...). What is important is that *you* created *meaning* by completing the narrative for yourself. When the wolf eats Grandma, dresses in her clothes and climbs into bed to await Little Red Riding Hood, we understand the narrative progression, but what it *means* is that Little Red Riding Hood is walking into a trap and is in mortal danger. Even at four years of age, our emotions are aroused and we are desperately projecting ahead trying to figure out the ultimate meaning and a route to a positive outcome.

There is a difference between what we are given and what we turn it into when we fill that gaps, and this is the key to the author's craft. Let's look at a more sophisticated example. Here is a novel, allegedly written by Earnest Hemingway and allegedly the shortest novel ever written, comprised as it is of six words:

FOR SALE. BABY'S SHOES. NEVER WORN.

Before you continue reading, just stop and think a little about the work you do in mind in interpreting these six words into what makes logical, human-cultural sense to you.

It is possible to simply read this text in a literal, 'readerly' manner, and build a narrative in mind comprising a classified advertisement in which a person is selling a pair of shoes. Fair enough. However, you did more than that, didn't you?! Driven by your personal cultural knowledge and experience, you did 'writerly' work. You did not just passively accept the basic meaning in the narrative. You joined in. Your imagination projected into the gaps in the causal logic and a storification emerged in mind. A story that is substantially different from and greater than the literal meaning in those six words. The six words are an *information* stream that is a vehicle for enormous gaps in *knowledge*. You projected into those gaps and you used your cultural understanding of classified advertisements and why people sell things to build a narrative scenario in mind that worked for you. Just look at the difference between the literal meaning of what you were given in the six words and what you built for yourself in mind. This is the power of story. Understanding how to create and manage gaps that work like this is the craft of story.

A story is any form of communication that involves knowledge gaps in the delivery.

If you think about it, at the beginning of a narration, a story is nothing but one enormous knowledge gap. The author knows everything and the receiver knows nothing. The author hands out knowledge, bit by bit, moment by moment, as the encoding and decoding take place over the period of narration. Knowledge — and gaps in that knowledge — are delivered and filled, bit by bit, until a complete story is created in the mind of the receiver.

2.1 What is a knowledge gap?

As established earlier, a narrative cannot become a story unless there is a human being there to perceive it. For this reason, all knowledge gaps are relative to the audience perspective. That is, the audience member either knows more than another participant in the story or they know less than another participant in the story. Logically then, a 'participant' is any entity in the narration that is capable of holding or withholding knowledge. Such as:

- A character
- The author
- The narrator
- A story event
- Impactful objects.

A safe can hold information and, therefore, potentially be a component of a knowledge gap. A playing card face down on a poker table in a wild west saloon withholds knowledge so potent that it can cause bedlam, gunfights, death and blood up the walls. A film's poster or trailer gives information but simultaneously withholds, thereby intriguing the receiver. A deluded man embodies a knowledge gap between his self-image and his reality. A character's plan contains gaps in knowledge (for example, between those who know of the plan and those who do not). A line of dialogue can both give knowledge and withhold it at the same time. If I tell you: 'Last night I was out with my mates.' I am both giving knowledge but also — quite possibly — withholding knowledge at the same time, so there is a gap.

A wrapped present — is there any more beautiful example of the power and emotional impact of withheld knowledge than a wrapped present?! The giver has knowledge that the receiver does not, and both are loving the promise in the knowledge gap.

The receiver of the story is not always 'in the know'. For example, if one character is lying to another, the knowledge gap exists between the two of them, however from the audience perspective they will either know about the lie (onside with the liar – a 'privilege' position) or they will not know about the lie (lacking knowledge, a 'revelation' position) putting them onside with the character being lied to. More on privilege and revelation shortly.

If knowledge is not held equally across all participants in the story a gap is created and the receiver becomes engaged. The art of generating grip through story is, in essence, as simple as that. However, knowledge gaps are one half of a duet. The author's half. The other half is provided by the receiver, and it is a magical, vital, critical element of story called...

2.2   Subtext

I don't know about you, but when I first heard about subtext I was baffled. The gurus tell us that a story must be delivered in subtext, and that if a scene is about what it seems to be about it is dismissed for being 'on the nose' and it must be cut.

I didn't get it. Well, I kind of got it — I knew that subtext was 'what lies beneath...' It is the unstated bit we get, like the moral message in a children's story or the way *Animal Farm* (Orwell, 1945) can be seen as an implicit criticism of communism in the 19th century. However, as a writer I was not sure how to use this in my general writing. I was being told I had to write my story without mentioning it, and I didn't see how.

If you feel a little foggy about subtext, lucky old you, because I am here to rescue you. All that stuff they say about writing in subtext is true... they just did not explain it accurately. The secret is this: *Writers do not work with subtext.* You will love me forever for this. I am excited to share it. Let me explain.

A story is made of knowledge gaps.
Subtext is the knowledge that goes into the gaps.

And it is the receiver of the narration who provides the knowledge that goes into the gaps. A writer works with knowledge gaps in order that the receiver can work with subtext.

See? I told you it was simple. As we discussed earlier, a story effectively has two sources of knowledge in mind: the knowledge delivered by the author (with gaps in it) and the knowledge provided by the receiver for themselves (the knowledge that goes into the gaps).

Subtext does not have to be huge and epic. Remember this dialogue:
"Oh, my God, she is SUCH a —!"
As the author I gave you an information stream with a gap in the knowledge. You did the interpretation — the readerly work to put together the basic sense of that narrative in your head. But that information, when formed into human logic in mind, includes a knowledge gap. Once you had put the sense together there was knowledge missing so you did the writerly work and you filled it in. YOU provided the subtext: The knowledge that goes into the gap. What is the meaning? Well, you are probably assuming that I am angry with this lady, and I am calling her names, so you frame up an

appropriate context in mind and begin to wonder what she did and why I think she is so bad.

In your assumptions, you might be right or you might be wrong but that isn't the point. Remember Santa Claus — it is not about truth, it is about *meaning*. You found your best-guess meaning so it became a valid narrative. It may change as more information arrives, it may prove to be something entirely different, or a big lie. It might well twist and turn as the narration unfolds but that does not matter from the viewpoint of building a story in mind. The point is that I gave you a narration with a knowledge gap and that triggers your mental activity. You applied your cultural knowledge and experience to fill in the gap. This is essentially the craft of story creation. As a writer, your job is to work with knowledge gaps to *create the conditions for subtext*. That is your craft, right there.

When the gurus tell us we have to write in subtext that wording is wrong because it is impossible. Only the receiver of the story can provide the subtext. The **writer** works with gaps so that the **receiver** has the space in which to work with subtext.

The writer works with knowledge gaps in order that the receiver can work with subtext. It's a duet. Writer and receiver working together. The writer encodes — creating knowledge gaps — and the receiver decodes — providing the knowledge that goes into the gap.

The skill of the writer is in creating the conditions for subtext. Not enough information and your audience will be confused or come to different or unwanted conclusions. Too much information and your audience will have no work to do and find the story boring. You have to craft your work so the audience does the writerly work in providing the subtext that completes the narrative in mind. If you get it right, the receiver will love every moment, because solving a story puzzle excited those visceral mental reflexes we discussed in section one. We feel a tremendous sense of satisfaction when we learn something new (that is, when we discover a new complete narrative).

Let's play a game with subtext. I am going to be the author, you be the receiver. I will use knowledge gaps to evoke a scenario in your mind by creating the conditions for subtext. I'm not going to mention what the scene is about, but I will give you knowledge gaps crafted in such a way that *you* deliver the meaning of *my* scenario to yourself, by yourself, from the abstract clues I give you. Up for it? Good. Let's go.

First, I'm going to plant an image in your mind. Here we go:

A parked car.

OK. Have you got the full narrative scenario yet? No. Of course not. There is no context for a gap in which any logical writerly work can take place. The audience is not framed towards loading a context in mind into which this car can sensibly fit, so different audience members would come to different conclusions. I have failed to create the conditions to trigger consistent subtext in an audience member. Let's expand the image.

How about a parked car, but parked at a funny angle compared to all the other cars?

Hmm. Now we are thinking around it, and we could decide on a couple of possibilities for what we think might be going on, because we have a little cultural information to leverage concerned with why someone might park at a funny angle. However, if you ask different people what is happening here they would still come to different conclusions. Hmmm. As an author I think I might be losing my audience. Let's add a little more.

OK. How about a car parked at a funny angle... outside a bank?

Aha! Bingo! NOW we are on the money! I have not told you what is going on in this scenario — very little has changed — and yet now just about everyone comes to the same conclusion from providing the subtext for themselves. I gave enough information for a framing to take place, and most people come to the same conclusion. THAT is the craft of storytelling. I gave you a parked car and you decided there is a robbery going on. The writer and reader working in harmony. The writer provides the knowledge gap and the reader provides the subtext. Boom. The receiver now loads up a context for a bank robbery. Balaclavas and shooters and 'everybody on the floor!'

Then sirens, a getaway and a car chase. We know how all these things go, so we readily load up a complete context (the author has provided the framing and oriented us). We have never been in a bank robbery or a car chase, but we know the context very well indeed.

What is the right amount of information a writer should give?
Another great question. You're very good at this. However, this is up to you. As the creator of a story, part of your craft is to decide if you have made the knowledge gap too big for your audience to build the correct scenario, or too small so the narration is too obvious and readerly. Your job is to think of your target audience and ensure you are in the right place for ninety percent of them. Many people give up on Shakespeare. They hate his stuff. It's too hard to figure out what is going on. This is because the knowledge gaps are huge. However, those who put the effort in will get a tremendous feeling of satisfaction because they will be rewarded with a story that is so significantly created by themselves through their writerly work. Similarly with poetry. The gaps are massive, and people either love it or hate it as a result. At the other end of the scale, many adults get bored reading children's stories. The knowledge gaps are small and obvious. There is not enough writerly work for an adult to do; it's all geared to the younger mind. You have to pitch yourself appropriately for your audience and for your intention, and within that audience likely range of writerly ability, just how much you want

to stretch them and how arty, complex and clever you want your work to be.

In many ways, this is the definition of your craft. This is how stories work as a conversation between an author and a receiver.

Stories are made of knowledge gaps.
Subtext is the knowledge that goes into a knowledge gap.

Knowledge gaps and subtext; the beautiful duet.

Now, wouldn't it be great if some idiot somewhere spent a decade of his life in a university studiously documenting a taxonomy of all the different types of knowledge gaps? (I know how to have a good time…)

My research showed that a story cannot exist without knowledge gaps. The more knowledge gaps there are, the deeper they run and the longer they persist the more highly rated that story will be compared to those with fewer and lesser knowledge gaps.

Understanding knowledge gaps is useful for writers because firstly, they are inevitable and unavoidable, so working with them helps make the best of your story ideas; and secondly, they let you understand the craft of story without anyone telling you how *your* story should go.

If you are feeling masochistic, you can go deeply into all aspects of knowledge gaps in narrative through immersion in my formal academic work on the subject, snappily entitled *Story in Mind: A Constructivist Narratology* (Baboulene, 2019). However, for our more applied and practical purposes I have distilled the list of knowledge gaps down to the essential gaps that are relevant to authors and from which I claim every fine story ever written is composed. Figure 4, below, provides the full list of the mainstream knowledge gaps.

Here they are! These are <drum roll...> **The Primary Colours of Story**.

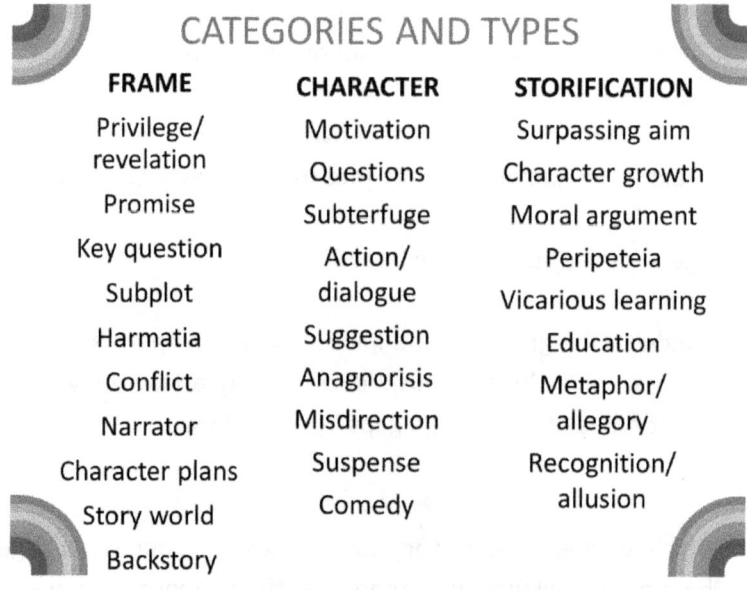

Figure 4: The Primary Colours of Story

Now that is a busy illustration, but if you think about it as a comprehensive understanding of every story — including yours — there is not a huge amount here to get your head around.

As you can see, knowledge gaps split out into categories that represent the three mental dynamics discussed in section 1. In broad terms:

- **Framing gaps.** The author orientates the receiver to the direction and intent of the story. Framing encourages the receiver to load up the appropriate context in mind for the beat/ scene/ sequence/ chapter/ story.

- **Character gaps** are present in the characters' moment-by-moment actions and interactions as their behaviours make a logical human narrative cause/effect chain in real-time in their story world.

- **Storification gaps** are the writerly work of the receiver. They cause the story to jump out of the story world and occupy the mindset of the receiver as they work to piece together meaning, as in the case of the children accidentally learning the Heimlich manoeuvre from watching *SpongeBob SquarePants*. Storification gaps demand writerly work from the receiver of the story to not simply complete the causal logic to the extent that we know what happened (narrafication), but to understand what it *means* (storification). That is, what it means to the receiver as figured out for themselves in their own mind. The Hemingway six-word story was not simply about someone placing a classified advertisement (narrafication). You decided it was about a couple suffering death in childbirth (storification).

2.3 Where Should you Focus?

We are going to work through framing, character and storification in order. However, it is important to recognise that developing a story is not a linear process. One does not frame the story, then overlay some characters, then pop a storification cherry on the top. If anything, it is the other way up. Our story seed — the originating idea and inspiration — is most likely to have its power and true potential somewhere on the storification level, however, it will be highly unlikely that you will be able to identify it at an early stage of story development.

If you have ever attended a creative writing or story guru course you will have been told that it is important to find your ending first. There is a lot of truth in that. Every story has a beginning, a middle and an end, that's for sure, and once you know the ending you can design the beginning and the middle to effectively head towards the goal. However, this is not where your focus should be as the author. It is the *receiver* who experiences a beginning, middle and end — because it is the narration you create which inevitably has these things — but as the working author trying to understand and organise the power of your story in order to *create* that narration, the most important component of your story is not the ending so much as the storification. This is the crowning glory that delivers ultimate story power to your audience, and it does not necessarily coincide with the 'ending'.

What. The hell. Are you talking about?
Ah. Sorry. Let's have an example. The **ending** of *Back to the Future* is act III and comprises the climax and resolution. The climax begins from the moment Marty McFly (Michael J. Fox) successfully re-unites his parents in love and heads off to his time machine. The climactic action has him get there just in time to hit the bolt of lightning and he makes it back to 1985. The climax gives us the answer to the key question: Will Marty get home to 1985? How will he do it? This climax is followed by the relative calm of the resolution in which Marty reunites with Doc Brown (Christopher Lloyd) and Jennifer Parker (Claudia Wells) in 1985, we see how the world has changed as a result of Marty's adventure and they all live happily ever after. A classic Hollywood formula act III.

However, this ending is not the storification. Indeed, the ending is the *outcome* of the storification. The major storification is the character growth of George McFly (Crispin Glover) in 1955 when he makes a fist for the first time in his life, overcomes his internal conflict and defeats the bully, Biff (Thomas F. Wilson). In that moment, George changes and he learns and he grows. The decision he makes leads to consequences that allow us to learn from his choices and we in the audience understand, in a human cultural terms, something about life and how it should be led.

The storification occurs when events force George into a difficult choice: either stand up to the bully (and get six bells kicked out of him) or avoid conflict (as every nerve and fibre of his being is willing him to do) and run away... leaving his beloved Lorraine to be abused by Biff in the car. George has a life choice to make. Stand and fight or run off and avoid the conflict. He digs deep inside himself, makes a fist for the first time in his life, takes on the bully... and punches his lights out. In this moment of triumph, George undergoes fundamental personal learning and growth. As a result of his decision to stand and fight, George gets the girl he loves, he gets status amongst his peers, he gains self-esteem and confidence that we can see in the consequences of his choice. We in the audience understand what happened and why. In purely narrative logic terms George won a fight (narrafication). However, in terms of life and how it should be led, George teaches us a lesson about life and how it should be led; the lesson that one must have the courage of one's convictions to lead a fulfilling life.

George's moment of character growth is the kingpin moment that is the highest peak of story power in *Back to the Future*. This is the moment of learning and growth that gives the story human meaning. It defines everything that happens and everything we end up thinking about afterwards. When I say it defines everything that happens, I am not exaggerating. As we shall discover, that is why storification is so important. Essentially, everything that happens before George's moment of growth is in service of it — boxing him into the pressure to make that life choice — and everything that happens after this moment is a result of it. George makes his decisions and there are consequences that make us think about how a person should lead their life. George's character growth is the storification that *causes* the ending. Once we go into the resolution with Marty back in 1985, we see how the world has changed as a result of George making a fist and using it — the character growth moment; the storification event. In this new version of 1985, the intervening 30 years have been characterised by a strong, assertive father instead of a weak one. Marty's life — indeed, all the characters' lives have changed significantly because of George McFly's character growth in 1955. Everything in the resolution is a consequence of the storification event. The power of the resolution material is not a function of the ending (Marty making it back to 1985). It is a function of the storification (which happened in the subplot with around a third of the film still to run).

As a writer, it is not so much the ending that you need to find in order to know how the beginning and middle should go, it is the storification you need to find in order to know the character behaviours required to deliver it and how to support those characters and behaviours through the framing.

And it is not the ending that you need to think about in terms of the climax and resolution. It is far more beneficial to the power of your story to understand how the character actions, reactions, decisions and their consequences lead to storification.

It is less:

> CLIMAX leads to RESOLUTION

And more:

> CHARACTER ACTIONS lead to STORIFICATION

For the writer developing the story, it is less:

> BEGINNING leads to MIDDLE leads to END

And more:

> FRAMING supports CHARACTERS taking ACTIONS lead to CONSEQUENCES drive STORIFICATION

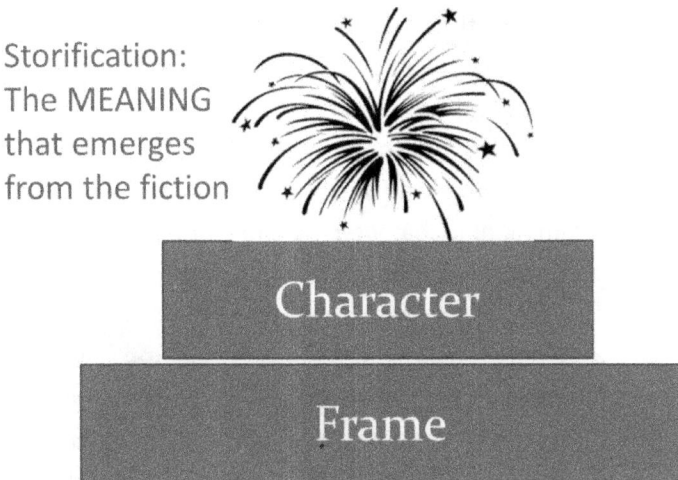

Figure 5: Supporting your storification

Here lies the most interesting puzzle for the writer. The storification is the kingpin that is central to everything else. It is the piece that you most critically need to get right. However, it is not possible to deliver a storification by itself. It is the most important dynamic in any story, however it only exists as a function of the framing and character dynamics. That is why it is not a linear process to develop a story. The author must work outwards from their idea to discover their storification, then work backwards from there to ensure that the storification is supported by appropriate character actions and framing.

This probably feels a little difficult at the moment, but do not worry. Things will get clearer as we go through the gears. For the moment, the point is that, as the story develops, your creative process is not linear. As a writer you must work backwards and forwards *along* the narrative (it will inevitably have a beginning, middle and end) but you must also work up and down the framing, character actions and storification to ensure *this* frame supports *these* characters in taking *these* actions leading to *these* consequences generating *this* storification.

How does this relate to knowledge gaps? Well, If there are no knowledge gaps then there is no space in which the mind of the receiver can project their own thinking. Storification gaps are the ultimate because they involve the receiver doing most of the work for themselves in their own minds after they have been orientated by the author and after they have interpreted the characters' actions and decisions and converted them into meaning. Storification is a function of framing and character, so the storification gaps arrive in their mind as an accumulation of framing and character subtext they have already provided for themselves.

The author frames using knowledge gaps and the characters take actions that are made of knowledge gaps. The receiver becomes a producer of story rather than simply a reader of a text. Every time a receiver puts subtext into a knowledge gap, that event (beat/ scene/ sequence/ chapter/ act/ subplot...) storifies. That is, it has meaning in mind. Your challenge as a creator of story is to learn how to encode knowledge gaps into a story and understand the effect this has on the mind of your receiver as *they* build *your* story in their own mind.

2.4 Framing Gaps

In this section, I will examine and give examples of each individual knowledge gap through framing. Firstly, a reminder of all the types of knowledge gap:

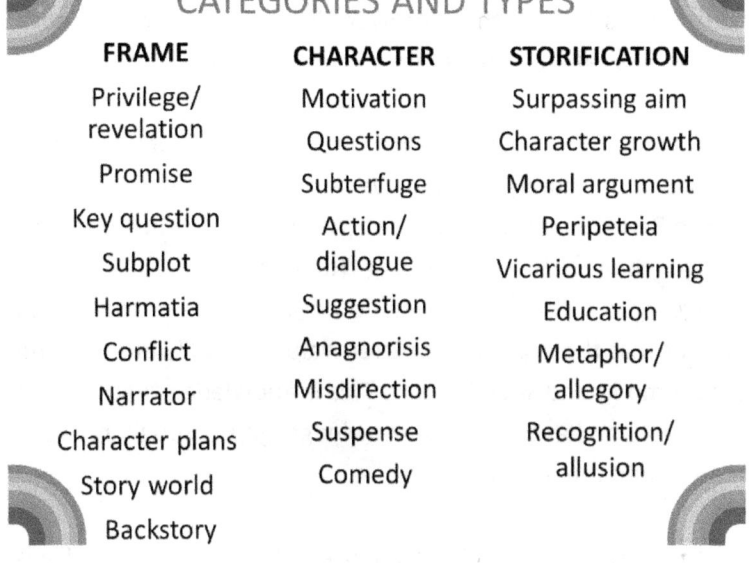

Figure 6: Types and categories of knowledge gap

We will begin top left and work through the detail of how each of the framing gaps works.

2.4.1 Privilege and Revelation

In truth, privilege and revelation are classifications of gap, not types, but what the heck. We only live once. Let's be wild and chuck them into the framing area so the picture is easier. Formally, they are a classification because all types of gap are either presented in privilege or revelation. If you get tense and sweaty about this kind of correctness, it is all done with full academic rigour in *Story in Mind* (2019). Either way, privilege and revelation work like this.

ALL knowledge gaps work from the perspective of the receiver. Stories are made to be told (remember that a narration must have a human receiver for a story to exist) so the receiver can always be assumed to be present and is always going to be at one end of a knowledge gap. So, if the receiver of the story knows more than another participant, this is called a **privilege** knowledge gap. (Good old 'dramatic irony', as you may remember from your English Literature classes.) If the receiver knows less than another participant, it is called a **revelation** knowledge gap.

In *Little Red Riding Hood*, we in the audience know that the grandma lying in bed with notably sizeable eyes, ears and teeth is actually the wolf. Little Red Riding Hood does not. We in the audience have more knowledge than Little Red Riding Hood so this is a privilege knowledge gap. On the revelation side, the author knows throughout that there is a woodcutter waiting handily in the garden, all set to jump in and save the day. This is knowledge that we in the audience do not have, so is a knowledge gap through revelation between us and the author.

In *Back to the Future*, we in the audience know that Marty McFly is a time-traveller from the future and no-one in 1955 knows. This is a knowledge gap in privilege. It is a deep, pervasive knowledge gap that persists throughout his time in 1955, bringing the story a baseline of continuous story power.

In revelation, the audience sees Doc Brown get mown down in a hail of machine-gun fire at the end of act 1. Doc knows that he is wearing a bullet proof vest and will survive but the audience does not and assumes, quite reasonably, that he must surely be dead.[iv] Doc knows more than the audience so this is a knowledge gap through **revelation**, one that is kept open for 75 minutes!

Most fine stories have a balance of privilege and revelation gaps. Aspiring writers tend to focus on revelation gaps because the impact is more obvious, whereas handing the audience privilege information is counterintuitive. Surely, we should not be telling the audience what is going to happen, should we?! More experienced writers trust that flagging knowledge forwards does not simply give away the plot. It *orientates* the audience, sets a path and makes them feel they are in good hands. It gives the story dimension, because the audience is evaluating everything that happens in the light of the fore-knowledge they have. Privilege knowledge raises the question: *how* is our hero going to get to there from here?

When you take a seat to watch a James Bond or a superhero film, or read a Harry Potter or Jack Reacher book, you do so fairly comfortable in the knowledge that the hero is going to win. They will bring down the bad guys and good will win out over evil. In a sense, we begin almost every story well armed with privilege information concerning what is going to happen. Good guy wins. Bad guy loses. Moral goodness will take the day.

Will Marty McFly make it back to 1985 or will he die? Of course, we assume Marty will get back to 1985, but the authors undermine that expectation by trapping Marty into situations from which the audience can see no possible route to the ending they want and expect. *What* will happen can be foreshadowed. *How* it will happen can be very unclear indeed! Knowledge gaps are often more about 'how' than 'what'. The receiving mind will constantly project forwards as information comes in, and the author must constantly battle against, mislead or twist this audience preconception. The writer needs to unsettle them; make them believe that this time... just maybe... this is the time it will not go quite to plan for the good guys. *Game of Thrones* is the masterwork for this. The authors set us up with a morally upright, strong, glorious hero... and then proceeds to have them lose horribly to the bad guy. They get back on their feet and we think: 'Aha! Here comes the big comeback!' And they get killed. The bad guy wins. Time after time. It is excellently unsettling.

As you get deeper into *Little Red Riding Hood* the question is not so much 'Will Little Red Riding Hood survive this story?' Because we are confident. Of course she will. However, as the story progresses it becomes incredibly challenging to see *how* she will squeak out of the situation. Particularly once she has been eaten by the wolf...

Almost any knowledge gap can be delivered in privilege or revelation and the choice (*your* choice) has a profound effect on the audience experience. To demonstrate the effect I'm going to give you the bones of a murder mystery, firstly in revelation and secondly the same story but in privilege.

In Revelation
In a mystery story, the audience follows the detective on his journey. We see everything he sees. In my example story, we begin with Detective Dave at the police station. Dave explains to his partner, Officer Billy Bob, that he just cannot find a pattern to the murders being committed all over town. Through describing his difficulties we get the backstory to the whole situation. But Dave is not a quitter. He is determined. He decides to get out there. Return to the scene. Shake the tree. Ruffle some feathers. But whatever he does, the killer stays one jump ahead. It seems almost as if he knows what Dave is going to do next. However, Dave then finds a murder weapon, roughs up a suspect, finds a footprint in the flowerbed, interviews The Blonde, dabs for some fingerprints, fights a shadowy figure who gets away... We in the audience see all the same clues that Dave sees and we know everything Dave knows. Then, suddenly, he arrests... The Blonde! We in the audience are shocked by his action: 'Whoa! Why would he do that..? She's not guilty! She's... surely, she's a victim?!'

And we reel back through everything we've seen, desperately trying to lock on to what it was that detective Dave picked up on that we did not. Dave pulls the blonde's prosthetic face off, just like they do on Scooby Doo, and the guilty party is not a blonde woman; it is Officer Billy Bob — Dave's own partner from the station. Up to no good from the start. It was the lipstick on Billy Bob's desk at the police station that gave him away. He noticed it and we didn't. Wowza. What a revelation. What a whodunnit! The power of a story delivered in revelation.

In Privilege

Now let's deliver the same story, but this time in privilege. Once again, we begin with Detective Dave at the police station. Dave explains to his partner Officer Billy Bob that he just cannot find a pattern to the murders being committed all over town. Through describing his difficulties we get the backstory to the whole situation. But Dave is not a quitter. He is determined. He decides to get out there. Return to the scene. Shake the tree. Ruffle some feathers. But whatever he does, the killer stays one jump ahead. It seems almost as if he knows what Dave's going to do next. We know Detective Dave is trying to solve the murder but this time, as he heads out into the city to rough up a suspect, we stick with Billy Bob. Once Dave has left, Billy Bob goes to the toilets, puts on his blonde wig and lippy and we go with him as he heads out a-murdering. We in the audience now know what Dave does not: That the blonde woman victim who gave excellent, helpful evidence… is actually the murderer and is also Dave's partner, Officer Billy Bob.

We fear for Detective Dave now, because the murderer, Billy Bob, is in Dave's life. Dave keeps telling him how the investigation is progressing and what his next move is going to be. The privilege presentation means that we know (and detective Dave does not) that the guilty person is a colleague and friend. As the author, we can now use this dynamic to really start ramping up the tension. We fear for people Billy Bob talks to as we know what they do not — that they may be the next victim. Tension. Billy Bob sends a shadowy figure to ambush Dave at the crime scene. There is suspense as Dave walks into the trap we know about. Detective Dave has Billy Bob round for dinner with his wife. They are buddies, after all. He asks Billy Bob to babysit the children. Oh, Jeez, Dave, don't do that! We know — and Dave does not — that Dave and his family are in mortal danger. Not only does Dave not realise this, but Billy Bob knows Dave is getting closer… so he takes Dave's daughter to the zoo. Just the two of them…

Hopefully you can see from these examples that the way you choose to use the knowledge gaps will bring your story a whole different style. When you have a scene to deliver, you can see the options for which gaps are offering themselves and how they can best be deployed. A range of choices and their impacts come into play each time you notice that every story event (beat, scene, sequence, chapter, act, subplot – whatever) has a knowledge gap — or set of gaps — that define it.

And just to clarify — *all* knowledge gaps are either in privilege or revelation. You can choose which you use, and most fine stories have a balance of privilege and revelation.

More to come on these options as we go through. The main point, however, is to take your plot and action, and look for ways to introduce knowledge gaps. A difference in the knowledge held between different participants turns an action sequence into gripping story.

The old Switcheroo...
When a revelation hits, it is important that this does not close off all the gaps and leave the story with no power. Unless it is the ultimate climax to a whole plot, a revelation should raise and many questions as it answers. A switch from revelation to privilege is a good way to achieve this.

The switcheroo occurs when a story event begins in revelation but switches over to privilege midway through. This is a wonderful way to maintain grip, because the switch is a compelling revelation event in itself when it arrives, and yet because the sequence is not yet at its climax, the grip goes on.

One of the finest examples is the opening sequence of Quentin Tarantino's *Inglourious Basterds* (2008). It lasts around twenty minutes – I mean, a single sequence of around 20 minutes — and it is masterful. One of the reasons it has such tension and power for such a long time is because the knowledge gaps do not close; the knowledge gap dynamics shift, such that different characters have different knowledge at any one time, and who knows what changes continuously.

Set in World War II, Nazi Colonel Hans Landa (Christopher Waltz) approaches the remote farmhouse of Perrier LaPadite (Denis Ménochet) and his three daughters. LaPadite invites the colonel into his home. They make polite, tense conversation and discuss the possible whereabouts of a family of Jews Landa wants to track down. LaPadite has heard rumours of what happened to them but doesn't know for sure. As their conversation continues, the tension builds… and the camera drops beneath the floorboards to reveal that the Jewish family is lying terrified under the floor, hiding right there under the colonel's feet. This revelation for us in the audience changes the knowledge gap dynamics. We now know what LaPadite has done and the huge risk he is taking. Now, with this privilege information we really feel the pressure LaPadite is under in keeping his cool. LaPadite and his daughters made a plan to help these Jews. But now the Colonel is playing hardball. He switches language with LaPadite to discuss the family without their understanding. He explains the consequences LaPadite will suffer if he is not truthful… the risk to him… and his lovely daughters… The knowledge dynamics change as LaPadite gently breaks down and admits what he has done. We know this, but the family does not because of the change in language. LaPadite owns up… sealing their fate… and they are under the floorboards, still unaware, as the SS colonel stands up and ushers his men into the house. The family lie there, still hiding, they do not realise they are sitting ducks. Since LaPadite broke down, we know they are in immediate mortal danger. We know it. They do not.

The knowledge gap dynamics have shifted, in a single, beautiful sequence, from the audience knowing nothing of LaPadite's plan (a revelation dynamic) to the revelation hitting, so the audience is now aware of it (a privilege dynamic) and hoping the colonel remains unaware. From there, the colonel also becomes aware. However, the family hiding under the floorboards are unaware that the plan and their secret has been laid bare. We know, but they do not, and we fear for them terribly as the soldiers march into the room and are silently signalled to take up their positions...

I urge you to watch it (overall, the story is a little on the violent side for some, but wonderful for all that). As you watch that opening sequence just keep noticing how the knowledge gap dynamics change because that is the source of the story's power. It's not what is happening in the plot, it is who knows what. A story is made of knowledge gaps, and switching the knowledge gap dynamics is far and away more important to story power than what is happening in the plot. All they do is sit at a table and have a conversation. They drink milk. Light pipes. Indulge small talk. BUT the knowledge gap dynamics keep changing... and we are gripped. Keep asking yourself: Who of the participants knows what? As you gain information, think about how the knowledge **you** have of the situation sits relative to the other participants in the sequence. Then as you get revelations, think back to consider which characters knew things that you did not know up until that point. It is these differences in the knowledge held by different participants in the story that give it such amazing grip, and when knowledge is revealed, it is still not held evenly across all the participants, so the grip is retained. It is through simply switching the knowledge gap dynamic that the sequence retains its power. Once the knowledge gaps are all closed, the sequence is finished. Tarantino closes it out and moves on to the next one.

Your One Takeaway
If you take nothing else from this book, understanding the power of knowledge gaps in privilege and revelation is a huge benefit. Many writers have fine plot ideas. Things happen in their stories, but their scenes do not truly grip as the writer hoped they might. The reason is right here. The knowledge gaps are all wrong.

It would be easy for a writer or director to look at a scene in which a Nazi Colonel decides the missing Jews he is after are hiding out at LaPadite's farm. He could take some soldiers, head up there, force his way in and search the house. LaPadite might have a go at lying about it, but the Colonel has overwhelming resources and simply ignores him. He finds the Jews and summarily executes them all.

It is easy, as a writer, to see a scene like this and decide it is good, meaty story. And potentially it is, of course. It has strong action, great characters, conflict and all the other things that the guru's tell you must be present. However, what elevates it into utterly gripping genius is that Tarantino took that scene and looked for ways to drive in differences in the knowledge held. He then kept switching those dynamics, gradually boxing LaPadite and the Jews further and further into difficulties. The sequence continued to grip, so he kept on going.

This is possibly the best tip I can give you in writing. When you have an idea for a story event, it is not simply 'what happens' that makes the story grip. Look at how you can progress the sequence with differences in the knowledge held by different participants; specifically, whereby the audience knows more or less than another participant.

2.4.2 Knowledge gaps through character plans

It is surprising just how often characters make plans in stories. In a way, every memory we have in our long-term narrative databanks is a 'plan' for getting the beneficial outcome of that narrative. Running a 'script' from your own memory is usually a very good plan, and we do it all the time, so when characters make and execute plans, it tends to resonate. This connection between story and life means a character plan is a powerful way to frame a story event.

Knowledge gaps are the secret to story power, and when a character makes a plan three knowledge gaps are implicit:

a) A question is raised: Will the plan succeed?

b) There is an implicit knowledge gap between those who know about the plan and those who do not. (So make sure some participants know about the plan and others do not.)

c) As the plan runs its course, there is a gap between what is hoped and expected to happen if the plan is successful and what actually happens as the plan plays out. (So, as the mischievous god of your story world, it is your job to make sure that things do not go to plan.)

Whenever there is a knowledge gap, there is story power and engagement, so every character plan carries that triple certainty of a certain level of story power.

There are six fully formed plans in *Back to the Future*, including the one Doc makes and explains in great detail to us using a model of Hill Valley he builds for a demonstration in which he acts out the plan. The authors took the time to take us through that plan because that is how powerful plans can be. Another plan involves Marty and George acting out a complete role play in front of us so we understand it. Let's go through that one.

Marty and his future father, George, make a plan to convince his future mother, Lorraine, that George is the strong, assertive type of man she desires. Lorraine is infatuated with Marty at the time so their plan involves making Marty appear thoroughly distasteful to Lorraine whilst simultaneously making George the hero of the hour for her. Marty and George role play the plan in advance so we in the audience understand it in privilege. Marty will drive Lorraine to the *Enchantment Under the Sea* dance. At precisely 9.00pm, Marty will make inappropriate sexual advances towards Lorraine in the car. George will turn up just in time, rip the car door open and say, "Hey, you. Get your damn hands off her."

George will drag Marty from the car, punch him in the stomach and rescue Lorraine, who will be so impressed with how strong and assertive George is that she will fall in love with him and the historical path necessary for Marty to be born in 1968 will be back on track.

The knowledge gap lies between those characters who know of the plan (Marty and George) and those that do not (Biff, Lorraine and everyone else), however the audience is always a participant, and in this case we have privilege knowledge of the plan. The audience understands the plan and its aims and they are, therefore, orientated to the intended path the story will take if things go to plan. However, things quickly go wrong. As the plan unfolds, George's nemesis, the bully, Biff, contrives to be in the car in place of Marty.

All three of the plan dynamics listed above are in play. As George approaches the car the audience is asking the question: Will the plan work? Will they trick Lorraine into thinking George is a strong man? As the plan unfolds, the audience is aware that things are going wrong. That is, there is a gap between the characters' situation as the plan plays out and where they need it to be for the plan to succeed. By the end, there is a gap between the intended outcome of the plan and what happens. And throughout the plan, there is a gap between those participants who know of the plan and those who do not. Their plan, in itself, fails. However, in a peripeteia twist (discussed in depth shortly) Marty and George subsequently get the outcome they were planning for, *but not in the way we expected*. (I highlight this in italics because it will become a recurring theme we will discuss in depth in section 3.3. – Aristotle's Principles.)

Plans may also be in revelation. A plan is deployed of which the audience is not aware. The plan's presence and intent are kept hidden until after it has succeeded or failed. In *Murder on the Orient Express* (Agatha Christie, 1934). <SPOILER ALERT!> It is not until the climax that Hercule Poirot reveals that the apparently disconnected passengers on the train were all colluding in a grand plan. They were not travelling together by coincidence. All twelve of them had been done wrong by Edward Ratchett and had made a plan together to book out the entire train and murder him on board. Hence his twelve stab wounds — they all stabbed him once each to share the responsibility. Poirot, ultimately, uncovered their secret plan, and we in the audience, in revelation, find out about it too, sending us back through all the events we have experienced, but now in the context of this plan and the knowledge gaps it delivered.

One more. In *Pulp Fiction* (Tarantino, 1994), the gang boss Marsellus (Ving Rhames) pays the prize fighter Butch (Bruce Willis) to deliberately lose the upcoming fight in order that Marsellus can cash-in through gambling on the fixed fight. This is a plan in privilege presentation that we in the audience know about. Butch agrees to throw the fight and takes the payment. However, what we do not find out until later is that Butch has a plan of his own. On the day of the fight, unbeknown to Marsellus and his men, Butch's girlfriend, Fabienne (Maria de Medeiros) moves all his belongings out of their flat in preparation for escaping from Marsellus and skipping town. That night, Butch does not throw the fight — he wins, and in doing so he makes a lot of money... and a very angry enemy in Marsellus, who has not only paid Butch but also, through Butch's betrayal, has lost a lot of money on the gambling side. At this point we become aware that Butch is in the middle of a plan of his own, and we see him follow a pre-set escape route. He meets his girlfriend. They are now ready to make good their escape. For us in the audience, Butch's plan was initially in revelation but is now in privilege, and the advantage of this switch is that, having had the excitement in revelation of realising that Butch had a plan, we now become aware that Butch's plan is going wrong. His girlfriend left his gold watch back at the apartment. It is of great sentimental value to Butch so he risks all in a single return visit to the apartment to get it back. As Butch sets off for his final visit to the apartment, in privilege presentation, we in the audience are shown that Marsellus has a hit-man at the flat... lying in wait...

Notice a Tarantino pattern here. In the *Inglorious Basterds* example, LaPadite had a plan, the intended outcome of which (saving the Jews) was in direct conflict with the intended outcome of the plan the Colonel had (to find and kill the Jews). In *Pulp Fiction*, Butch had a plan, the intended outcome of which (winning the fight and taking Marsellus' money) was in direct conflict with the intended outcome of Marsellus' plan (to throw the fight and make himself a lot of money). Later, when Butch plans to make one final return to his apartment, the intended outcome (to grab the gold watch and get away) is in direct conflict with the intended outcome of the plan Vince has as he lies in wait at the apartment (to capture Butch and prevent his escape). Hopefully you can see that character plans are a major tool that brings significant power to Tarantino's work.

As writers, the use of character plans is a terrific mechanism for embedding knowledge gaps which frame a story or story event. By using privilege plans, we frame the story, but plans in revelation are a powerful method for re-framing and surprising your audience, and of course the use of both privilege and revelation, sometimes within the context of the same plan, can be a powerful tool of audience engagement.

Later we shall go into some depth on characters and in particular on the critical component of character motivation. Giving your characters plans is a simple way to give your story strong characters. To push ahead with a plan gives a character an agenda and clear motivation.

I recommend you take a look at a story event of your own. Look at the plans the characters have within that plot. Then look at the potential for the knowledge differences I have discussed here and maximise them. Introduce new ones. Look at privilege and revelation. Switch the dynamics around. You may well find yourself just a little bit amazed at the impact this simple technique can have on the quality of your story telling.

2.4.3 Knowledge gaps through key question

The key question dynamic is possibly the most common knowledge gap in all storytelling. Indeed, it is the basis for the fabled Hollywood Formula. For a long time, I tried to distance myself from the key question and diminish its importance in order to shun the ubiquitous formula, however I have grown to accept that although it is possible and reasonable to reduce the key question out of a prominent position in the telling of a story, it is rare that a story does not have one at all. The main difference between a story that majors on its key question and one that does not is the extent to which the key question is in privilege or revelation. For this reason, it is well worth your time in understanding what it is and how it works.

It is also important to distinguish between a key question and other questions, because the same dynamics exist in all the various types of question. The difference is that there is usually only one key question in a story and the knowledge gap that is opened remains open across the widest arcs of the main plot storyline, creating what is known as the major dramatic arc. Because of this, the key question often provides the most important framing. It does not have to be there — stories do exist without one — but it is the most common mechanism for orientating your audience.

In functional terms, the key question dynamic is a 'triplet' of story elements comprising, firstly, an **inciting incident**, secondly, the **key question itself** and thirdly, **the answer to the key question**. Generally, it works as follows: An event occurs, known as the inciting incident, which raises a question in the mind of the audience. The question is held open across the course of the telling before being answered through the events of the climax of the story.

For example, in *Back to the Future*:

> **Inciting incident:** Marty McFly is accidentally sent back in time to 1955. Events make it clear that he did not intend for

this to happen and that he does not want to stay there; his life has been thrown out of balance. This inciting incident raises a...

...key question in the mind of the audience: 'Will Marty get home to 1985?' And, given that the time machine is broken and the necessary fuel (plutonium) cannot be sourced in 1955: 'How will he do it?'

This key question is...

...answered at climax: Marty and Doc Brown make a plan to get him home by harnessing the power in a bolt of lightning to fire the time machine back to 1985. It works, so the key question is answered: Yes, Marty will get home to 1955. How? By harnessing the power in a bolt of lightning.

Every question raised is, of course, implicitly a knowledge gap between the question and the answer. This means that the key question sets the goals and motivation of the protagonist for the entire story. This orientates the audience to the direction of the story. The audience knows what the story is about from the moment the key question is raised until the point at which it is answered. Logically, this means that answering the key question is also the end of the story. Once the key question is answered, the audience is satisfied. We are done! It is time to get out of there!

The key question is: 'can Marty get back to 1985? And how will he do it?' Once Marty uses a bolt of lightning to power the time machine and he makes it safely back to 1985, the story is finished. There is generally a period of story **resolution** whereby we understand the lasting impacts of the actions taken by the protagonist, and we get a satisfying view of what the world looks like now the key question has been resolved, but then we get out. Any further exposition will serve generally to irritate the audience, who feel that the story is finished now the major gaps have been filled, and they are ready to leave. If you have a key question it is well worth remembering this. Closing the key question knowledge gap is closing the story.

It is worth noting that it is fairly common for people to mess this up. Production companies do it on purpose because they do not want the story to end. If we close the key question, there can be no sequel or season two, so the story is bent right out of shape to keep the key characters and arcs alive to facilitate more story. This often causes audience dissatisfaction, although we generally see through it and, in the spirit of the author/audience pact we shall discuss in the next section, we let it go. We know they want a sequel, so we see why they spoiled the perfect ending to *this* story. However, for the purposes of this book, I am talking about pure stories, so let us assume that all stories complete to absolute endings and that the aim is to achieve audience satisfaction.

Before we look at less clear key questions, here are some examples of key questions from classic stories in different media.

2.4.3.1 Breaking Bad

The inciting incident occurs when Walter White (Bryan Cranston), a high school chemistry teacher, is diagnosed with terminal cancer. He has a wife, a disabled son, a baby on the way, financial problems and a second job, so he worries about how his wife will cope after he is gone. He decides to use his chemistry skills to make and sell top quality methamphetamine in the hope of making enough easy money from drug dealing to provide for his family after he has gone. The key question is raised: will he make enough money from drugs to provide for his family after he is gone? This key question is addressed to satisfaction at the climax.

This is a fine key question and, whilst we are here, notice the implicit knowledge gaps. The key question is, of course, a knowledge gap (as is every question); one which remains open across the full course of more than 60 episodes. Note how Walter opens this gap by — guess what, making a plan — and he keeps his plan a secret. This means there is a second deep and persistent knowledge gap through this subterfuge; a difference in the knowledge held between those who know about the plan (us in the audience and Jesse Pinkman) and those who do not (Walter's wife and son are unaware of the plan — as is his brother-in-law who works for the drugs enforcement agency).

2.4.3.2 Citizen Kane

Citizen Kane (1941, directed by Orson Welles) is an enigmatic film because it is regarded as one of the greatest of all time, and yet most 'normal' people who watch it seem to struggle to see why it holds such status. It is an interesting case study for a knowledge gap theory of story.

One of the things it has is a very clear key question dynamic. The opening of *Citizen Kane* has Charles Kane (Orson Welles) utter his last word on his death bed: 'Rosebud'. He has lived his life as a major public figure so the media of the time are intrigued. The utterance is the inciting incident, and the key question is raised: why did this great and influential man say, 'Rosebud' on his death bed? What does it mean?

A journalist, Thompson (William Alland), sets off to investigate the significance of the word 'rosebud' to Charles Kane. The majority of the story then follows Thompson on his journey through a series of interviews with significant people from Kane's life. We get a clear understanding of the events that shaped him and we also get a clear idea that Charles Kane died an unhappy man. Despite all his money and power, Kane did not find fulfilment.

The final scene in *Citizen Kane* has Thompson admit to his fellow reporters that, despite his forensic examination of Kane's life, he has failed. The key question is answered: No, they could not establish the significance of the word, 'rosebud'. The reporters shrug their shoulders, give it up and go their separate ways. The focus shifts to workers at Kane's mansion, Xanadu, as they close down his life and sort through the objects Kane accumulated in his lifetime. A worker picks up a toboggan from Kane's childhood. It was all he had back then, before the family had money. Indeed, we saw him playing with it in the opening sequences of the film when he was a child. Raymond, the butler, labels it as junk, and directs the worker to throw it on the fire. The fire burns the paint off the sledge, revealing the name inscribed on the sledge: Rosebud.

Only we in the audience receive this information, thus answering the key question for us in the audience. Rosebud was his childhood sledge, but we are all over the significance of this. In the same way as we built a meaning for 'FOR SALE. BABY'S SHOES. NEVER WORN' we now build a meaning atop this single word, 'Rosebud'. We realise that, despite all his money and power, his childhood, symbolically represented by a beloved sledge, was the only time he felt happy and fulfilled. His power and money brought him only frustration, anger and sadness. He was happiest when he was poor, when he was with his parents and when life was simple before he had fame and fortune.

Part of the reason *Citizen Kane* is regarded as a classic is this rather unusual knowledge gap at the very end. We in the audience find out the significance of 'rosebud', and get the insight into Kane's personality and character that the journalists so craved and worked so hard to get, but never found out. A knowledge gap for which the audience deduces the answer but which will remain open forever for the characters in the story world... It also makes us think (i.e., the story storifies) about how the things we might aspire to in our lives (money, fame, power...) have the greatest potential to destroy our lives. The story has this hugely powerful storification and this is why *Citizen Kane* is genuinely a classic and wonderful story.

2.4.3.3 Romeo and Juliet

The inciting incident in Shakespeare's classic is when Romeo and Juliet meet and fall in love. However, they are from different sides of two warring families so although their passions run high, theirs is a love which cannot be. The key question is raised: will Romeo and Juliet be united in love? Through possibly the most famous dramatic act of all time, the key question is answered. No, they will both end up dead. Yet somehow there is the happy irony in death because we also feel they are now united in perfect love forever. Ultimately, the families could not keep them apart.

Note that with both *Citizen Kane* and *Romeo and Juliet* the realisation of the truth of events lies only with the audience. The protagonists never knew the truth. It is an extraordinary skill to shift some of the main story dynamics onto the audience in this way and it has great impact. We will look at this more in the section on Aristotle's *Anagnorisis* ('Realisation') in section 3.3. When I talk about the work a receiver does, these are great examples because, I feel sure you can see, they only truly complete in the mind of the audience.

Note also that both Romeo and Juliet make a plan. A further knowledge gap is introduced because each does not know the other's plan. The plans are perfectly designed to defeat each other and each of the lovers unwittingly takes the other to their tragic deaths.

2.4.3.4 *The Giggler Treatment*

For the novelists amongst you, the inciting incident in Roddy Doyle's children's book, *The Giggler Treatment,* comes at the end of Chapter 1 when we are told that the protagonist, Mr Mack, is four paces away from treading in a large dog poo on the pavement; a dog poo that has been placed there deliberately for him to tread in. The key question is raised – will he tread in the poo? Who put it there? Why would they do that? The rest of the entire book covers these four paces and the events causing, surrounding and leading up to the climax when this key question is answered. Wonderful.

This is a fine example of what we are after. It doesn't matter what the story is about but if you are sure you have an inciting incident, and manage to raise a clear key question in the mind of your reader or viewer, you definitively have the essence of a story. And no, I'm not going to tell you if he treads in the poo.

2.4.3.5 Tom and Jerry

The inciting incident occurs almost instantly: A mouse comes running frantically around the corner of a house. He is followed hot-foot by a cat wielding a frying pan. The key question is raised: will the cat catch the mouse? And we're off! We have all the knowledge we need to orientate ourselves to the story and we sit back to be entertained. The key question is answered at climax: No, the cat will not catch the mouse. The cat will end up with a head the shape of a frying pan and with a pan handle sticking out of his ear.

2.4.3.6 Oedipus Rex

In Greek mythology, the parents of a new born baby boy, *Oedipus*, are warned by an oracle that their son will grow up to murder his father and sleep with his mother. The oracle's message is the inciting incident. The key question is raised: will the prophesy come true? The key question is answered at climax. Despite the parents knowing of the prophesy and taking action to prevent it from ever coming to pass, the actions they take simply serve to fulfil the prophesy and yes, the prophesy does come true. Oedipus does end up killing his father and sleeping with his mother. *Oedipus Rex* is a wonderful, extraordinary story. A relentlessly tragic story, but a real beauty all the same! I recommend it.

2.4.3.7 Toy Story

In *Toy Story* (John Lasseter, 1995), the inciting incident is the moment that the new toy on the block, Buzz Lightyear, is discovered on the bed of Andy, the young boy who owns the toys. This occurs at around 13 minutes. The toys are surprised, because Buzz is in the place on the bed usually occupied by their current leader, Woody, who has always been Andy's favourite toy. Until now... The toys start chattering that Woody might have been replaced. They are then doubly surprised — and mightily impressed — to find that Buzz is apparently not a toy. He is a real live space ranger. He is packed with gadgetry and titanium wings. He is modern, digital and capable. Woody feels inadequate with his string-pull voice and lack of bells and whistles... and Andy loves his new toy. Woody is jealous and decides to take action to get rid of Buzz. The key question is raised: Will Woody get rid of Buzz and regain his status as Andy's favourite toy?

2.4.3.8 La Boheme

Opera and musicals fascinate me. How is it that a story delivered in song — even those sung in a language we do not understand — can bring people to tears more readily than any other medium? What is it about music that heightens our reception and triples our emotional responses?

The story is so difficult to ascertain, perhaps it is this that forces us to make more of our own interpretations of what we see and hear; fill in huge knowledge gaps, and build an idealised version of a perfect story for ourselves in our own mind?

Puccini's *La Boheme* has been working this magic since 1896. The story concerns the carefree but poor lives of a group of bohemians in Paris in the 1840s. One of them, Rodolfo, falls in love with a girl called Mimi. She is unwell, and desperately needs medical care which Rodolfo cannot afford. Rodolfo decides to leave Mimi so that she can accept the advances of another suitor who is rich and can help her. He will let another man into the life of the woman he loves to help her; an extraordinary act of devotion. At the same time, Mimi, realising she is going to die, decides to leave Rodolfo so he does not have to be put through watching her die. We in the audience know that they are both leaving each other for practical reasons, driven by adoration, and not for the reasons they give each other. The story key question is raised: Will they realise that they both want to be together, and they should be together to share their love in the limited time they have? The key question is answered at climax (if you can see through the tears).

At resolution, we in the audience are strongly storifying what we have experienced, and how it applies to us all in our time-limited lives.

2.4.3.9   The Big Sleep (Hawks, 1946)

This is a work that I will explore with you in some depth later because it storifies very powerfully despite the story not really making sense. An interesting case from a theoretical viewpoint.

However, it does have a clear key question. The inciting incident occurs when General Sternwood (Charles Waldron) commissions a private detective, Marlowe (Humphrey Bogart) to find out who is blackmailing him for money. The key question is raised: Can Marlowe solve the crime and save the Sternwoods from the blackmailers? The key question is answered at climax: Yes, he can.

2.4.3.10   Key question options

There is a sliding scale associated with the key question that is rather interesting. It is a scale of key question prominence. How obvious you choose to make it. This visibility can fundamentally change the type and perceived sophistication of your story. At one end of the scale, it is possible, as is the case in most of the examples above, to lay it out on a plate for your audience. Superhero stories are about as clear as it gets. A key question on a plate with neon lights and arrows pointing at it: Will the good guy superhero defeat the psychotic Dr. Evil bad guy and prevent him from taking over the country/world/universe?

There is nothing wrong with this much-loved basis for entertaining but relatively simple stories. However, there are alternatives. A key question can be dropped into the background and require writerly work from the audience before it comes to light. The Scorcese Oscar winner, *Hugo* (Scorsese, 2011) is a beauty for this. The story appears to be about a child's mission to fix a mechanical man his father was working on before his death. Hugo (Asa Butterfield) believes the automaton holds a secret his father either planted or was attempting to uncover. This mission is the one connection he still has with his father. The story retains our interest beautifully despite jumping between many threads: his life living behind the walls and clocks of a Paris railway station; His difficulties with his uncle — now his formal guardian; His need to escape the 'child catcher' in the station; His run-ins with shop-keepers from whom he steals in order to live; His burgeoning relationship with Isabelle (Chloë Grace Moretz); Their adventures together as they dig into film history; Hugo's capture by a shopkeeper (Ben Kingsley) who is not only Isabelle's father but also turns out to be George Méliès — the filmmaker — a man who is becoming personally lost through his own lack of confidence and recognition and whom Hugo and Isabelle revitalise as a person and as a legend of film-making.

Ultimately, once the story completes, we in the audience realise that, despite all the different threads to the story and the challenges Hugo faces, the puzzle with the automaton and the climactic action which seems to centre much more strongly around Méliès, Hugo's real underlying desire is simply to have a family and a sense of belonging. Ultimately — and to some extent in retrospect — we realise that the key question was this: Following the loss of his father, can Hugo find a family and a sense of belonging? However, this question is not given to us. We have to find it for ourselves as the true desires of the characters becomes evident through the telling. For many audience members, the full implications of the story will not arrive in mind until after they have left the cinema and thought about it. This is writerly work delivering subtext to ourselves after the event. This is beautiful story telling.

The film *Atonement* (Joe Wright, 2007), from the novel by Ian McEwan, is another example of how to create a more sophisticated construction through dropping the key question into revelation. It appears to be the story of a 13-year-old girl, Briony (Saoirse Ronan), who makes a false rape allegation against her sister Cecelia's (Keira Knightley) boyfriend, Robbie (James McAvoy). It is an accusation which is believed and which leads to Robbie being found guilty and imprisoned. The story then cuts to some five years later, during the war. Cecilia is working as a nurse in a London hospital and Robbie is away, a soldier at war. He has been allowed to leave prison on condition that he joins the army. At this point, the story appears to lose its way a little, because the key question is apparently answered. Briony did get away with the rape allegation, and despite the misery she caused, the story appears to be over. We continue, now primarily following Robbie off to war, but with a slightly unsatisfactory sense of story meander. (A factor which is very interesting from a story theory perspective. Once the key question has been answered, the story feels like it is over. It is not clear at this point what the story is about.)

Briony, now 18, goes to London to make peace with her sister. To her surprise she finds Robbie is there with Cecilia. He is on leave from the army, and he and Cecelia are together. Despite their reunion, they remain angry with Briony for the trouble she caused with her lies. Briony persists with her apology, but they refuse to accept her; obligating her to go to the authorities, confess her lies, and set the record straight for Robbie. Cecilia promises him a time when they will be at peace and in love, a romantic union at a cottage she knows by the sea.

We cut now to contemporary times. Briony is now 77-years-old and a successful author being interviewed about her new book, *Atonement*. She admits that although the book is largely autobiographical truth, the scene in which Briony apologises, and in which Cecilia and Robbie meet all those years later, and share romantic time together and in love, is fiction. Both Cecelia and Robbie died during the war. They never had time together. Their love never blossomed. Once Cecelia left home, Briony never saw her again. Briony, as an author, has rewritten history. Unable to fix things in her life, she tried to bring all of them together in fiction, in love and in forgiveness (for herself); to give them all what they never found in life. The key question was always there, but it was unknown to us in the audience for 90% of the story. Can Briony as a fiction writer in adulthood atone for her behaviour as a child? Once we in the audience get this key question, so late in the story, we re-visit everything we have seen in the light of what is now known, and we reflect on what Briony's guilt-filled life must have been like. The story ends with Cecelia and Robbie playing around on a beach, then disappearing into an idyllic seaside cottage together to consummate their love. An event Briony reported in her book and longed for in her head, but which never actually happened.

Other stories render the key question close to impenetrable within the text. The film *Pulp Fiction* (Quentin Tarantino, 1994) delivers seven narrative threads, chronologically out of order, that intersect into essentially three storylines. There is apparently no key question, however, in retrospect, if one digs deeply enough, a spine can be found that links these narrative threads and a key question can be divined. The central story is the one we discussed earlier. It involves the gang boss Marsellus bribing a boxer, Butch to take a dive in his next fight in order that Marsellus can cash in through fixed betting. Butch decides to double-cross him, cash in on the illegal gambling himself and make good his escape. The key question is: Will Butch successfully trick Marsellus and get away with the money? This is the key question, however, the way the story is delivered means we only glimpse this core tangentially as we receive the satellite stories that orbit around it. The key question is almost impossible to pick out and is certainly not recognisable on first viewing.

Beyond this, at the furthest end of the scale, there are many stories without a key question at all. These tend to be stories that focus on the character journey towards some life lesson rather than the 'action' that goes around it. So, for example, the film *Almost Famous* (Cameron Crowe, 2000) follows the coming-of-age story of William, a teenager who gets commissioned by *Rolling Stone* magazine to tour with and write about a rock band in the 1970s. The magazine editor does not realise William is only 15. William accepts the commission, runs away from home and the story follows his boy-to-a-man journey on tour with the rock band and their groupies. The story has no key question, but does have the all-important storification gaps which, I argue, characterise all great stories, whether they have a key question or not. Similarly, other biographical stories, such as *Bohemian Rhapsody* (director, Brian Singer, 2018) or *Rocketman* (Dexter Fletcher, 2019) do not have a key question as such.

Never out of print since 1843, the classic novel *A Christmas Carol* (Charles Dickens) is a great story, but it has no key question. It has an inciting incident, when the ghost of Ebenezer Scrooge's ex-business partner, Jacob Marley, visits him, but no key question is raised beyond 'what will happen next?' (which should always be the case, so does not serve as a key question). However, we are primed by the ghost to expect three spirits to visit Scrooge. The foreshadowing of these future scenarios keeps us gripped, and in the end it is Scrooge's character growth that satisfies us at resolution. Scrooge journeys from a greedy, bullying, selfish man to a generous, society-appropriate, warm-hearted person, fulfilled by his own generosity. Once again, it is the presence of this storification that grips us, not any driving need for a key question. The story is powered by Scrooge's personal journey and his learning of life lessons. Indeed, the resolution to the story does not involve ghosties at all; that's all done with by that point – the climax and resolution are all about Scrooge's personal growth.

The principal knowledge gap in *Groundhog Day* (Harold Ramis, 1993) is huge and fascinating. Weatherman Phil (Bill Murray) is having the worst day of his life — and is reliving that same day over and over again. We in the audience know that he is stuck in some sort of time loop, but the people he meets do not, so they behave in exactly the same way every day. There is a gap in knowledge between what we, the audience, know (along with Phil) and what the other characters in the story know. This is a fine example of a deep, persistent, continuous knowledge gap, but there is no 'question' arising from it. Again, we can project forwards to future sequences — we know he is going to relive the same day again and again, and we are interested to know how he is going to handle the same day multiple times. There is no key question and we do not know where the story is heading.

With all stories, irrespective of their key question dynamic, it is the **storification** that defines the ultimate power in the story. In the case of *Groundhog Day*, that is the personal journey of learning and growth that Phil goes through. Once Phil realises he is going to be reliving the same day time and time again, he sees selfish opportunities to take advantage of the predictability of the people around him. He uses his fore-knowledge of daily events to steal money, gain gratuitous sex, even commit murder; and yet despite these opportunities he becomes less and less happy with his lot. His character and the story move forwards when he changes his approach to society. He gives up the hollow dissatisfaction he gets from self-centredness and experiences personal growth and learning when he changes to altruistic, society-benefiting behaviours. He becomes a finer person, using his fore-knowledge of the day's events to save lives, learn piano, indulge romance, help the elderly and so on. Once he becomes a genuinely good person, the spell is broken, society gives him his rewards and he is free to move on with a happy life.

Many writers become something of a slave to the key question dynamic principally because it is such a defining component of the Hollywood formula (which we shall come to shortly). However, it is often the stories with a less clear key question that have the most sophistication and win all the Oscars. To add the most recent winner, the film *Parasite* (Bong Joon Ho, 2019) does not have a key question.

When there is a key question, it tends to relate to the *action* of the story, rather than to the real power of the story, which is a character journey leading to storification. This is why looking at knowledge gaps is so important in elevating an event into a compelling story. The key question is part of the framing, not so much a part of the emotional power.

What do I mean by that? Well, think about *Back to the Future*. If you ask people what the story is about, they will most likely tell you all about the key question dynamics. They will tell you it is a story about a kid who goes back in time and his battle to get back home again. The inciting incident is his accidental time-travel back to 1955; the key question is raised: Will he get back to 1985 again? How will he do it? And this question is answered at climax. For most, that is what *Back to the Future* is about and it is true that this provides for a highly effective 'major dramatic arc' across the course of the story. And yes, it is powerful in that it is a knowledge gap and it remains open for the majority of the story. However, the real power in the story is concerned with George McFly's character growth journey. The storification dynamic in George's transition is the most important dynamic in the story. Everything else is there to serve and support this storification.

The key question dynamic provides the framing that pressures the characters into the situation in which they take their actions. The storification dynamics *emerge from* the characters' decisions and it is the outcome of these decisions that deliver the emotional power that affects the receiver through storification. The key question is about *what* happens. It is a framing which gives context for the character agenda and actions. The decisions the characters are forced to make under pressure as a result shifted them through into storification. The key question rarely defines the true power of a story; it defines the framing.

In *Three Billboards Outside Ebbing, Missouri* (directed by Martin McDonagh, 2017), the framing through key question dynamic is through Mildred (Frances McDormand) putting up three massive billboards outside Ebbing, using them to criticise the police (and the police chief personally). Mildred's daughter was raped and murdered and she feels the police have not done enough to find her daughter's killer and bring the criminal to justice. So she rents the billboards to publicly expose the police for their negligence. This action provides the context that pressures all the characters into the same moral argument in which the character agendas, interactions, decisions and the outcomes they harvest can deliver the storification power of the story.

In *The Shawshank Redemption* (Director Frank Darabont, 1995) the framing through key question dynamic is the action in which Andy Dufresne (Tim Robbins) is caught and imprisoned for a murder he did not commit. This provides the key question (can Andy get justice and freedom?) a framing and context that pressures all the characters into the same moral argument in which the character agendas, interactions, decisions and the outcomes they harvest can deliver the storification power of the story.

In basically any James Bond film, (indeed, most hero or superhero stories) the framing through the key question dynamic is the action in which a power-mad bad guy sets a plan into action to take over the city/world/planet/universe. This provides the context that pressures all the characters into the same moral argument in which the character agendas, interactions, decisions and the outcomes they harvest can deliver the storification power of the story.

Top tip...
This is important, because when you are stretching your brain over a story idea and sweating and struggling to make it work for you, the chances are you are over-fretting on the key question; the action and plot dynamics. You are turning circles, driving yourself crazy asking yourself: 'What can happen now? What happens? What is this story *about*?!' You need to adjust your thinking towards the characters and the choices they make. Focus your thoughts where they will bear finer fruit: putting the characters under pressure to make decisions; the learning the characters may make through their choices; the learning the audience might make through the

outcomes; and, of course, the differences in the knowledge held by various participants as the characters make their choices and drive their agenda. You are fretting over the framing (what happens) when the power of your story will be in the characters choices (how it happens) and the outcomes the character choices reap (causing the story to storify). Find the storification and work back from there to find a framing through which you can pressure your characters so the consequences of their action generate that storification.

This is probably a little sketchy at present, because we have yet to discuss storification, but hopefully you are getting a glimpse of some interesting concepts. I will revisit this and make things a lot clearer as we embrace storification later. The point for now is that the key question is an important component of almost every story. You can choose to make your story clear and obvious or more subtle and sophisticated by putting your key question more in privilege or more in revelation, or by not having one at all.

2.4.4 Knowledge gaps through promise

Remember, a story exists only in mind and is a communication between a human mind and another human mind. The medium used is simply a mechanism — a conduit — for communicating the narration. A story is a knowledge exchange (story) wrapped inside an information exchange (narration).

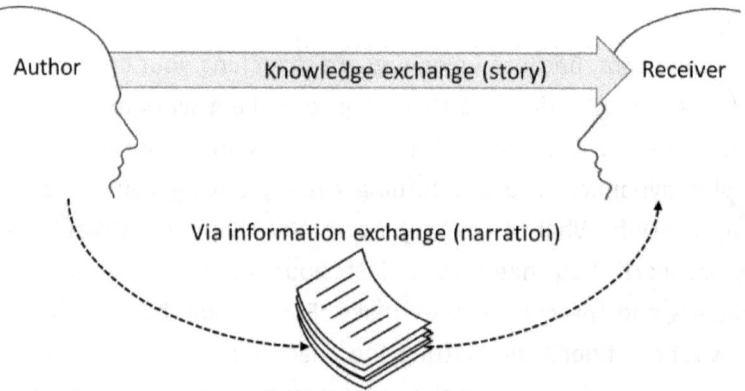

Figure 7: A story is a communication between people

This is important, because both parties are aware of the interaction that is occurring and enter into a 'pact' that sets the rules for the exchange. A receiver of story is looking to receive the knowledge that the author is ultimately going to deliver. However, the process is knowingly fighting against simply telling the 'truth'. A story is made of subterfuge, deliberate delay, distraction, red herrings, misdirection and all the other tools of the storyteller's trade introduced deliberately as part of the entertainment. What is included in the narration will be a puzzle that will lead the receiver on a merry dance — a dance that the audience demands and hopes for — that will exercise the receiver's skills at compiling and re-compiling narrative logic but will, ultimately, make sense and be worth the receiver's time, even if the value is not readily apparent moment by moment. A story is enigmatic and must be indulged before it reveals its secrets.

Solving the story puzzle is a satisfying exercise for a human mind. At its best, receiving and figuring out a story is preparation for dealing with the world. Like a kitten plays with a ball of wool in preparation for hunting, a human grows up figuring out narrative logic in stories to help them understand and thrive in our peculiarly advanced society.

This pact between author and audience is especially beneficial to writers in the early stages of a story unfolding. The receiver knows that you are building the story, so they give you a break. If you put a banana skin on the floor next to a character's desk the audience is all over it. This is relevant. You've opened a knowledge gap, and because of that, intrigue is alive and present in the receiver's mind. Your audience does not think, 'What on Earth?! This is rubbish! What kind of stupid story shows me a banana skin next to a desk?'

    They think: 'Ooooo! I wonder why that's there? Who is going to slip up at a critical moment?!'

This dynamic is called a **knowledge gap through promise**. The disconnected object, character or event is banked for later. The receiver holds on to it and will expend mental energy attempting to fit it into the causal logic of the story (close the knowledge gap) and they feel a surprisingly powerful sense of positivity and achievement when they do. So use this. Every character, every item, every object and every event is there for a reason and carries a knowledge gap within that inherent promise. Do not give facts, give holes. And let the intrigue pile up as the receiver tries to fill the gap with accurate knowledge.

Mise-en-scène
The term mise-en-scène comes originally from theatre. This is the term for everything that appears on the stage — props, actors, costumes, lighting — and its arrangement. The literal translation being 'placed into the scene'. An audience knows that to put up props and include characters and to have them do specific things is costly. Producers would not include anything in the mise-en-scène that was not relevant. Why spend the money on something pointless? Everything is assumed to have relevance, otherwise, why is it there? (Indeed, when you do get a film deal, the producers will ask you precisely that… Then they will ask you to do it more cheaply, but perhaps this is a conversation for another time.)

The question will be asked: Why pay to include something in the mise-en-scène if it has no reason to be there? For example, in *Back to the Future*, the opening sequence delivers an enormous amount of 'promise' as they show us around the mise-en-scène. It opens with the sound of ticking. Then the first visual: Clocks. Lots and lots of different types of clocks, all set to 7.53. Then some pictures on the wall and an unmade, unoccupied bed. Some of the clocks are part of mechanisms — a clock radio, a coffee maker, a toaster, a dog-feeder — some of which trigger… and fail, because nobody has been there to set them all up properly. Whose house is this? Where are the occupants? Why so many clocks? We know there must surely be significance in all this. The subjective pact between the author and the audience means it surely is relevant, otherwise why show us these things? A television turns on and the camera focuses on a newsreader. She explains how some plutonium has been stolen from a research laboratory. Why are we being given this focus? A moment or two later, we are shown a case of plutonium tucked under a bench. This repetition piques our interest. The plutonium is significant. We do not know why, but we do know we must carry it forwards into the plot. We trust that the authors are giving us this information for a reason and we rise to the challenge of integrating this into the narrative puzzle as soon as we can find logical patterns to lock it into.

These are knowledge gaps through promise. As story creators, we can use the enormous opportunity provided by a knowledge gap through promise in every character, object or event, but do not abuse this trust; ensure everything has a reason and a relevance (even if that reason is to misdirect your audience). Just hide that relevance for a while. It creates a knowledge gap and it works. Do not rush to explain everything. Your audience likes the potential and loves to be teased with the prospect of discovery and building the story puzzle for themselves.

2.4.5 Knowledge gaps through subplot

A subplot is a mini-story, nested into a wider plot. Although a subplot is likely to be interconnected with the main plot, it will also have its own internal logic and should stand alone as a story in its own right. As a writer, it is often worthwhile analysing and understanding your subplot story dynamics independently of the wider plot in which it is embedded. However, the point of this as an independent type of knowledge gap is that a subplot can generate powerful gaps through its relationship with the storyline of the main plot.

The main plot outcome is usually dependent upon the events and/or the outcome of the subplot. It is this interrelationship that generates knowledge gaps. Once two plotlines are active, what we understand in the subplot makes us think about the impact it may have in the main plot, and vice versa. When both plots are running we get very busy in the work we do in speculating, projecting scenarios, angsting about impact and so on. The gap between the projections made due to events in one plotline and the outcomes in a related plotline is a knowledge gap through subplot.

In *Back to the Future,* when Marty interferes with the meeting between his parents in 1955, the audience realises that there is no point in him achieving his overarching story aim (to time-travel his way back home to 1985) because if his parents did not meet in 1955 then even if he does make it back to 1985 he will not exist when he gets there. Hence, there are now two plotlines:

a) The main plot storyline, with the key question: 'can Marty successfully get home to 1985?'

b) The subplot storyline, with the key question: 'can Marty re-unite his parents in love so that he will exist in the future?'

The two plotlines are inter-dependent. As Marty sets about contriving his parents' meeting, the audience are interpreting events in this subplot storyline with half an eye on the implications for the main plot storyline. Similarly, progress in the main plot storyline is interpreted in the context of its impact on the subplot storyline. For example, the knowledge that the bolt of lightning which will power his journey back to 1985 in the main plot line is at a fixed point in time on the Saturday night drives a level of urgency into events in the subplot in which Marty is failing to reunite his parents in love. As the clock ticks down, every subplot event is overshadowed by the time pressure imposed from the main plot which has fatal implications for Marty.

Similarly, as and when Marty makes it back to 1985 in the main plot storyline, his fortunes are inextricably linked to progress in the subplot. For example, Marty's actions in the romantic fortunes of his parents in the subplot in 1955 have an unexpected and profound effect on his life as it is eventually revealed to be when he gets back to 1985 because the manner in which George finally does hook up romantically with Lorraine renders him as a strong, assertive man, rather than the weak and unassertive man who characterised the first version of 1985. In the intervening 30 years this new, strong George lived his life more assertively, so the 1985 to which Marty arrives home is dramatically higher quality than the one he left because George was forced to face his daemons and confront Biff when they were 17 years old, leading to a difference in the way George conducted his life the second time around.

Subplots of this nature provide dimension to the story and add beautiful complexity. They are also generally highly impactful gaps because they tend to run deep and remain open for a long time. Quite often when I am consulting on a full-length story that is struggling to retain interest across 100,000 words or 2 hours of movie, the problem is essentially that there is no subplot and the writer is struggling to get enough meat from a single plot story of that duration.

Game of Thrones (created by David Benioff, D.B. Weiss) is possibly the finest example of how to generate sophisticated story through the deployment of literally dozens of subplots. The main plot storyline is based on a good old classical key question: Who will win the Iron Throne and control the whole of Westeros? We then follow the intertwined and yet separate subplots of the nine noble families — the Starks, Arryn, Lannisters, Baratheons, Tullys, the Iron-born, Tyrells, Martells and Targaryens.

Within these threads are the additional subplots concerning individuals and other groups, such as the Wildlings, the Nights Watch, Arya Stark (Maisie Williams), Bran Stark (Isaac Hempstead-Wright), the religious thread through The High Sparrow (Jonathan Pryce) and the precarious individual paths of Lord Baelish (Aidan Gillen), Sandor "the Hound" Clegane (Rory McCann), Jorah Mormont (Iain Glen), Sam Tarly (John Bradley), Tyrion Lannister (Peter Dinklage) and so on. It is quite remarkable — and a lesson for us all

— how pretty much every character in the huge list of characters has a meaningful arc.

The lack of a single protagonist and the presence of so many separate subplots through which any of the characters may rise or fall is one of the major differentiators of *Game of Thrones*. Nobody is safe and we in the audience have no idea who may be dead by the end of the next episode.

A major writers' tip in *Game of Thrones* is that each subplot is begun and taken to the point of hooking us in; by which I mean, a character is taken to a point of serious jeopardy with grave doubts for us over the likely outcome. Then, at this point when we are thoroughly engaged, the writers leave us hanging there and take us off to begin (or re-join) another character journey somewhere else. They take that one to a point of precarious engagement… and begin another one with other characters somewhere else. Then another. Then return to the first one and move it forwards a few steps. Then to subplot 3 and move that one a little. Then 2. Then 4. Then 6 and so on. We become enthralled because we are trying to retain so many incomplete narratives; that is, there are so many gaps continuously open across so many separate subplot storylines, we are engaged forever!

Genius. And a simple example of the powerful grip asserted by an open knowledge gap. As human beings, we cannot stand to feel unsafe. George R.R. Martin, who wrote the books for *Game of Thrones* gave this advice for gripping an audience: Make them unsafe. Keep them unsafe. In my terms, this means introduce knowledge gaps and keep the knowledge gaps open.

In my experience, aspiring writers often look to make themselves feel comfortable, whereas the best writers take an almost sadistic pleasure in the awful things they do to their characters. Writers often write because it helps them; it is therapeutic. However, this often means they are writing about themselves; they are writing for self-help; they are writing to find resolution, so they undermine their bad guys and stamp them to death as quickly as possible with their good guys. This is counter to the best way to write compelling stories. If you can unnerve yourself, there's a good chance you will engage your audience.

As I say on Twitter: 'Writers are peace-loving pacifists. Until you give them a pen, at which point the good ones turn into ruinous bastards.' [v]

Think about this. Can you do it? Are you undermining your bad guys? Can you unsettle *yourself*? Could you write something that would shock your own family to the point that they would be seriously worried about you?! For many writers I work with, the dark side of what they do is their biggest problem — it simply isn't dark enough. Remember, your good guys can only be as heroic as the dark side demands of them. Underpowering your bad side is to undermine your whole story. More on this shortly, in section 2.4.10 — Meaningful Conflict.

2.4.6 Knowledge gaps through narrator

Every story is narrated, and every story delivery (narration) therefore has a narrator. There have been grand studies done into what are known as 'narrational modes'. I do not intend to go deeply into this topic because, from the perspective of a story creator, the only important point is that a narrator is another participant. A narrator can hold or withhold knowledge and therefore can be used to form a knowledge gap.

The narrator may effectively be the author. If you think about it, a narration begins as one enormous knowledge gap in which the author knows absolutely everything and the receiver knows nothing. The author then begins to trickle out information to the receiver, who starts to build a story in their own mind.

In between the author and the receiver, there may be a narrator who may or may not be identified and who may or may not be reliable in the accuracy of the information they deliver.

They could simply be a 'voice'; unidentified and 'uninterested', in the sense that they have no part to play in the story world, as is common in classic French films such as *Amélie* (Jean-Pierre Jeunet, 2001) or *Jules et Jim* (François Truffaut, 1962), or in more Hollywood terms, *Casablanca* (Michael Curtiz, 1942) or *The Royal Tanenbaums* (Wes Anderson, 2001). The narrator reports authoritatively but is unidentified and is not a character in the story world. More commonly, the narrator is personalised to the audience as one of the characters. For example, *Betty Blue* (Jean-Jacques Beineix, 1986) or, for a more recent example from television, the narrator in the Netflix series *You* is the lead character, Joe Goldberg (Penn Badgley), who talks us through his thinking as he sets about his obsessive and murderous life choices.

The Christmas story, *Elf* (2003, director Jon Favreau) begins with a book, which opens on a picture of an Elf. The voice of the elf is heard, and then comes to life, talking to us directly, telling us interesting facts about life as an elf, and introducing the story. Our narrator is Papa Elf (James Caan) who will regularly step out of his story world to provide a narrational perspective to us throughout the story. When the narrational mode acknowledges the presence of an audience this is known as a self-conscious narrator. You may also have heard it referred to as 'breaking the fourth wall'. This expression comes from the way a stage is set so a room in a house, for example, has a wall missing so the audience can see inside. If a character turns and speaks to the audience directly, acknowledging that the audience exists, they have broken the pretence that there is a wall there. A very fine example of this is the excellent comedy series *Fleabag* (2016, written by and starring Phoebe Waller-Bridge) in which the eponymous lead character not only breaks the fourth wall but does so during conversations between characters and even during sex. It works wonderfully.

In the Willy Russell play *Blood Brothers*, a character steps out of their story world and speaks directly to the audience whenever necessary. Willy Russell told me that he wrote it like this because they had to keep the costs down and he was allowed a maximum of seven players. The use of the narrator in this way becomes a humorous component as the audience gradually realises that the same actor is playing multiple secondary roles in the story but is always the narrator. (My conversation with Willy Russell can be found in *The Story Book*.)

Citizen Kane (Orson Welles, 1941) has no fewer than six narrational positions in addition to that of the author. One is an unidentified voice, the others are characters, who, mostly through being interviewed, narrate flashback sequences providing insight into Kane's life.

One final example, then, which demonstrates the key point: A narrator must hold or withhold knowledge to be an effective tool for the story. The narrator in *The Usual Suspects* (Bryan Singer, 1995) withholds key information and plays a critical role in the story. Initially, we understand the narrator to be Verbal Kint (Kevin Spacey) a criminal gang member who has been caught. He is at the low-end in the gang hierarchy, meek and disabled, but may have critical information for the police investigation. Verbal's narration is delivered in the form of evidence to the police interrogator as they pump him for information regarding their real target, the master criminal, Keyser Soze. Through the course of the interrogation, the story is delivered in flashbacks that illuminate Verbal's version of events.

However, the twist in the final moments of the story is that the narrator is not who we believed him to be. The meek and annoying Verbal *is* the feared and elusive master-criminal Keyser Soze, who has therefore been our narrator throughout, sat right in front of the police officer searching for him. This revelation causes us to reel back through everything, now understanding it as a fabrication designed not only to facilitate his (Verbal/Keyser's) escape but to toy with and humiliate the police as he does. As Verbal/Keyser walks from the police station his meekness and disability disappear from his persona. The narrator has lied to the police interrogator (and therefore to us) the entire way through the story. This is a prime example of the narrator providing the largest, widest, deepest — and most satisfying — knowledge gaps in a story. This is also an example of an 'unreliable' narrator. He is talking to us — delivering an internal monologue throughout — but is not telling us the truth.

One of the more common questions in story is 'Why are novels so much better than the film of the book?'
Good question, and the answer is in the narrational mode.

Novels are different because they can take us into the head of a character and deliver a mindset and motivation straight from the characters thoughts and feelings. However, in films, we mostly get to look on at characters from the outside, just like we do in the real world, and can only guess what they are thinking and can only judge them on their actions. A narrator, particularly if they are one of the characters, can give us insights into their thoughts and feelings in ways a camera cannot.

This is a hugely valuable tool in the film story box. Getting into a character's head and truly understanding them is one of the most difficult things to do and one of the most valuable things that happens by default in a book. A narrator facilitates this in a visual medium. In *Memento* (Christopher Nolan, 2000), the protagonist Leonard (Guy Pearce) is an example of a personalised narrator who, through his internal monologue, is delivering us his truth throughout the story. A 'reliable' narrator, getting the psychology of a character across.

It is rumoured that the film *Apocolypse Now* (Francis Ford Coppola, 1979) had the narrator added afterwards as the story was struggling to make sense without one. This turned out to be a masterstroke, providing insight into Martin Sheen's troubled character and adding enormously to the story's power and appeal.

As you get deeply into your own story it is well worth sitting back and having a think about what a narrator might do for you and your story. It can be a surprisingly powerful tool in the armoury. A specifically useful application is with backstory. If you have a good deal of essential information to deliver and cannot find a slick dramatic way to do it, the quickest way is to put up a narrator and simply have them tell us. It is not ideal (as we shall discuss in section 2.4.9 – Knowledge Gaps through Backstory) but it is a fine way to deliver a huge quantity of information quickly.

It is also worth noting — and you can quote me on this to anyone who tries to tell you otherwise — that using a narrator is a perfectly valid and acceptable story mechanism. I have no idea why some people look down on the use of a narrator as some sort of unacceptable and lowly form of storytelling. I disagree. It is a fine and powerful tool and a perfectly valid option for you. If it works for you and you think it is fine, then it is fine. It worked just fine for *A Clockwork Orange* (Stanley Kubrick, 1971); and *American Psycho* (Mary Harron, 2000); *Annie Hall* (Woody Allen, 1977); *Double Indemnity* (Billy Wilder, 1944); *Taxi Driver* (Martin Scorsese, 1976); *Fight Club* (David Fincher, 1999); *The Shawshank Redemption* (Frank Darabont, 1994); *American Beauty* (Sam Mendez, 1999); *Goodfellas* (Martin Scorsese, 1990); and *Sunset Boulevard* (Billy Wilder, 1950). Use it if you wish.

And the same goes for flashbacks. Using flashbacks is powerful and excellent. Imagine trying to tell the story of PJ Travers relationship with Walt Disney regarding his attempts to get her to approve his film version of her book, *Mary Poppins,* without the flashback sequences. The resultant film, *Saving Mr Banks* ((Dir. John Lee Hancock, 2013) is a masterpiece *because* of the flashbacks. The story simply would not carry that wonderful, dimensional power without them. The series, *Patrick Melrose* (played by Benedict Cumberpatch) spends more than half the time across the whole series in flashback. Imagine what Patrick would be, as a character, if we did not have the flashbacks to his childhood to give him depth and to create empathy. He would be more like a slapstick Mr Bean type character than a deeply troubled, empathic soul for whom the flashbacks *cause* the story. You are the master of your story universe, so if you think it is right, then it is right. If it works for you then go for it and damn them all!

I cannot resist offering you one more. For a good laugh, look up *The Gunfighter* (2014, Directed by Eric Kissack). The old Wild West movies also had a tradition of unidentified omnipotent narrators, and this wonderful short film has a lot of fun with that. It is under ten minutes and at the time of writing is freely available on Youtube.

2.4.7 Knowledge gaps through the story world

One of the most powerful and wonderful things a writer can do for a receiver is to take them to another world and show them something they are unlikely to find in their own lives. By doing so, vividly and with compelling detail, they are filling a knowledge gap for that person concerning what that world is like and giving them a new experience that feels surprisingly real (remember, stories that fill gaps can create actual memories). It can be a fictional world or it can be a part of the real world, either way the visit there is an experience for the receiver that feels as powerfully real as a genuine memory.

For example, many people in the western world opened a book, became enthralled and are now able to close their eyes and recall the time they went to Hogwarts School of Witchcraft and Wizardry. We have all been there. We can hang out there in our memories, live and breathe and move around and feel what it is like in just as much detail as any holiday we ever had. We all know how to get there, we know what it looks like and what it would be like to be a pupil. How amazing is that?! JK Rowling took us to a place and made it come to life. She gave us knowledge and experience of that place. I can imagine my time at Hogwarts more readily and more vividly than I can remember the real school I actually attended! This is serious story power and you should not undervalue just how compelling and important the story world you create is to your chances of making stories that grip. This is one of the biggest factors in the grip of Harry Potter; that and the deep and persistent gap between those of us who are muggles and those of us who move among us but secretly are not. If you see what I mean. (Nearly gave myself away there...) This is a wonderful, perfect persistent knowledge gap which jumps out of the story world and becomes active for us in the real world.

Your fictional world can be more closely aligned to the real world but still take us somewhere we would not normally go. *Breaking Bad* takes us to the underworld of drug dealers, big money, murder, dangerous, unstable people and makes it all very real for us. I believe one of the many reasons *Breaking Bad* is so popular is that it was filmed in Albuquerque. We see Los Angeles or New York so often, we unconsciously drop into 'fiction mode' the moment we see those familiar streets. However, by shooting it in New Mexico, we found ourselves experiencing somewhere new and bought into it more readily as a result. *Breaking Bad* felt more like documentary truth because it was an unfamiliar story world.

The story of *Saving Private Ryan* (Dir. Steven Spielberg, 1998) brings us the reality of war as we go behind enemy lines in France during World War II through the eyes of Captain Miller (Tom Hanks). A similar brutal reality is brought to life for us in 1917 (Sam Mendes, 2019) which takes us to the trenches of World War I; *Black Hawk Down* (Dir. Ridley Scott; 2001) which takes us on a dangerous mission with a small group of soldiers in Somalia and makes us feel what it is like to be vulnerable, trapped and exposed in hostile territory when a mission goes wrong. An amazingly powerful film, largely because of the story world to which we are transported and the vulnerable situation in which we would hate to be placed. *Homeless Ashes* (Marc Zammit, 2019) takes us into the world of a homeless man on the streets of London. A vivid exposure to a life most of us see on our streets every day and yet avoid. The story shows us how, in a couple of moments of bad luck or twists of fate, any one of us could end up there.

Back to the Future shows us what it was like to be a teenager in a beautiful (if idealised) version of 1955. *Tron* (Joseph Kosinski, 2010), *Wreck-it Ralph* (Rich Moore, 2012), *Ready Player One* (Steven Spielberg, 2018) take us inside computer games. *Star Wars (George Lucas, 1977)*, *Avatar* (James Cameron, 2009) and *Star Trek* (J.J. Abrams, 2009) take us to other parts of the cosmos. *The Shawshank Redemption* (Frank Darabont, 1994) leaves us to rot in a prison. *The Martian* (Ridley Scott, 2015) abandons us to die on Mars. *Game of Thrones* (David Benioff, D.B. Weiss, 2011-2019) gives us a flavour of the brutal reality of medieval politics when one bad choice could mean death. Soap operas take us into other people's lives. It is still compelling, and it is still a story world, because it takes us to a new place and gives us experience of relationships.

Of course, a story (including many of the examples above) does not necessarily bring us the *truth* of a world. Stories are escapism and stories are not 'truth'. We will look more deeply at the relationship between truth and stories shortly, but for now, suffice to say, trying to keep to 'the truth' is rarely useful to a writer, even if you strongly desire to deliver with integrity. In the same way that we can learn some human 'truth' about life and how it should be led from the actions of a girl in a red riding hood interacting with a cross-dressing wolf, so the world to which we take our audience is bound to be metaphoric. It doesn't matter if you take your audience to genuine events from the real world or a clearly made-up sci-fi world, neither is real; they are both representations. The only meaning we gain is from the actions and behaviours of the characters and the outcomes they yield, so free yourself from the truth. Do not be a slave to it. This is why stories are often 'based on' a true story rather than being an actual 'true story'. It's a better story that allows your imagination and skill as a writer to express itself, and the story world is a huge part of that.

Transport your audience to a place of terror, humour, beauty, adventure, love and hate, hope and fear — and make it vivid. A story world is a deep and pervasive knowledge gap. Get this right, and you have your audience feeling emotional not just through the character journey that happens there, but through that slightly unsettling sense we get by going somewhere — anywhere — that is not familiar to us.

2.4.8 Knowledge gaps through backstory

Backstory is tricky. We do not want the story to tread water whilst we drone on and on about some apparently irrelevant stuff that the audience will need to know later when the story gets interesting. However, if that information is necessary we do need to find a way to get it across. The good news is that backstory is all knowledge going into gaps, so it can be designed in intriguing ways. A little thought about how to deliver backstory can make a huge difference. The best answer is to look at the material you wish to deliver and turn it into meat. Use it as source material for dramatic sequences.

Back to the Future had a very large problem here. If you think about it, that first 30 minutes or so — almost a third of the story — is backstory that is necessary to make the main body of the story in 1955 magical and compelling. Gale and Zemeckis used a number of techniques. Firstly, they made that first 30 minutes a story in itself. In that way, even though it was largely backstory, it functioned more like an episode that is left on a cliff-hanger. Act I is a whole story about a teenager called Marty getting involved in a crazy inventor's time travel experiment. At the same time, when Lorraine tells her family in 1985 the whole necessary backstory concerning how she met their father in 1955, she tells them (and us) a story. A story which just happens to be made out of backstory and packed with historical information that is relevant to the later events. The fact that Marty and his family sit around a table talking about the past and planting huge quantities of backstory for several whole minutes is not boring old exposition because it is a story in itself. It is also character development and also relies greatly on lots and lots of knowledge gaps through promise — section 2.4.4.

The second major way to deliver backstory is in flashback. This may become rather confusing to discuss in the context of *Back to the Future*, so let's use a different example. In *Pulp Fiction*, the boxer Butch appears to have made good his escape from the brutal gang boss Marsellus. He and his girlfriend Fabienne (Maria de Medeiros) should shortly be rich and living the high life in Tennessee. But when he discovers that Fabienne has left his gold watch at the apartment, he gets highly emotional and decides to go back to get it. We in the audience are begging him not to do it. It's just a watch. Going to get it is a massive risk and given that they are happy, free, rich, in love and making good their escape — it's simply not worth it. Leave the stupid watch! Buy another one with your new-found wealth! Go live your life! But he goes back... And we are tearing our hair out. Why would he DO that?!

To answer this question (that is, to deliver Butch's motivation and backstory) Tarantino makes an entire story about it in a flashback sequence to Butch's childhood. We do not know that this is what he is doing. It just seems initially like another random story in *Pulp Fiction*. Butch remembers an event when he was a child at home in 1973 when an army officer, Captain Koons (Christopher Walken) visited Butch to bring him a family heirloom: a gold watch. The watch had belonged to Butch's great-grandfather, who took it to World War I with him. Butch's grandfather had taken it to World War II, and Butch's father had taken it to Vietnam. Butch's father and Captain Koons had been prisoners of war together. Before Butch's father died, he gave the watch to Koons along with his dying wish that Koons finds Butch and passes it on to him. The sequence's humour is another factor helping to keep audience interest through the delivery of backstory. Koons' lack of sensitivity in delivering the fact that he and Butch's father had to hide the watch in their rectums for some seven years to keep it away from their captors does not serve to make it appealing as an heirloom. However, Butch reaches up and takes the watch from Koons... and is snapped back to reality. He's about to go into the ring to fight the fight he must throw. The backstory is now in place, through a very entertaining sequence, so the significance of the watch to his motivation is now understood for what is to follow. Note that this backstory involves nothing but Captain Koons talking. There is basically no action, just Koons telling a story. But that is fine. Because even though it is just backstory and it is just dialogue it is, in itself, a really good story, and that is the very best way to deliver backstory.

Quick tip — comedy is a great tool for delivering backstory in a drama. *Breaking Bad* is a superb example of cleverly timing the use of comedy. The more serious dramatic sequences are kept powerful by ensuring there is no comedy, and yet *Breaking Bad* is very funny in places. That is because much of the humour in *Breaking Bad* is used in between the drama sequences to ease the pain of delivering backstory while positioning all the characters for the next major action sequence.

There is excellent use of flashback in *Saving Mr. Banks* (Dir. John Lee Hancock, 2013). The story is effectively divided into two. Firstly, the contemporary story concerning Walt Disney's (Tom Hanks) attempts to get PL Travers (Emma Thompson) to allow him to make the film of her book, *Mary Poppins*. Secondly, the backstory — delivered entirely in flashback — of Travers' traumatic childhood in Australia, from which we gradually understand why she is so brittle and difficult in her dealings with Disney in the contemporary story and why she is so precious about the treatment of the characters in her book. Her backstory is a story in itself, hugely powerful and significant when combined with the knowledge we have from the main plot storyline. Again, the tactic here is to elevate the backstory into an entire subplot. The backstory is upgraded from tedious exposition into a knowledge gap through subplot. We in the audience understand Travers' motivation because we get to understand her past. Disney does not have this knowledge. This privilege gap is intriguing for us as we watch Disney flounder around desperately trying to figure out Travers' difficult attitude to his wonderful ideas. He is a smart man, desperately trying to work her out. Here is the gap: we know what is going on for her and Disney does not. We wonder if he will get there.

When you recognise that you have backstory to deliver, if you cannot turn it into a compelling subplot, then the important thing to do is to go to the opposite extreme: reduce it out and make it as economical as possible. Take the shortest time and space to get the important messages across. Decide what needs to be communicated and find a way to deliver it without ceremony. The quickest way to get backstory across is through a narrator, an image or in dialogue. Every time I do a script analysis, I always, always consider the value a narrator might bring to the story. They are so useful sometimes and can bring a whole new dimension. Writers often forget the narrator and the possibilities opened up by using one in terms of swift and clear delivery of backstory.

Using an image, if the audience absolutely must know that a woman used to be at Oxford University, put a photograph of her graduating in full cap and gown on the dresser with 'Oxford Graduation – 2019. Congratulations Anna!' written across the picture. Three seconds. Job done. If it is really important to nail it home, turn it into a beat with some dialogue. Say, the woman is trying to find space on the dresser. She picks up the photograph, looks at it with sentimental smile, then goes to pack it in a drawer. Her son stops her: 'No, Mum! No. You went to Oxford and you must be proud of that. Leave it right there for everyone to see.'
    Job done. In ten seconds.

The main message here is this: Backstory is still story. Try to convert it into story and develop it in its own right.

2.4.9 Knowledge gaps through harmatia

The harmatia is one of Aristotle's core principles, which I shall address separately. I mention it here to note that it is a framing element. The harmatia is an error or mistake or a problem — something which sends the protagonist's world out of balance. More on this coming soon in section 3.3. – Aristotle's Principles.

2.4.10 Knowledge gaps through conflict

Conflict is the life-blood of the vast majority of stories. it is *possible* to create a story without conflict but it is very unusual and most stories without conflict are often more like a beautiful work of art than a story. Given that conflict is so important, and that there are four forms of conflict and a particularly important definition and understanding for *meaningful* conflict, I have given it a dedicated section later in the book. For the moment, notice that every conflict implies winners and losers or success and failure and therefore embodies a knowledge gap or gaps in the question every conflict raises: Who will win and who will lose? Hence there is always an implicit knowledge gap between the different parties involved or between the presence of a conflict and its outcome. Much more detail coming shortly, in section 3.1.

2.4.11 Practical Application

As we finish with framing gaps, the key point I would like to emphasise is that whatever you are trying to do in orientating your audience to the direction of your story can be done using a knowledge gap. Do not think about the plot element ('what happens') in obvious terms. Think about it in terms of how you can present it using a knowledge gap.

Think holes, not string. Ask yourself: In the course of this plot event, how can I punch holes in this obvious narrative progression? How can I create gaps in knowledge between the different characters? How about if they make a plan? Who knows about the plan? Who does not? Who else has a plan that is secretly in conflict with this one? Now the two plans are in conflict. Excellent. What is my story's key question? How obvious shall I make it? How can I create more meat using a subplot? How can I make my story world new and wondrous or unsettling for my audience? How can I introduce conflict into this story?

On my website, you will find the story of *Bella* (Baboulene, 2019). A story about a funeral. How can you turn a story about a funeral into gaps in knowledge? Go to my webpage and take a look. The very best thing you can do as a writer is to begin thinking about how to put knowledge gaps into your story.

2.5   Character Gaps

Let us remind ourselves where we are in the scheme of things with a reprise for the categories and types of knowledge gap:

CATEGORIES AND TYPES

FRAME	CHARACTER	STORIFICATION
Privilege/ revelation	Motivation	Surpassing aim
Promise	Questions	Character growth
Key question	Subterfuge	Moral argument
Subplot	Action/ dialogue	Peripeteia
Harmatia	Suggestion	Vicarious learning
Conflict	Anagnorisis	Education
Narrator	Misdirection	Metaphor/ allegory
Character plans	Suspense	Recognition/ allusion
Story world	Comedy	
Backstory		

Figure 8: A reminder of the gap types

We have been through all the first column, and now we are getting into the meat of any story because we are going to allow our characters to move and talk, interact and take decisions, suffer and benefit from the consequences of those decisions. Before we go into the detail of the gap types, it is interesting to address one question I get with this slide: Where is 'the plot'?

2.5.1   Plot and character – one and the same

There is a perennial argument regarding which is most important, plot or character. While there is some validity in forcing a distinction between them, the main thing to get your head around is that when your writing is beautiful and brilliant, and you wonder how it is that you did that and why it does not happen all the time, it is almost certainly because you have gained the magical dimension to your writing that comes when plot and character become essentially one and the same thing. Let me explain.

Firstly, let's separate them out. In simple terms, the plot is 'what happens' in the story. I also like to see it as 'the plan for a narration'. If you take a story such as *Romeo and Juliet*, the script written by Shakespeare around the year 1590 has the same **plot** as the play that goes on the stage somewhere in the world today. That play has the same plot as the 1936 film version starring Norma Leslie. Which has the same plot as the hip suburban film version of 1996 starring Leonardo DiCaprio which has the same plot as the BBC radio dramatization in 2015. The plot stays the same, however the characters deliver different versions of that same plot. It is rather like a football match. The 'plot' remains the same every time in the sense that the rules provide a route map that characterises every match. However, the way the characters are defined and behave within that plot frame mean that every single match is unique.

So, in a sense plot and character are separated, like the rules of football are contrived separately from any given match, so the 'rules' for delivering a version of *Romeo and Juliet* are separate from the unique qualities of the characters and events that make up any one of the individual versions. Hence there are dozens of versions of the same story — *Romeo and Juliet* — each version jumps through the same plot hoops but the characters speak differently and do different things in different ways in each version.

This is why, when people respond to the question 'What is the plot of *Back to the Future*?' the answer is that it's about a kid who gets sent back in time and has to find a way to get back home. However, this is just the plot. The framing that facilitates the real power of the story, which is in George McFly's **character** growth journey. What the characters do is where the real story lies. Ironically, what the characters do delivers the true power of the story AND in doing so, they jump through the hoops provided by the plot. This is where the secret blending of plot and character takes place. The plot is **what** happens. The characters depict **how** it happens.

To make a story you need both plot and character and they need to be blended into a single entity called a story in which each is magnified by the other. What a player does — the actions they take — defines who they truly are. However, what a player does also defines what happens. In other words, character is the source of both plot and character. Like this:

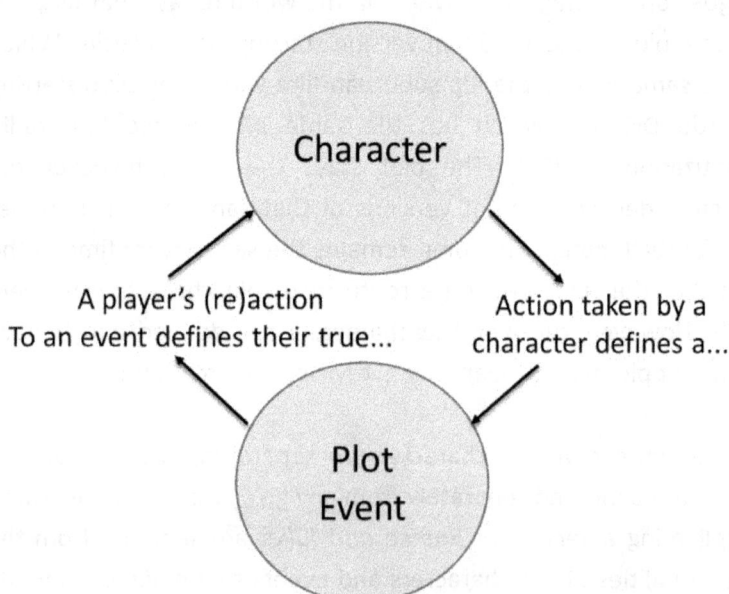

Figure 9: Plot and character - one and the same

Your characters define both plot and character; i.e., everything in your story, so let's be in no doubt, character is fundamental to story. Your plot is what happens. Your characters are how it happens.

Framing, character and storification
The framing of a story equates broadly with the plot. The characters take action and deliver the story events. The receiver creates a meaning in mind from interpreting the character actions. The plot is foundational, but that transition from character actions to meaning in the mind of the receiver is the major power of your story.

Look at it like this. This is interesting:

> **From a <u>writer</u> perspective, the story emanates primarily from the storification. However, from the <u>audience</u> perspective, it all comes from character, because from the audience perspective, it is the characters that deliver the storification.**

So, the job of the writer is to sit in a dark room and establish the storification in secret, then work back from there to create characters and actions that deliver it. When things need extra clarification, framing elements can be used to provide that support.

As we shall establish more thoroughly later, the audience works forwards through the narration from start to finish. They journey from the framing through the characters to finally discover the storification. The writer works backwards from the storification to create the character interactions that deliver that storification and to provide the necessary framing. Once that is perfected the writer will have created a narration that takes the audience forwards from start to finish on that journey to storification.

This is the secret code a writer works with, and this is the key. YOU — the writer — secretly and privately discover your storification, you understand it completely, you create characters and you put them under pressure to make decisions, and the outcomes of the decisions they make deliver a narrative into the mind of your audience that storifies into their mindset.

Wow. That was profound. I kind of impressed myself there, because that is an important lesson, but I do understand it probably makes little sense right now. Do not worry. By the end of this book you will understand what I just wrote (imagine that!) and you will have learned something fundamental about being a creator of story.

2.5.2 Protagonist and antagonist

Is Walter White a protagonist or an antagonist? Is he a good guy or a bad guy? If he is the protagonist, does that make Hank, the policeman, the antagonist? If there are multiple protagonists, for example in *The Magnificent Seven,* whose story is it? Who is the protagonist in *Game of Thrones*? Who is the antagonist?

Stories often involve more than one key character with aims, ambitions and an interesting journey, so how can one decide? Who is the protagonist?

In simple terms, the protagonist is the entity whose story is being told and the antagonist is the entity who is blocking the progress of the protagonist towards achieving their ends. However, of course, nothing is ever that simple.

Firstly, note that the term 'protagonist' does not mean 'the good guy'. It means **the character whose story is being told**. Yes, this is usually the main character, and usually the good guy, but here is the secret:

> **The protagonist is the character who carries the storification dynamic.**

The storification defines the major power of your story, so the character that carries the storification is the one whose story is being told. And make sure you get this: Everything else in your story is being crafted into place to ensure the storification is being delivered successfully. The storification delivers the magic and power of your story. Everything else is in service of the storification.

In *Back to the Future*, the storification is delivered through George McFly's character growth. George is the character who changes and grows and teaches/learns the moral imperatives of the story through the actions and decisions he takes under pressure of conflict. He is the one who makes the choice that drives the storification outcome (George's character grows as a result of his decision to stand up to Biff) so **George McFly is the protagonist**. Marty might be the star of the framing and several individual scenes and story events. Marty might 'bookend' the film with his time-travel adventure, and he is there throughout, but Marty's protagonism is all plot. The storification defines the real power of the story, and George is the bearer of the storification, because it is his character growth that defines the story. The story is therefore George McFly's story. Everything Marty does is there to *create the conditions* for George's storification arc. (More on storification and this example later.)

It is interesting to note that Marty McFly is present in every sequence of *Back to the Future*... with one exception. The scene in which George McFly's character grows. Marty is locked away in the boot of a car for that one. George has to learn for himself.

Once you have identified which character is carrying the storification, then you know whose story you are telling, and that is a huge help in getting everything right on the character journey that will deliver the magic and power of your story. If the main storification is not clear to you this may be an indicator of problems in your story. It may be that you have two stories to tell around two different characters. It is important that you understand each story and divide the whole into a plot and subplot, or two different books, or several episodes, a trilogy, or maybe you have...

2.5.3 Multiple protagonists

A protagonist certainly does not have to be an individual or indeed a person. It may be a Lassie dog, an ugly duckling or a Skippy kangaroo, an anthropomorphic car, an iron giant, a friendly ghost, a Butch and a Sundance, three musketeers, four horsemen, five who go a-hunting, a big hero six, a magnificent seven, a hateful eight, a class of 91, an ocean's 11/12/13, a dance troupe, a full monty, an orchestra, sports team, choir, regiment an army or a planet's population. In each case of multiple protagonists the members of the group work together as an agent of change and although there may be plotlines that revolve around individuals in the group, it is the group as an entity in itself that functions as the protagonist in these stories IF that *group* is put under pressure and goes through storification.

Find the storification dynamic and work out how and who delivers it. That is where the focus must lie in creating your story.

2.5.4 Antagonism

Antagonism is the term for the forces ranged in opposition to fulfilment for the protagonist. Again, this will most often be a person — the 'bad guy' — in conflict with the good guy protagonist, but you may have a criminal as your protagonist (Robin Hood; Tony Soprano, Butch and Sundance; Jack Sparrow; Delboy Trotter; Walter White; Norman Stanley Fletcher...) and the antagonistic forces to such a protagonist might therefore be 'good' people; the victims or the police. Forces of antagonism do not have to be a person; they could be the weather, a dog, the protagonist's own insecurity, jealousy or delusions, acts of God and many others (as we shall see in section 3.1 on Conflict). Equally, there are plenty of excellent full-length stories that don't have a 'bad guy' at all. *Toy Story*, (1995, Director John Lasseter), *Juno* (2007, director Jason Reitman), *Mary Poppins* (1964, directed by Robert Stevenson) and many, many others are stories in which there is no 'bad guy'. The principal conflict is a 'good' person standing in the way of their own fulfilment. Indeed, this is the case with George McFly whose internal conflict — his cowardice — provides the key antagonism that must be overcome in the process of storification. He is both the good guy and the bad guy. This might sound strange, but internal conflict is an extremely common and a highly effective story tool (more on this in section 3.1 on Conflict as well).

Do not worry if this is not clear right now, but hang in there! We need to understand storification and conflict to truly understand what I am saying here, and we have not covered those topics. I recommend you make a note to come back and re-read this section after you fully appreciate storification, because character gaps are fundamental to everything and storification is a function of character motivation and actions. Unfortunately, I can only present topics one at a time!

2.5.5 The five components of character

What is it that defines a character? Characters in a good story are likely to embrace most or all of the following five things:

> Motivation (section 2.5.5.1)
> Meaningful conflict (section 2.4.10)
> Decisions under pressure (also section 2.4.10)
> A character arc (section 2.5.5.2)
> A moral argument (section 3.4)

Each of these components delivers story power when crafted into a story in the form of a knowledge gap. Let's begin at the top.

2.5.5.1 Knowledge gaps through motivation

Even the most passive character must want something and this drive towards fulfilment — whatever that means for the individual character — is the source of your story.

Motivation is fundamental. A character's motivation causes them to channel their energy into a narrative progression that will deliver consequences. That energy, driven by a character's desires, beliefs, aims and ambitions is the well from which your story springs. Story generally comes from what someone wants and their passion to drive towards achieving it.

So, you must understand your characters deeply. Get behind their eyes and nail down their motivation by asking your character these six questions:

- What do they want?
- Why do they want it?
- What are they prepared to do to get it?
- Why now?
- What does **fulfilment** look like for this character?
- Why do we care?

These are the elements of motivation. Each is a knowledge gap that can bring power to your story. Let's go through them one by one, and let's build a character called Walter White, from *Breaking Bad* to exemplify each point.

What do they want?
Imagine a story about some characters who don't want anything. How will that go?! Not so compelling, right? Character drive is story drive, so understanding what characters want is fundamental. And not just for your protagonist. Every character is important. The clash of one character's aims in conflict with another is the basis for most stories and story events, so once you know where your protagonist journey is driving them, then the design of other characters can be crafted to set their aims against those of the protagonist. This is conflict 101.

So here is a rule for you which is a surprising liberation for a lot of writers: You are the God of your story world, and your characters are not fixed. CHANGE your characters' drives and motivations to ensure they do the right job for your story. Many, many writers write their stories with their characters 'pre-set'; either because they thought their characters up in advance of coming up with their story or the creative writing class told them to define their characters in great detail. No, no, no. You can and must redesign the personality of your characters continuously if they are going to do the right job for your story. Free yourself from fixed character definitions. Change them to get in the way properly!

It is not a coincidence that Perrier LaPadite's motivation and consequent plan are in direct conflict with Colonel Lander's motivation and consequent plan in *Inglourious Basterds*. It is not a coincidence that Butch Coolidge's motives and plan are in direct conflict with Marsellus' motives and plan in *Pulp Fiction*. It is not a coincidence that George McFly's motives and plan for Lorraine are in direct conflict with Biff's motives and plan for her. These characters are designed to be a conflict of motivations. Character actions and behaviours are a function of their motivation (they should drive towards what they want). You can design your characters so that their agenda forces them into conflict with others (who are driving towards what they want). The conflict forces them to take action, and the actions they take in response to the conflict causes the story. If the conflict of motivations is not aligning, you are free to change your character so that it does.

Give your characters motivation. Then put other characters in their way. Simple, basic story.

Walter White
In *Breaking Bad*, what does Walter White want? Well, he wants to provide for his family after his death. He wants to make an extraordinary quantity of easy money in a short period of time and he's going to do that by manufacturing and distributing illegal drugs.

A good, clear plot basis. He sets off with single-minded determination along that path. So, the writers *designed* the other characters to put obstacles in his way. What does Walter White definitely not need in his story life? Well, I guess he desperately does not need a clever and highly motivated and experienced drugs enforcement agent determinedly working against his best interests. OK. So let's give him a policeman for a brother-in-law. Even better, let's make him a drugs enforcement agent who is passionately committed to his work and let's make sure that the case of Heisenberg is the top one in his in-tray. Who else might be problematic? Well, I suppose Walter White desperately does not need there to be a brutal, murderous drugs-dealer who is absolutely motivated to get this new player out of his postcode... so let's make sure there is one of those. Walter needs a wife who is supportive and helpful... so let's make sure she is the opposite of those things. When his wife Skyler (Anna Gunn) finds out what he is doing, she is not pleased with all the money he is making. If they are in agreement, that wouldn't be great story, would it? So the writers make her disgusted with his life choices. She doesn't want his dirty money. Her decisions make life difficult for Walter, put him under pressure to make further choices under pressure and the story is forced into decision-driven wonderland around a huge knowledge gap through motivation.

In this way the writers ensured that all the other characters are motivated against Walter's aims; even the ones who love him.

Why does he want it?
Digging deeper into motivation, understanding why a character is driven the way they are is much more important than it might initially appear. In real life, as in story, it is a character's motivation that stirs us into an emotional response. If we see someone crying, we don't start to cry. We need to know *why* they are crying before we can cry ourselves. Once we can relate to the cause of their upset, then we can become emotional ourselves. It is the same with characters. Once we know what drives them, then we find ourselves

becoming emotionally engaged. Indeed, we cannot help but become emotionally engaged. This is related to the other question here:

Why do we care? If we know a man wants lots of money, we don't necessarily like that character, and we certainly have no reason to care. However, if we understand his motivation it will affect our feelings towards that character. Walter White wants to make a lot of drugs money *because he is dying of cancer*. His motivation is *to provide for his family after his death*. These are admirable ambitions and we want him to succeed in these terms. We know how we *feel* about this. This is why we continue to root for Walter long after he becomes a ruthless, murderous drugs lord.

It is important to recognise that emotional engagement is not about *liking* a character, it is about empathising. As long as we understand their motivation and we know why they behave the way they do, then we become engaged. We don't only engage with good behaviours and positive emotions. In real life, if you know someone is being naughty or taking a risk there is a part of you that feels they should be stopped, but there is also an even bigger part of you that loves it because it makes life juicy and interesting and we can learn from what befalls them without the dangers of taking that risk ourselves. We say they must be stopped, but we are loving watching events unfold. We want to see *how* they will be stopped — there could be drama and emotion — and we will be secretly sad when it is over. We want to know what happens when people set off on new and different narrative tracks in life. This is an important point for your antagonist. Bad guys are often rather one-dimensional; a moustache-twirling scoundrel or an evil psychotic who wants to take over the world — but if we don't know *why* they are like that — the motivation behind who they are — their character lacks dimension and, even though we might know *what* they want, we don't care as much as we would if we understood *why* they are driven to want it. They may be misguided or morally skewed, as can be argued in the case of Walter White, but understanding what is driving him brings empathy and engagement.

When an audience knows a character wants something *so* much and when they know the difference it will make to them and the outcome it might bring... they want them to get it too. When we see a character *strive*, and we see their endeavour in the face of huge forces of antagonism ranged against them, we want to see how much they want it and how they are going to get it and what will happen... and this is true of the antagonists as much as it is of the protagonists. Think of the simple example of a sports person trying their very, very hardest to win. We get emotional through exposure to the sheer endeavour. Remember, it isn't because they win or lose (we do not cry because we see someone cry) it is because they are trying so hard and we know what winning or losing *means* to this person.

The 'bad guy' in *Toy Story* is Woody. Andy's favourite toy and the loveable, respectable leader of the toys. His problem is the arrival of Buzz Lightyear and the loss of his status. Andy loves his funky, gadget-packed new toy, and Woody is jealous. This brings him fine motivation. He begins to take action against Buzz Lightyear and do bad things. He tries to lose him down the back of the drawers, and actually ends up getting him knocked out of an upstairs window into the garden. We cannot condone his actions, however we totally understand his child-like jealousy. His motivation. We do not dislike him for it. We empathise. Buzz is also a source of antagonism, but the problems he causes are because he is deluded. He genuinely thinks he is an actual space ranger and acts accordingly. Much of the antagonism in *Toy Story* comes from this, and we don't hate Buzz for it, of course. We don't think he is stupid. We *understand*. Why does he want what he wants? Because being a space ranger is what (he thinks) he was born to do and we love him for being so true to himself and we empathise. He is well motivated. That is terrific, dimensional, sophisticated antagonism. How is that a knowledge gap? Well, we know he is not a real space ranger, but he believes he is. A basic knowledge gap providing terrific story power.

So addressing the question *why do they want it?* Allows you to generate empathy and therefore arouse an emotional connection with the audience.

What are they prepared to do to get it?
Story comes to life when you box your characters into difficult decisions and force them to make hard choices under pressure. As the writer, your side of this question is: How can you set conflicts and obstacles in the way of your protagonist to prevent them from simply getting what they want? How gummed up and boxed in and screwed over and soundly impaled on the horns of dilemma can you make your character... and still find a clever way out?

Walter White knew full well from the start of his drug-making adventure that he was breaking the law. We went with him through that decision-making process because we supported his aim — to provide for his family after his death. What was interesting for us from an audience perspective is that it did not stop there. At the point at which it all went a little too far, where he crossed moral boundaries and began to hurt other people, we still stuck with him. We told ourselves the guys who were getting blown away were proper bad people — criminals and drug dealers exploiting our children and getting them addicted for their own gain. Walter was acting illegally, sure, but his actions could be seen as good old vigilante justice, wiping out some lowlife for the benefit of society. So we made excuses and forgave him and continued to hope he could win out and get back to a decent lifestyle once his aims are achieved. However, things do not quite work out. He makes money, but not nearly enough and it was a world of pain and murder to get him to that inadequate point. He is in a really difficult situation... but he chooses to dig deep and go further still. He begins to find himself responsible for the deaths of others who are not enemies of society and he does so with reducing justification, increasing obsession and without much apparent conscience. When he becomes responsible for the death of Jesse's girlfriend and later the poisoning of a small boy surely now some people in the audience are beginning to squirm and rethink their feelings about him.

These dynamics are an opportunity for writers. When a character is so passionate that they will not stop at the point where most people would stop, then the stakes go up and your story finds new heights. If you are writing action adventure or any form of suspenseful story, your job is to continuously hold your character(s) under pressure to make tough decisions to carry on at a point where most people would stop. That creates a gap between the choice the character has made and the choice the receiver of the story would make (a knowledge gap through suspense). Your job is to create the conditions that put them under that pressure. If a character begins to break moral codes in single-minded pursuit of their aims, like Walter does, we like this. Even if the aims are society-negative we are rubbing our hands because the prospect is that there will be consequences and interesting, original events.

Most fine characters reach a point of no return where the stakes become so high that ultimate success or failure is inevitable. Once he has become a murderer, Walter cannot apologise and back out to where he started. It is all or nothing now. Once Marty McFly has interfered with his parents' original meeting, he is now all in. He must get them to reunite before the bolt of lightning strikes, or he is dead.

Many writers struggle to deliver convincing conflict because they do not like it. they are too nice. However, conflict does not have to be negative. Conflict creates and reveals — and *tests* — motivation. It is the motivation that drives the character into situations that require them to make difficult choices, and sometimes it is the positive choice that is the hardest one to make. Which is also great for writers because even positive motivation can go too far. If there is a bully and you decide to fight them, you are now as bad as them. You have got into the gutter with them. If you beat them up does that make you a winner? Or are you now a bully as well? If the answer to that is too easy and comfortable for your audience (hooray! The good guy beat up the bully!) then ramp it up! You are the God of your story, so tweak it to make your audience think again. Your good guy is fighting a bully and this action is justified. Let's rethink it to remove that justification. What if your good guy is an adult and the bully is a school kid. The good guy beats them up. Still OK with that?! In that case, let's go further. Let's say he beats them up... and then keeps going — pummelling them long after they have been subdued. He stops for a breather. Then wades in again, punching and punching this defeated, almost lifeless person. Now what is he?

This is a good way of generating a strong story. Have someone with the moral high ground go too far. Now their own friends, family and allies begin to abandon them and even actively turn against them. They become more isolated, more vulnerable, more unsure about whether what they are doing is correct; and they have more people lining up in opposition to their aims — both friends and foes. The conflict and pressure is building, but they have gone too far to turn back, so they push on. The splits amongst the good side bring tension, empower the antagonist and greatly increase emotional engagement as we try to figure out what is right, what is wrong, and what is wrong but kind of OK if it ends up making things right. If you see what I mean.

Walter White's illegal activities eventually come to light for his wife, Skyler. Walter shows her his money. His power. ("I am the one who knocks.") She makes it very, very clear that she disapproves entirely. She is not impressed and she has no interest in ill-gotten gains. He is exasperated. He is putting in all this effort essentially *for her*, taking huge risks in the face of great danger from both the drugs world and the authorities and Skyler is unimpressed. Now he is in conflict with the very person he is trying to help. The forces ranged against him are mounting up... does he stop?! Go back to a decent, law-abiding life..? Too late for that...

How is this a knowledge gap? Well, it is a powerful point in the story because it is the moment that a huge knowledge gap closes. The gap between what we know of Walter's illegal activities and what Skyler knows. A momentous story event. The writers made sure that even though Skyler now knows (her position moved from revelation to privilege) Walter's son and his in-laws (including Hank) still do not, so the gap remains open and story power is retained.

Understanding the morality in your story and understanding your characters' positions relative to the moral argument is extremely valuable and can greatly inform your story. Much more on morality coming soon in section 3.4 – Stories and the Moral Argument.

For the moment remember that all your characters must want something and your story will be progressed by those who are prepared to go the extra mile in pursuit of fulfilment.

Note: Many writers get their characters from observing people. Oh, there's this hilarious Greek guy in the kebab shop or this incredible hottie at work or that movie character I love so much — I'm going to use them in my story. This is kind of fine — your characters need some basis, a starting point, some characteristics — but do not make the mistake of locking down who your characters are until you know what they are required to DO. If you have a protagonist like Walter White pushing determinedly towards making lots of drugs money, then your other characters must be designed to put him under pressure. I cannot tell you how often I see writers who are so wedded to the characters *they decided in advance* that they cannot move their story forwards because these characters are totally unsuited to what this story requires them to be.

If you are the writer of *Breaking Bad* and you have in your mind a hottie from work and a hilarious Greek guy from the kebab shop... your story is going to struggle. They are not characters who are motivated in ways that will put Walter under pressure. Sure, they might have gorgeous, enchanting *characteristics*, but that is not the same as having character. You are the God of your story so you need to have the flexibility in your mind to simply change the personality and ambitions — and *motivation* — of your players to cynically make sure they get in the way and do the job that is required of them to cause your story. To do that you must motivate each character and have them drive towards what they want, making absolutely sure, as you do, that what they are driving towards will cause problems.

Even a character's friends and allies must interfere. Watch an episode of *Friends*. Every episode is an adventure between six 'good guys' and every episode sets these friends in opposition with each other's aims. Walter and Jesse are on the same side and share the same aims, but that does not mean they are happily in agreement all the time. Quite the opposite! They are constantly and endlessly in conflict with each other.

You get the point. Characters must be designed to ensure the narration is driven along the spine that generates the story you are trying to tell. More on this later in section 4.4 — Crafting characters.

Why now?
The question 'why now?' originally came from David Mamet, and I must confess I did not initially see the relevance. Who cares why now?! It turns out there is a very good reason for asking this question.

As we have discussed, more often than not, a story is compelling because the characters are placed under pressure to take action and make difficult decisions. However, there will normally be some compelling reason that these decisions must be addressed 'now' and these reasons will be of great interest to us, the writer, because the answer to 'why now?' is often the reason the story exists and that can be useful to know!

It is not always the case, but when there is a clear answer to 'why now?' for the protagonist, that knowledge can help you to identify the spine of your event and stay in touch with it. If you can find ways to force your protagonist into making a difficult decision, that is the moment your story exists, and that is the 'why now?' imperative. As soon as there is a 'why now?' you have the material for story power.

What is the 'why now?' pressure on Walter White? Well, he has terminal lung cancer. He needs to make money *now* to provide for his family after his death. He has no choice but to take on all the forces of antagonism now because his time is limited. If you think about it *Breaking Bad* could have been made without Walter White having a terminal illness. He could have just wanted easy money. But then the imperatives driving his decision-making would not have been there. There would have been no reason 'why now?' and all of that lovely urgency would have been removed from the story.

For the majority of *Back to the Future*, George McFly is weak and unassertive. When faced with a decision to make, he has no dilemma; he avoids the conflict. He freely admits he is 'not very good at confrontation', so every time he is faced with a difficult choice he turns and runs.

'Why now?' No reason. He avoids the confrontation. Ah. OK. In which case, there is no story. It is all just preparation for when there is a 'why now?'. That comes when he is faced with a confrontation from which running away is not an easy option. He stumbles across Biff abusing Lorraine in the car, and *now* a decision must be made. Sure, he can turn and run, but if he does, he is leaving Lorraine to be raped in the car. However, if he stands his ground, he will get beaten up by the huge, muscle-bound bully he has feared throughout. Now George must make a decision under pressure. Bingo! Now we have the 'why now?', because it is now that Lorraine will be raped if he avoids the confrontation. There are only two choices — stand and fight or run away. Both are horrible, and one must be chosen 'now'. That is why there is story power to be had in this moment, because the why now has the imperatives that pressure the character.

Marty's story has a similar recognition of the importance of 'now'. If he cannot get his parents reunited in love, he will not exist in the future. He will die if he cannot get history back on track. He must also get it done in time to hit the bolt of lightning. Once again, the writers have ensured there is a 'why now?' imperative driving the characters under pressure. Marty cannot put things off, because the clock is ticking.

So, the question 'why now?' really means 'why is there a story in this particular event?' This is not a rule book and there are plenty of stories out there that do not have clear and helpful 'why now?' imperatives. However, if you can find (or create) 'why now?' imperatives, it will help you to identify the kingpin moments and events that define the power in your story or story event and the elements that can bring the characters to life through pressure. This brings vibrancy and urgency to your story. If you cannot identify any 'why now?' imperatives in your story, it might be worth trying to design some into the picture or it may be a clue that you are focusing on the wrong character or events.

Catharsis
In explaining the emotional connection of an event to the audience, Aristotle used the word 'catharsis'. There is much argument concerning what he meant in story theory terms. Catharsis is the feeling of 'relief' we get when we learn or experience something vicariously. The empathic response that gives us a *feeling* for that experience without actually having to go through the emotional mill ourselves. We feel purged even though the experience was someone else's. When we slow down to look at a car accident, although we feel for the unfortunate souls involved, we also experience something deep and fundamental inside ourselves about our relationship to death and suffering. We feel relief that it was not us, and we get a natural, visceral glimpse of our own mortality, along with a certain emotional release. We feel fortunate. We don't want to find ourselves getting close to death, but we want to understand it. We distance ourselves from it and yet we know it is always there

for us, and we are drawn to it. Empathy and catharsis are connections deep within us. Stories bring us insights into these parts of us without the danger that normally goes with such experiences in real life.

We live in ivory towers and distance ourselves from the animal within. Catharsis is a connection to the fundamental, raw truths of our life that we can only avoid for so long. Life is, ultimately, a tragedy and death is inevitable. By following a character in a story, we can get in touch with these parts of our souls and investigate areas of our own consciousness without risk.

> As an author, you can lock your audience on to a character by getting them to empathise with their motivation and then with their endeavour. Then you can take them somewhere they would not comfortably go in their own lives and you can, through storification, make them find something deep inside themselves.

That was true. And useful. I would read that last paragraph again.

We find out who someone really is and what they are truly capable of when they must battle to get what they want. A character can only be as heroic and admirable as the forces of antagonism demand of them, so make us care by setting up an aim we can relate to, then giving them strong, credible, perhaps overwhelming forces of antagonism to overcome in achieving their aims. Give them passion and determination to try, despite the odds. Succeed or fail, we will love them for trying.

Much more on this shortly, but these are the things that make us empathic and bring us catharsis. These are the things that make us care deeply.

What does fulfilment look like for this character?

This is the quietly important component of motivation which pulls it all together and connects it into the whole story. What fulfilment means for your character will drive all the other elements. Fulfilment for a character is going to define your story, because that fulfilment will be strived for in a way that not only brings all the other characteristics into the game, but fulfilment then goes on to drive out the all-important storification dynamics.

Ask your character: what does fulfilment look like for you? Define that (mostly using the other subheadings in this chapter), set them off to strive for it and your story is underway. Now set up forces of antagonism to make it difficult for them, spicy and complex. Test their resolve. How far *will* they go? Box them in so they must make difficult choices under pressure. Now you have compelling story.

Note that fulfilment is deeper than the earlier question: 'What do they want?'. Fulfilment is a component of a character's deeper and even unconscious drives, which we shall discuss shortly in section 2.5.5.2 – Character Arcs.

Example knowledge gap through motivation
I am going to tell you a story now which is a very fine example of a knowledge gap through motivation. I show this film in my seminars — a 90-second trailer for the Disney film *Frozen*. I recommend you have a look at it online, partly because it is built around a knowledge gap through motivation, but also because it is a phenomenal piece of work. Ninety seconds of film story that has just about every story theory dynamic in the book. If you didn't like *Frozen*, fear not; this trailer is like nothing in the movie. And nobody sings. The trailer can be found via my website at http://www.baboulene.com/clipsanddata/ or my company website at www.dreamengine.co.uk. If you are reading this in 2060 and my website or the link isn't there anymore — give me a break, I'm 100 years old. Have a search on youtube for 'Frozen first look trailer'. It's the one with the snowman and the moose.

For those who cannot access it right now, the story opens with Olaf the snowman alone in a beautiful Winter scene. He sniffs a flower, gets pollen up his nose, sneezes and accidentally blows his own carrot-nose off. The sneeze has such power his carrot-nose is sent scudding across the iced-over pond. His motivation is instantly clear for us. What does fulfilment mean for Olaf in this story? It means he gets his nose back. So, we have our protagonist, we have set his ambition and he sets off to fulfil it. Now, if you were paying attention earlier you will know that it is now the job of the writer to make fulfilment hard to achieve. We must introduce complications that test the protagonist's motivation. We are the God of our story, so how can we design a situation that will cause conflict for Olaf?

Enter stage right: Sven. A ton of moose who has also spotted the carrot on the ice and his reaction says it all. A crunchy fresh carrot in this wintry scene is not something a moose is going to pass up. Sven's ambition is clear: he wants to eat the carrot. We now have motivation for the moose, and we know what fulfilment looks like for both characters.

We now have all the story basics in place: a protagonist with motivation in pursuit of fulfilment. Forces of antagonism with clear motivation for *their* fulfilment. The antagonist (moose) motivation is in direct opposition to the protagonist (Olaf) achieving fulfilment. Two characters. If they both drive with passion towards fulfilment they will go into conflict. They can't both have the carrot, so the question is raised: Will the snowman get his nose back? Who will win?

Let's take a trot through the character basics for Olaf:

- **What does he want?**
  Olaf wants to get his nose back.

- **Why does he want it?**

He wants to look normal. Nobody should have to live without a nose. (We empathise with this desire.)

- **What is he prepared to do to get it?**
  Fight a moose.

- **Why now?**
  Because if Olaf doesn't crack on and get his nose back it will be eaten by the moose. Perhaps he has sneezed his nose off many times before. None of these previous times was a story, because he rolled his eyes at himself for doing it again and says: 'what am I like?!' He picked it back up and shoved it back in his face. All sorted. No drama. However, THIS is the time when it turns into a story because THIS is the time when there is a 'why now?' that makes it interesting. A moose also wants the carrot so this time, we have a story.

- **What does fulfilment look like?**
  When we answered the question 'What does he want?', the answer was for Olaf to successfully defeat the moose, get his nose back and live on in peace. However, this is his outer arc ambition. True fulfilment is on his inner arc, and in this context we need to dig a little deeper. He begins the story as a lonely snowman. He's talking to the flowers. By the end he has a friend. This is satisfying his inner arc ambition. More on this shortly in section 2.5.5.2 — Character Arcs.

- **Why do we care?**
  Because we empathise with the snowman's position — we all want to keep our noses — however, we cannot see an easy win here. A small snowman versus a ton of hungry moose? How can this possibly resolve to a happy ending?

So it all looks pretty solid as a story setup because the protagonist is well designed and the forces of antagonism are overwhelming. As the story unfolds, the moose is clearly winning. Fulfilment is clearly beyond Olaf's reach. We cannot see a win for the hero here. And that is a beautiful, winning story setup.

The framing is in place. Let's move up to the character action. Off we go. What happens in the story?

Olaf and the moose both rush to get to the carrot first, and both instantly go into conflict with the ice. It's hard to make progress and the second act of the story is the to-and-fro as each of them tries to get to the carrot first. It looks like Olaf will win; then the moose; then Olaf... then the moose. Then even more the moose. In the end, the moose is clearly on top, and then... the moose wins out. The moose gets the carrot.

We focus on poor Olaf. He has lost and now has no nose. We can see no positive outcome here. It's a sad story with a sad ending. Can it really be that this is the time when the good guy loses?! Really?

No. Not really. In the midst of Olaf's despondency, the moose reappears, shoves the nose back into his face and lies down like an excited puppy, with his tail in the air and a 'do it again!' attitude, hoping Olaf is going to throw something else for him to fetch. There was a knowledge gap between the motivation we overlaid on the moose (he wants to eat the carrot) and the actual motivation of the moose (he wants to play and make friends). That knowledge gap through motivation provides the kingpin power of the entire story.

The storification is strong for us in the audience because each of the characters progresses up the ladder of life. As a result of the decisions they make under pressure of conflict, they both journey from lost and alone in a winter's scene, to making a friend. Their personal values and fortunes have changed. We fundamentally like this. We also feel a little ashamed at the way we judged the moose. And so we should. The life-lesson is there: Never judge a book by its cover. Shame on you!

What we did not do and should have done is profile ALL the characters. In this case, we have the moose — our antagonist. It is very important we do not only focus on the good guy protagonist. As we saw from the 'why now?' piece, it is the antagonism that actually causes the story to exist. The protagonist can only be as strong and resourceful and impressive as the antagonism demands of him. So we must focus on the antagonism. We need to craft all our characters beautifully, so let's profile the moose as well:

- **What does he want?**
  He wants to make friends.

- **Why does he want it?**
  Nobody should have to live alone.

- **What is he prepared to do to get it?**
  Run and fetch the snowman's nose back to help him in life and make friends.

- **Why now?**
  Because the stranger threw the carrot. Now is the opportunity to do something fun with this stranger and hopefully make a friend.

- **What does fulfilment look like?**
  No longer being alone in a bleak wintery scene.

- **Why do we care?**
  Because we empathise with characters who are lost or alone.

Story lives in the conflict of motivations. The snowman wants the carrot to bring his life back into balance and the moose wants the carrot to help him make friends. Note how the writers know of both motivations and hide one of them. They trick the audience into misreading the situation. This is a fine example of an author knowing everything about their story before writing it and using that privilege knowledge to create a knowledge gap in revelation that is the basis to the story. In this case, that is a knowledge gap through motivation and it is the kingpin to everything that happens in the story.

Often the conflict of motivations is within the character themselves. As with Sven the Moose, there is a different motivation apparent from their actions on the outside from the internal secret agenda they have for themselves. This conflict of motivations within the same character is a wonderful mechanism for story. I will go into it in some depth soon in section 2.5.5.2 — character's inner and outer arcs.

All characters must want something. Even a character whose ambition is to do nothing would have to work at that as a fulfilment aim. All characters must have an impact on the spine of your story (the journey of your protagonist) otherwise, why are they there? What are they for? For this reason, it is well worth going through the above criteria for all your characters and understanding what they are for in the context of the story spine and how you will use their motivation. A good way to practise how this can work is to pick a story you know and profile some of the characters in the above terms. It should be very clear who they are, what they want, why getting it is complex and interesting, and why now? How do their actions lead to conflict and difficult decisions under pressure?

Later, in the section on the story development process, we will go through the process of crafting some characters.

Finally for the moment, let us take a look at the knowledge gaps in play in the Olaf story.

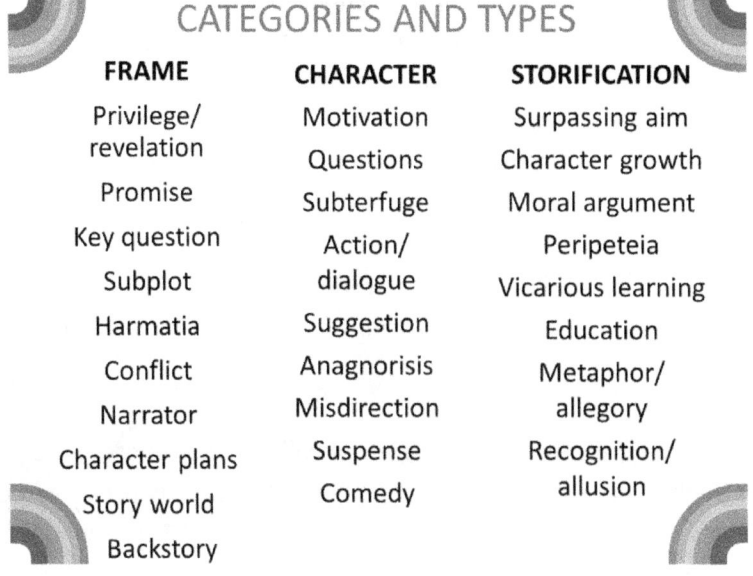

Figure 10: A reminder of the primary colours

OK, so starting top left. We have a mix of privilege and revelation. There is a key question: Will Olaf get his nose back? This provides a privilege basis that orientates us to the plot — what the story is about. Once the moose appears, that same key question also carries a revelation component because the moose brings with it a clear conflict so there is a revelation knowledge gap that brings a 'part two' to the key question: Will Olaf get his nose back? And how will he do it? What happens (plot) and how it will happen (character decisions).

The main gap providing the revelation (how) is the motivation of the moose. He knows he wants to play and make friends. We think he wants to eat the carrot. A knowledge gap through motivation, presented in revelation form. Excellent. The key question is answered at climax: Yes, Olaf will get his nose back, but not in the way we expected.

However, on the **storification** side, there is also a **surpassing aim**: He didn't just get his nose back, he made a friend as well, so his quality of life has gone significantly up the ladder of life, and in doing so, it could be argued that **character growth** has taken place. There is also a **moral argument** in how we pre-judged that moose. Shame on us. We thought he was a bad guy, but he wanted to play and make friends. The moral argument is that we should not judge a book by its cover.

There is also a complete set of Aristotle's principles — indeed, two complete sets — in this story. I shall work through those when we explain Aristotle in section 3.3.

That is not all the knowledge gaps — we will address others as we go through the character-specific list. However, I think you can agree this is already not a bad haul for a 90-second trailer! This is why it is so wonderful. Lots and lots of knowledge gaps, with a mix of privilege and revelation and powerful storification.

2.5.5.2   Character arcs

First and foremost, it is important to recognise that character arcs are not the same thing as character growth. Character arcs *lead to* character growth (if there is any) which is addressed separately under storification coming soon.

Character arcs are a function of the duality inside us all. We have our internal drives — our motivation — within us, and we have our actual behaviours on the outside. This creates two separate arcs: an inner arc and an outer arc. When there is a difference between these two arcs there is strong potential for story.

Let's say you work in an office. Your boss asks you to work late. She asks you: "How would you feel about an increase in responsibility? It won't initially be a promotion, but who knows? If you do well…?"

You are delighted: "Yes! Thank you! That's wonderful! I've been looking for an opportunity to prove myself to you. I will not let you down!"

All the while, deep inside, you are wondering just how long you are going to have to put up this façade until you can afford to tell that horrible boss that she can shove her 'increased responsibility' where the sun don't shine, and you can dance out into the sunshine and go open a bar on the beach of a Greek island — your ultimate dream.

The beach bar is fulfilment on your inner arc and the enthusiastic worker is your outer arc doing what has to be done in pursuit of the secret inner arc. The potential for story lies in the gap between the two.

Walter White's outer arc asserts his image as a decent man in society. He is a fine upstanding, law-abiding, school teacher holding down two jobs and battling with cancer. However, his inner arc is defined by his determined ambition to illegally make a large amount of money to provide for his family after his death. Compelling story is sourced from the difference between the inner arc and the outer arc because it is here that many of the strongest knowledge gaps can be found. When Walter is helping the police to try and profile the chemist who is making the drugs that are flooding the market, we can see him being very helpful, however at the same time we know that Walter White **is** the infamous chemist the police are trying to find. The knowledge gap is a function of the difference between his inner and outer arc and the knowledge gaps make the story.

Generally, the inner arc and the outer arc have the same destination: the character's fulfilment, whatever that is for them. However, while a character's motivation and fulfilment destination may be clear and simple on the inner arc, the outer arc defines the route the character is obliged to take in negotiating the forces of antagonism to get to that fulfilment out there in the story world.

For Marty McFly, fulfilment means getting back to 1985. However, achieving that inner arc ambition requires that he keeps that a secret and spends his time on the outer arc trying to get teenagers (his future parents) to meet and fall in love in 1955. The difference causes story potential. When the inner arc and the outer arc are one and the same thing, the story potential is reduced. If Marty had simply marched up to his future parents in 1955 and explained that he was their son, a time traveller from the future, and helped them to believe that by talking to Doc Brown and showing them the time machine then the inner arc and the outer arc would have become aligned and the story potential is reduced out. There would be no knowledge gap. Everyone would know everything, so the story disappears.

The main point to take away from character arcs is that if the outer presentation and inner truth of a character are the same, it can be a sign that the story lacks power. Such a character is likely to be 'on the nose' and shallow. This is not a rule book and many characters do not have inner and outer arcs; indeed, many of your peripheral characters will need to be 'obvious' to do the job they need to do for your story. Not every character will have a difference between their inner and outer arc, but the character whose story is being told almost certainly will. An interesting character will know what they want but will most likely have to find a convoluted route to achieving that end without revealing their inner truth to other characters. A narration is often the story of how the protagonist's inner and outer arcs were brought together.

2.5.5.3   The Deep Fulfilment Arc

There is another dimension to this which is worth noting at this point. Quite often, in the very finest stories, the protagonist has a third layer of almost subconscious fulfilment they are pursuing. Finding this can be solid gold for an author because it is linked closely to the storification that a receiver will take away in the context of 'deep subtext' from the story.

Walter White is trying to provide for his family after his death, right? We like this. It's a good inner arc desire that brings empathy to the character, drive to the story and subtextual messages to the

receiver. All good. However, when Walt's wife, Skyler, tells him she massively disapproves of what he is doing, dismisses his efforts to provide for her after his death and tells him she wants nothing to do with his dirty money... he does not stop. He carries on with his criminal ambitions even though his justification is now gone. And when Jesse asks him outright: 'Why are you doing this?' he does not talk about his family and his death. He says:
"I am awake."
By the end, the smile on his face confirms our suspicion — he has done all this for himself. He opens the story at age fifty. He's bored. His actions are not so tightly driven by his commitment to his family — he is doing this for himself. He loves it. He wants his final months to be exciting. To stretch his brain and give him something interesting to deal with. This is his deep fulfilment arc.

Marty McFly wants to get back to 1985 and he wants to get his parents to meet and fall in love. However, let's take a look at his face in the first version of 1985. He's ashamed at the low quality of his family. The drinking, the obesity, the lowly jobs... Look at his face — he wants them to do better. To BE better. By the end of the story, when he returns to the new version of 1985, all those aspects are fixed. His family are high quality people with high standards, and this satisfies Marty's deep fulfilment arc.

Note how the subtext this brings us is not about the content of the story. It has us jumping out of the story world and thinking about ourselves, life and how it should be led. Walter might make us think about whether we could be more fulfilled in our own lives if we took a few more risks and lived a little more on the edge. Is 'live fast die young' better than having a dull life but living to be 100?

The changes on the deep arc for Marty in *Back to the Future* might make us think about how we might stand up for ourselves and have the courage of our convictions in our own lives.

There won't always be a deep fulfilment arc in your story, but when there is, it brings a whole new layer and dimension to your story and is well worth embracing. This is a storification dimension, so we will talk about this more later on.

For the remainder of this section let's look at other forms of knowledge gap that can be embedded through character behaviours.

2.5.6 Knowledge gaps through action and dialogue

An audience will judge and evaluate every action and every word, searching for meaning in the moment and pumping it for subtext that might help to reveal the wider narrative context in which the knowledge gaps are embedded. You provide a tiny snapshot of action or words, and the receiver instantly pattern-matches it against the best-guess complete narrative they have in their knowledge banks. If I give you a car parked at a funny angle outside a bank, you load up a context for a robbery. If I say the words: 'Ashes to ashes…' you load up a context for a funeral. This is the game we play. Writer's leave gaps which exercise the visceral human skill to load a narrative context in mind.

If you see someone pointing up in the sky, that **action** carries with it a knowledge gap. Similarly, if you get a few words of **dialogue** come your way, as the words build into a sentence, you want to know the meaning as it emerges and you project forwards to fill the implicit knowledge gap in every incomplete sentence.

"Oh, my God. She is SUCH a –!"

This sentence is instantly alive with knowledge gaps into which we project where we think it might go. Each word and the attitude and expression with which it is delivered stimulates our senses. The signifieds rush our brain, which automatically pattern-matches significations and narrafications (meaning in the context of change over time) trying to lock on to a life context that brings the most narrative sense.

If the incomplete sentence was: "Do you take this man to be –?"

Your mind instantly searches for patterns... and finds a match. There's enough there for you to be pretty certain, so your mind loads up a context in working memory for a wedding ceremony, a bride and a groom, in a church with a priest and a congregation. You took a minimal amount of information and constructed a framing for it. You used your personal experience and filled the knowledge gaps to create a best-guess narrative scenario.

It can be simple: An airport customs officer snaps on a thin rubber glove and a receiver (of the story, not the glove) pattern-matches a context and possibly begins to map out an inevitable narrative sequence (actually, the receiver of the glove will gulp and see where this is going too...). Your brain is a brilliant pattern-matching machine. The match is to a moment in a known narrative and the context that is loaded up into mind is the complete narrative containing the matched element. Remember the car parked at a funny angle outside a bank? You instantly structured up a robbery scenario all around a badly parked car.

Or it can be complex: In *Back to the Future* Marty McFly meets his future father when he was 17 in 1955. He sees an accident about to happen, so he runs into the road and saves his future father from being hit by a car. Marty is knocked unconscious by the impact and his father runs away from the scene. Through this character action, wide-ranging knowledge gaps are opened up for the audience to project into. We know from the backstory that Marty has now replaced his father in his father's life. Marty is about to meet his own future mother instead of his future father meeting her. Lorraine falls for Marty instead of George and now, projecting forwards, we can see that Marty will not exist in the future unless he can get history back on track. How will he do it? What will happen? From this point, every moment of *Back to the Future* is alive with knowledge gaps because of this contextual frame. There is always a gap between what happens in real time for the characters in the story world and our thoughts on what has gone before and what may come next.

Holding your audience in the middle of an incomplete narrative that you have caused them to build in mind creates gripping story.

2.5.6.1 Knowledge gaps through dialogue

A narration is an information stream that assaults the senses of a receiver. Dialogue is simply another tool for delivering information to senses.

Once delivered, dialogue works on the receiver's mind in just the same way as everything else we have spoken about. Words are signifiers; they can be joined into narrative progression; they can be absorbed into mind where they become narrafications that make sense; and finally the narrative logic in mind can be joined with existing knowledge and experience from the receiver to storify into meaning.

Dialogue also tells us a good deal about the character delivering that information and will almost always create a direct or indirect knowledge gap. 'Direct' because there can be a knowledge gap implicit to the meaning of the words: 'You know what? I'm going to kill that bastard if it's the last thing I do.'
Or 'indirect' because it is in the nature of the receiver to doubt or question the veracity of what someone says.

>'The cheque is in the post.'
>'Oh, no, Biff. Of course I wouldn't want you to get thrown out of school.'
>'Yes, yes. Of course I love you.'

As with so much of what we have done so far, each of these lines carries a clear knowledge gap between what we are given and what we find it means.

True character is more certainly established through a character's actions. Their words are more open to doubt and interpretation. This is especially true of dialogue for the screen, where the audience generally looks on our characters from the outside and it is more difficult to gain insights into a character's mindset than it is in a novel, but it can still be done. Characters can speak to themselves, to other characters or directly to the audience. If characters talk to themselves, we can understand how they are thinking. Joe Goldberg (Penn Badgley) in *You*, for example. If a character in therapy speaks earnestly to their psychologist, we can gain insights that may be considered more reliable. *The Sopranos* (1999, created by David Chase) is a series about the mafia, however Tony Soprano (James Gandolfini) spends a significant proportion of every episode talking to his therapist, and the dimension this brings to both the mafia boss and to the story overall is a defining factor in the series' excellence.

Not forgetting, of course, that a character can 'break the fourth wall' and speak directly to the audience to tell us what they are thinking (*Fleabag* being a wonderful example) or a narrator — who may or may not be one of the characters — can speak to us (as discussed in section 2.4.6 — Knowledge gaps through narrator). In any of these cases, they still may not be giving us reliable information but that is not a problem. They are contributing to the story's progress using dialogue that you, as the author, can manage and use in the knowledge gap domain.

So, although the saying goes that actions speak louder than words, the key thing to remember is that dialogue IS action, and the fact that it is more unreliable is fine. More than fine; Unreliable information is a huge part of a story puzzle. It makes it even easier to use to create knowledge gaps. It is less easy to read the immediate impact of dialogue than physical action, however dialogue still affects others, it still introduces knowledge gaps and it still moves the story forwards.

Ultimately, the key to effective dialogue is to treat it like action and a vehicle for knowledge gaps. Ask yourself: What is this line of dialogue actively doing? Does it progress or define motivation, raise a question, deliver subterfuge, lies, misdirection, suspense or comedy? Like any other item, object, character or event, the question to ask of any line of dialogue is: What is it *for*?

Which knowledge gap is it opening, extending, changing or closing? Which essential aspect of a character is it delivering? Motivation? Agenda? Conflict? Raising a question? Backstory? Part of a choice or decision? Developing the character's inner arc or the moral argument? Is it helping us to understand what the character wants, why they want it, what they are prepared to do to get it, or why now?

All of the elements of character development we have discussed are potential areas where dialogue can be brought to bear, and if a line of dialogue is not delivering against any of these areas, you must ask yourself the purpose of the words and whether they can be justified.

The key thing to look for is a knowledge gap. The receiver must hear dialogue, but that dialogue should demand that the receiver provides the subtext that completes meaning. In *Back to the Future*, Marty's future mother, Lorraine, is watching Marty outwit the bullies in their chase around the square. She turns to her friends and declares: "he's such a dreamboat!"

These four words seem like a simple statement. On-the-nose, even. However, the audience are all over it. These words are evidence of motivation and her drive towards fulfilment (a romance with Marty) and now we know something in the context of her drive towards fulfilment that she does not: we have privilege knowledge that the person to whom she is romantically attracted is her own son. Quite a gap. The more Marty stands up to the bully to help his father, the more Lorraine becomes infatuated with Marty instead of George and the further Marty moves from existing in the future. Thus, through these four spoken words, a gap is introduced between what the audience knows and what Marty and Doc know. Lorraine says: "he's such a dreamboat!" but these four words:

- Define her motivation and let us know what fulfilment means for her.

- Give her an agenda that carries conflict into the upcoming events.
- Develop the character arcs of Lorraine specifically, but all the characters by implication.
- The scene storifies through recognition: the *meaning* we get in our minds is that Lorraine's attraction to Marty (and the implicit rejection of George) is taking Marty one step nearer to dying.

Similarly, with framing gaps, dialogue can deliver the orientation that creates a context. When the detective says: 'You know what? I'm going to dedicate the rest of my life to bringing that crook to justice...' this works like an inciting incident. The key question is raised and we are orientated to the intention of the story.

If a character says: 'Right! Car park, you! Let's settle this the old-fashioned way...' A conflict is set in motion and we are orientated to the scene.

When Marty and his future father discuss the detail of the role play they will use to trick Lorraine into thinking that George is a strong man, their dialogue may seem a little on-the-nose. However, it carries with it the implicit knowledge gaps that come with their character plan (Will the plan succeed? Who doesn't know about the plan and it's intended outcome?) and there is a difference in the motivation implicit to the conversation. We know that Marty is using this plan to unite his future parents so he can exist in future. George does not know this. Their plan is delivered in dialogue, and there are knowledge gaps alive within that dialogue, both in the plan that is developed and in the differences between what the audience knows and what other participants know, so it is valid, effective dialogue.

Speaking 'in character'
One particular area in which dialogue has an advantage is in expressing a gap between a character's inner and outer arcs.

The character says: 'I would love to take extra responsibility at work. Thank you sooo much for this opportunity!'

While we know, on her inner arc, that plans have been made for her to elope with her lover and go open a bar on a Greek island. If you can establish the inner and outer arcs of a character, it is through dialogue that the gap between the arcs can be expressed, and when this happens it is almost impossible not to speak from the soul of the character, because a person is in many ways defined by their inner arc drives and their outer arc expression of those drives.

Dialogue will generally be revealing of the outer-arc drives and the knowledge gap that is inherent in the dialogue will be in the way it hides the inner-arc ambition, and yet we in the audience will perceive it in subtext. You can make a conscious choice about what a line of dialogue is intended to do in these terms before you choose the words that are said. If the dialogue says one thing (outer arc) and yet means another (inner arc) you can be sure it is terrific dialogue. It is also through understanding the dual arcs that you can find the character's 'voice' and speak as they would speak, using the gap between their thoughts and feelings and what they have to say on the outside to create dimension through subtext. They say one thing, they mean something else. Simple subtext.

Dialogue tips

As you write dialogue, think carefully about the character's motivation and ambition. That is, dialogue should generally be agenda-driven. By understanding the character's motivation, dialogue will be 'in character' if it is agenda-driven and, of course, it will be helping to move the story forwards. This is the sense in which dialogue IS action. It should almost always be relatable, in the sense that it is an expression of a character's motivation and their drive towards fulfilment.

Once your dialogue is written, try to find ways to make it more metaphoric. Not so much that you lose your character's integrity, but within their character, try to be more abstract. Your first go at a line of dialogue will almost certainly be directly truthful, too long and possibly clichéd. Your second attempt will be the same thing but cut down in length. Your third attempt will begin to become original and authoritative. Work with this. Accept it. Look for the improvement that will shorten the speech and make it more owned by the character's personality.

For example, a character might say: 'You know what? That's brilliant, that.' And it gets the message across.

But when you get behind their eyes and think about it, the character is a cocky Londoner, so you change it to: 'Solid, mate. That is knockout.'

However, once the actor comes along, they will take that cockiness and put it into their attitude and reduce the necessary dialogue. The character nods with a confident grin: 'All day long...'

We have the same meaning in a more abstract and economical delivery that delivers the character of the character. The actor will greatly appreciate the space that is left for them to show what they can do.

One of the most powerful experiences I had when I first had actors reading my words and acting my characters was to have an actor barge through my door slapping the script and saying: 'What the hell is THIS?! How is anyone supposed to deliver this..?!'

It was a sobering education.

In creating fine dialogue, the very best thing you can do is act it out and speak it out loud. Take out words that do the job a physical action can do, as I did with the character's 'cockiness' above. I moved it to the acting.

A great deal of the dialogue I see is not considered with the character-of-the-character in mind. Get behind their eyes, think as they would think, put on their accent, attitude and class, pull all the right faces and speak as they would. Putting yourself in the position of the actor is a wise thing to do, and ensuring that your dialogue is alive with subtext is the best way of ensuring they will be happy bunnies.

Some Do-Nots
Do not have two characters tell each other things that they both already know. And if we in the audience already know it too, this is likely to be awful. This is often a good sign of a scene that can be cut.

Do not have characters who simply agree with each other. It is very unlikely — unless we are fully aware that one of them is lying — that this will be an interesting exchange.

Do not use excessive dialogue. Quite often a lot of what a character might say is self-evident or, as we have shown, will be best delivered by the acting. This is more important in a film story, or course, but the same applies to prose. Have a character state something we can already divine from the action only if there is good reason why you absolutely need to assert that point very strongly. Don't forget, a story is made of gaps in knowledge. Do not tell us everything. In life, people do not generally express themselves in crystal clear, well-articulated ways. We grope our way through spoken interactions. Then the other person sees where we are going with it and interrupts. We speak in clipped, agenda-driven ways that are rarely well formed. Ensure there is value in every word, and understand the purpose of every sentence. Dialogue can be long, that's fine, but only if the words are all justifiable.

There is a general instruction out there to keep clear of dialogue as much as possible (again, particularly in the film industry). You write your story using action alone and then you add the minimum necessary dialogue. I do not wholly subscribe to this approach, particularly for other media, but it does help to end up with something closer to the right dialogue if you think of it as a separate layer. For example, when Marty and George make their plan, we know what the dialogue is for. Its purpose is to deliver a knowledge gap through character plan, so we can design the dialogue to work with the action and to do what is necessary. We know that it is compelling because of the gap between Marty's outer arc aim (match-making fellow teenagers) and his inner arc aim (to exist in 1985). Both the characters express their motivation within their words and both are pushing towards what fulfilment means for them. The dialogue sequence therefore has power. (And it would be very hard to deliver this character plan in privilege without dialogue...)

So think about the knowledge gap the dialogue is delivering or is an essential part of. Think of dialogue as firstly, an expression and magnification of a character's motivation and their drive towards fulfilment, and secondly, as a mechanism for planting a knowledge gap, and you cannot go far wrong.

A note on detail
Creative writing classes often have their students indulge exercises in long passages of exposition and description. This is fine in terms of use of English in the same way that doing scales is good for learning piano. However, when you read a masterful work of fiction, you possibly do not realise that the detail you are reading is not simple description. *It is description of the holes, not the net.* It is glorious exposition of the knowledge gap, not the information that frames it. It may be detailed, but it is delivering the gaps.

Let's say you want to get across that someone has died. Your first idea might be a big, wide shot (or in a novel, a detailed description) of a funeral. A bleak, winter's day; crows caw and wheel around spindly leafless branches; mourners in black; a hearse; a hole in the ground with a priest standing next to it. This is fine, but it is lifeless in more ways than one. It is cliched and it leaves absolutely no room for the receiver to do any of the work. It might be gloriously prosaic description, but there are no knowledge gaps. OK, so there are two things to do from here.

1. **Abstract away.** As we did with the car parked at a funny angle, what is the minimal symbolism of a death that we can give that will have the receiver load in the appropriate context all by themselves? How about a church bell tolls. How about the dialogue: 'Ashes to ashes.'

   OK. That all works. Simple and effective (and a lot cheaper than the outdoor location shoot with a cast of 50 we had for the funeral…). But it's still a little obvious and unoriginal. We want our writing to have more flare than that. Our third idea will begin to have a little originality.

2. **Go Metaphoric.** What can we deliver than implies or suggests a death without stating it so obviously? How about a pair of empty shoes? We pull out to a wide shot and the apartment is empty. The phone rings, unanswered. Now we're thinking, right? NOW we have something original.

It is in the delivery of this kind of abstraction, implication and metaphor that characterises the finest works. This is also the opportunity for you as a writer. We can let our artistic selves loose to deliver glorious, beautiful, crafted, arty material. Sure, it's exposition, but because it is delivering a big old knowledge gap your receivers' eyebrows will go up as they appreciate the glory of your writing.

When you love a writer's (or a director's) detail, it is because it is detailed delivery of abstracted, metaphoric implication that you have to interpret into knowledge in your mind.

2.5.7 Knowledge gaps through subterfuge

One of the most common gaps in any story is a subterfuge. If one participant knows more than another, there is a good chance it is because there is some skulduggery going on, and knowledge is deliberately being held back or manipulated. Of course, any form of subterfuge is a gap in knowledge.

Gaps of this nature are not always lies and deceit (although these are, of course, excellent examples). Every superhero's alter ego is a subterfuge. All muggles are unaware of the half-bloods and pure-bloods that move amongst you. I mean us. (Nearly gave myself away there...) Every mystery story is one big subterfuge.

Every move that Marty McFly makes through the main body of *Back to the Future* carries the implicit, deep and persistent knowledge gap through subterfuge between us in the audience, who know that he is a time-traveller from the future, and the people of 1955 who do not. Every move that Daphne and Josephine make in *Some Like it Hot* (Billy Wilder, 1959) includes the implicit, deep and persistent knowledge gap that they are really men dressed as women. Every moment of *Breaking Bad*, we in the audience know that Walter White is not a fine, upstanding chemistry teacher. He's the infamous Heisenberg — a brilliant and brutal drugs lord making dirty money and prepared to murder anyone who stands in his way. This is an implicit, deep and persistent subterfuge that brings a baseline knowledge gap to almost all 60+ episodes.

As with all gaps, the presentation can be privilege as well as revelation. In *The Truman Show* (Director Peter Weir, 1998) it is an interesting inversion in the sense that the protagonist is the only participant who is unaware of the subterfuge. Only Truman (Jim Carrey) is lacking knowledge. Everybody else — all the other characters, the television audience as well as the film audience — the whole world — knows the truth and everyone is complicit in the subterfuge against one person — the protagonist.

In *The Usual Suspects*, it is the other way up; that is, the protagonist withholds knowledge from everybody that is finally delivered in revelation at climax. The subterfuge is that our narrator, Verbal Kint knows throughout that he is the feared master-criminal Keyser Soze. We in the audience, along with the police interrogator — everyone — only find this out at the very last moment — just when it becomes too late to react. A beautifully crafted knowledge gap through subterfuge in revelation that has been held open across the entire course of the story.

As you can see from these examples, a good solid subterfuge at the heart of your story can bring a level of knowledge gap power as a 'given' to your whole story. My research has shown that the public rating of a story correlates with the number, depth and duration of overall knowledge gaps, so it is very handy to have a deep and persistent baseline gap like this.

2.5.8 Knowledge gaps through questions

In the framing category we recognised the value of a key question in defining an arc that holds a knowledge gap open across the story-wide plots and major subplots. But of course, all questions are implicitly a knowledge gap and they can be raised at every level and for any duration. In my research I split questions out into **simple**, **compound** and **complex** categories, depending upon the knowledge gap complexity, but as a writer you really do not need to be concerned with all that. Simply be aware that when you are addressing a story event — a plot, a subplot, a chapter, a sequence, scene, sentence or beat, any sort of question that is raised — has an implicit knowledge gap, and therefore carries a degree of story power.

To give you an example, act II of *Back to the Future* has questions at all levels of complexity. As we go into act II, Marty has just been accidentally sent back to 1955, and has the story-wide key question at the forefront of his mind: Can he get back to 1985? How will he do it? He wanders into Hill Valley. In the diner he finds a telephone booth and finds an entry in the phone book for Doc Brown. Now we see his plan and the question is raised for act II: Will Marty find Doc Brown in 1955? Will Doc be able to help him get him back home to 1985?

On the way through this act, a number of smaller, scene level questions are raised: Can Marty find where Doc Brown lives? Can he escape the caring clutches of his future relatives who want to take responsibility for him? Can he escape the romantic advances of his future mother, Lorraine Baines? And within these scenes, there are many beat-level, smaller questions: Will he successfully answer their questions over who he is? How will he explain his clothes? How will he explain that he's already seen *The Man from Space* episode of *The Honeymooners* even though it was (genuinely, in the real world) first aired in 1955? (Actually, that episode was first aired in December 1955, around 2 months after the date of Marty's visit to his future grandparents' house, but we obsessives can forgive the filmmakers for such failings, right?!) Is Doc at home? Will Doc answer the door?

Questions are being raised and answered continuously and on many levels in all stories. Some clear, some less clear. Some direct, some indirect. Some in privilege, some in revelation. Some in the framing, some in the character elements. As a writer, knowing the power of questions on a receiving mind and endlessly raising them at small, medium and large is a simple and powerful method of ensuring your story is compelling.

2.5.9 Knowledge gaps through suggestion and implication

This type of gap refers to knowledge that is implied or assumed rather than certain. As mentioned earlier, not only do we slot new information into the accumulated causal logic that we have gathered so far in a narration, we also project forwards. We cannot help ourselves. We do it automatically and we do it all the time.

There are many tools of implication and suggestion. The clothes someone wears may suggest their profession, wealth, personality, recent or intended likely behaviour. The soundtrack or lighting can tip the audience towards thinking a certain way. A facial expression or a movement of a curtain can have the audience infer information and project forwards on that basis (which may turn out to be true or false). Just because a man is wearing a policeman's uniform does not mean he is a policeman. Even if he can prove he is a policeman, that does not mean he is necessarily honest. Or even a man! However, we unconsciously and automatically make assumptions and build scenarios and project forwards on the basis of these assumptions until further information confirms or denies our hypothesis.

> So ongoing and insistent is the perceiver's drive to anticipate narrative information that a confirmed hypothesis easily becomes a tacit assumption, the ground for further hypothesis. (Bordwell, 1985b, p.38)

Not only does this happen all the time, it is part of your job as the writer to *make sure* it happens all the time. Lead your audience to make an assumption, then confound it. Set it up one way, then twist out to an unexpected new direction. The gap between the audience's projected scenarios and what happens is a knowledge gap through implication or suggestion. The assumption may turn out to be true or false.

An example of a gap of this nature which is reliable occurs when Doc Brown asks to view the photograph of Marty standing with his brother and sister. Marty's older brother, Dave (Marc McClure) is fading from the photograph. The *implication* is that the decreasing likelihood that George and Lorraine will ever become romantically involved and have children is gradually beginning to erase the family from existence, one by one in order of birth. This photograph is used regularly throughout the story, filling a knowledge gap through implication that grows and not only provides a context for the possibility of Marty existing in the future but helps to ramp up the tension as the children disappear from the photograph, one by one.

(Incidentally, when Marty is saying goodbye to his future parents just before he finally leaves 1955, he has reunited them in love and his future mother says thoughtfully: "Marty… such a nice name…" The implication is that this is the moment when she decides the name they will give their future son. It is somewhat incongruous then, that their first-born was named 'Dave'. We nerds can be jerks about stuff like this.)

Another simple example of implication is the monster terrifying the occupants of the spacecraft in *Alien* (Director Ridley Scott, 1989). The monster does not actually make a physical appearance until three-quarters of the way through the film. Most of the time its presence and awesome powers are all implied rather than spelled out and that means it is left for us to create a totally terrifying monster, perfectly attuned to our personal insecurities, all by ourselves. Our own imagination will do a far, far better job of building a monster that genuinely unsettles us than any purveyor of computer-generated mayhem and teeth. For most of the film we see nothing but ceiling tiles rattling and images on radar screens, and because the knowledge is so lacking, we have to build the beast out of subtext, and because we are making it from our own fears, it will be a perfect monster.

Implication and suggestion can also work strongly on the false side. A writer can use these receiver tendencies to mislead, then twist them back to reality through revelation. In the *Frozen* trailer, the implication is not reliable. The authors coax us to believe that the moose wants to eat the carrot, and we go galloping off along this train of thought, beautifully coerced into the channel that the authors wanted us to take. As soon as we take this bait, we are primed for the revelation at climax which brings such fine power and cleverness to the story.

As the author, by making the implication strongly in the opposite direction to the one you know the story event will end up taking, you build strong turning points and revelations.

When Doc Brown is mowed down in a hail of gunfire as Marty is leaving 1985 at the end of act I, the *implication* is that Doc is dead. When Marty eventually gets back at the end of act II, he comes back in a different part of town, he fails to get to Doc in time and we see the same tragic incident a second time. We are left in little doubt: Doc Brown is dead. The writers have taken us to a point where we can see no positive outcome from this, no alternatives or possibilities, and the tragedy is only compounded by Marty's stupid mistake in not giving himself enough time to prevent Doc's death. He had a time machine and he still failed to make it in time. However, the writers built us into this place on purpose, to heighten the impact of the twist they now spring upon us, which is that Doc Brown read the note Marty left him in 1955 and is wearing a bullet proof vest. He is fine.

And, of course, the implication can be in privilege or revelation. As Bordwell observes:

> More often than we are usually aware, narratives invoke expectations only to defeat them, plan and time our encounters with information that will upset our assumptions, encourage us to extrapolate and then chide us for going too far, parade a host of positive instances before trotting out the single and crucial exception. (Bordwell, 1985b, p.39)

Every time you, as a writer, suggest or imply a likely possible future, you are raising questions in the mind of the audience and opening a knowledge gap between the current position and an imagined future projection, as well as another gap between that projected future scenario and what actually happens.

2.5.10 Knowledge Gaps through suspense

Very much related to suggestion and implication is the creation of suspense. Branigan, in his discussion of hierarchies of knowledge, explains how Alfred Hitchcock created suspense:

> Using the example of a bomb placed in a briefcase under a table, he explained how he could create feelings of

suspense, mystery, or surprise in the audience. If the spectator knows about the bomb, but not the characters seated around the table, then the spectator will be in suspense and must anxiously await the bomb's discovery or explosion (Branigan, 1992, p.75).

Suspense is created using, need I say it, a difference in the knowledge held by different participants in the story. Suspense occurs when there is a predictable likely outcome, and the audience is hoping or fearing that it will come to pass. For example, if the audience is made aware of a bomb placed in a briefcase, the predictable outcome is that the bomb will, at some point, explode.

More often than not, the simple use of privilege is the cause of suspense. If we in the audience know there is a ticking bomb in a briefcase and our protagonist does not, it is this knowledge gap that causes the intrigue and the privilege knowledge which renders the event suspenseful.

When the wolf eats Grandma, dresses up in her clothes and settles back in bed to await the arrival of Little Red Riding Hood, we sit in horrified trepidation for the question — what will happen next? — to be answered.

Suspense is usually a function of privilege presentation, however do not forget that you can choose the dynamic you prefer. For example, if a detective is climbing some rickety stairs in an empty old house, creeping cautiously up into the attic, we project forwards with a certain anxiety. What is up there? What's going to happen? If there is a madman waiting with an axe behind the door at the top and we do not know about it, this is a revelation presentation that will come to hit us (as it will the detective) when he gets to the top of the stairs, but you could equally write this in privilege. As the author you can let the audience know that there is an axe-wielding maniac behind the door at the top of the stairs waiting to greet the detective. We know it, but the detective does not. Now, that privilege information brings simple, powerful suspense. The detective is walking up towards that door... and he does not know what is behind that door... Nobody is going to walk away from this story now, right?!

2.5.11 Knowledge Gaps through anagnorisis ('realisation')

Anagnorisis is a moment of realisation for a character. A moment when the truth dawns. This is traditionally (that is, in Aristotle's Greek tragic terms) a stomach-churning realisation that things are much, much worse than they thought. Realisation is a powerful device and one to which most writers do not give nearly enough attention. Anagnorisis is listed here because it is a knowledge gap through character. However, it is also one of Aristotle's dynamics which I shall discuss in depth in section 3.3 — Aristotle's Principles, so I will not go into detail here.

2.6 Storification Gaps

Our audience has been orientated to the direction and intent of the story event through a contextual framing. They have been introduced to characters in their story world. They have seen and heard their actions and words and are evaluating the characters' choices and the outcomes they reap. We now come to the crowning glory of story: **Storification**.

Storification occurs in the mind of the receiver. Having taken in all the information in the narration and interpreted it into a logical progression in mind, storification is the receiver's process of combining the sense of that logical progression with their own existing cultural knowledge and experience in order to create **meaning**.

Note the two parts to the knowledge stream in mind. Firstly, it is assimilated into a narrative that makes sense. A leads to B leads to C — and the causal logic hangs together. This is known as the

narrafication. A set of objects and events are linked by change over time. It does not have to be truth; it just has to be a progression of change over time that we can shrug and accept (more on this shortly). It is 'what happened'. Then it is considered at an intellectual level as that narrafication is searched for what it *means*. A fishing net. It's a thing. A sign. I know what it *is*. It is attached to a boat, dragged through the water and things get caught in it through change over time. This acceptance into mind of a logical progression for what it *does* is narrafication. I then get to eat that night and now I understand what it *means*, at the human cultural knowledge level, and this is storification.

So, for example, there is a narrative progression in *Little Red Riding Hood* that builds into a logical series of actions and words. The causal logic hangs together. Then the receiver thinks about it and decides on a human cultural meaning: that children should not talk to strangers.

In the Hemingway short (For Sale. Baby's Shoes. Never Worn) there is the narrative progression that can be deduced. Someone posted a classified advertisement to sell some shoes. The causal logic hangs together, and this is the narrafication that is interpreted into mind. However, the receiver thinks about it, and decides on a human cultural meaning: That a couple tragically lost a baby.

Storification is the dynamic that creates the ultimate power of a story. Storification causes the events in a narration to leap out of the story world and impact the mind and thoughts of the receiver in ways that receivers like very much. It is a satisfying mental process. Do you remember the first time you divined the moral message from a children's story? If you can get your head around the process of storification, you are armed to create stories that blow people's minds. Storification is the device that turns a narrative into a story, a story into a mind-altering memory and an author into a master of the universe. This is the one, folks!

Every narrative script we have in our long-term memory from learning about life in the real world was new at some point, from learning to walk and use a toilet through paying for things in a shop and playing games, to driving a car and getting a job, and when that memory was laid down it was learned through storification. The receiver may be six years old and discovering a narrative that is perfectly common amongst most adults but new to them. For example, that the cheese on a mouse trap is not yours; that looking down the end of the hose to see what's making the interesting gurgling noise is a bad way of finding out; and that sunscreen only *looks* the same as ice cream (I didn't enjoy that day). Such voyages of narrative discovery lead to a storification meaning. We learn what something is. We learn what it does in a narrative context. Then, ultimately, we learn what it means when that narrative context runs its course. We fill in gap after gap after gap, at the sign, signification, narrafication and ultimately storification levels. Now we have knowledge.

As we discovered with the Heimlich manoeuvre example, this same storification process can be triggered through the delivery of a well-crafted fictional narration.

However, although storification is the ultimate story dynamic, it is also the most difficult to explain in story terms, for three reasons:

1. Storification is a function of the communication between the author and the receiver, and is ultimately a mental dynamic within the receiver. It is not a structure that can be found in the text.

2. Every storification is unique to the individual receiver. It takes place in the mind of the receiver, it relies on their capability and mindset, and it is personal to them. A person may be able to read and understand a series of words, it does not mean they will be capable of storification in the way the author intends.

3. Storification requires the building blocks of framing and character gaps before it can happen. A storification cannot be isolated in itself. It is a product of the framing and character elements.

The author frames the narrative and orientates the audience to the context of the narrative. The characters interact and react in their story world, playing out a narrative. Even though the framing and characters are fictional the outcomes of the decisions made by characters cause a narrative progression to lead to an outcome. What this means can cause storification to take place in the mind of the receiver; that is, 'meaning' is potentially delivered to the mindset of the receiver through understanding the human costs and benefits of the narrative containing those character actions and decisions.

How can there be any reliable meaning when the framing and characters generally form an acknowledged fiction? If a kid goes back in time to provide dating services to his future parents or if a playroom full of toys come to life when nobody's looking or if a cross-dressing wolf convinces a little girl that he is her grandmother how can these things deliver any form of reliable meaning?

The answer lies in the critical distinction between truth and meaning. I have touched on this a few times so let's nail it down.

2.6.1 True lies and fictional truth

It is important to understand the role of storification in the delivery of a narration. In these terms, telling a 'true' story is no different from a work of fiction. Telling a true story is still not the truth, it is a *representation* of a narrative that is built in the mind of the receiver. The only absolute truth of a 'true story' was the real event in the moment it happened, and only witnesses who were there experienced that truth. Those witnesses build a representation of that event in mind — what we call a memory. That representation will also be an approximation. It will be coloured by the receiver's personal mindset, history, experience, age, gender, mood, concentration, existing knowledge, conditioning, cultural and political preferences... and who knows what else. It is a version of that event held in mind. It is not the truth.

As soon as that reality is passed it is gone forever. For every receiver who get to know about it after that, it is the representation of events that is recounted. Even if a person intends, with all their heart, to narrate the truth of an event with absolute integrity, it is still not the truth. It has been uploaded into mind through the limiting lens of the human senses, interpreted through the tools of human mental understanding, reshaped into human causal logic, coloured by the receiver's personality and experience, formed up into a sequence made from the strictures of language, and may or may not be anything like an accurate representation of the truth. As a story emerges into the air as a narration, it is not truth and it is not knowledge, it is narrative.

But narrative contains *meaning*, and narrative is what knowledge is made of. If a narrative makes sense in terms of human causal logic it can be rebuilt in a receiving mind like any other narrative progression. A work of pure fiction can still deliver valuable and reliable meaning. Think of all the myriad of stories that are out there which, when it is all boiled down, carry the meaning: Crime does not pay. Whatever the extent of fiction, fact or fairy tale in the drama which delivers that message, it is still human meaning that is delivered. That is why we can *know* how time travel works in Hill Valley just as readily as we understand how nuclear fission works in the real world. We understand the lifecycle of a zombie as readily as the lifecycle of a butterfly; we understand the narrative involved in a horse race just as readily as when a hare races a tortoise; the narrative integral to Jesus as readily as the narrative integral to Santa Claus as readily as the narrative integral to George McFly. They are all forms of *meaning*, because, to us, logical narrative progression *is* meaning, and that meaning is not truth. It is contextualised by our personal evaluation. Santa Claus, for a four-year-old, is absolute truth. It's a narrative that makes sense and hangs together perfectly when contextualised into the young mind, and when that narrative script runs, it has significant meaning in their life. To a child, it feels like truth. It is absolute and reliable. As our ability to provide a more sophisticated framing develops with age and experience, Santa Claus does not simply disappear or become filed under 'LIES'. The mental context changes, but the narrative remains the same, and the meaning simply changes. Santa Claus still has meaning to us in adulthood, however that meaning is nuanced to situate Santa more appropriately into our broader mindset and greater knowledge. The Santa narrative becomes more about our holidays, families and children. What it means becomes 'edited' in our mind over time. The narrative remains the same, the meaning is changed to make it more usable in the context of our personal knowledge and experience as we change and grow.

Story is context and meaning, not truth or fiction.

This is very important for writers who are often so anxious to communicate the 'truth' that they don't allow themselves to tell their stories to best effect. Apart from anything else, we *want* our story-tellers to lie to us. We want to be entertained and puzzled and led a merry dance before we find out the meaning of the story. We demand that storytellers do this for us. Imagine if Agatha Christie came in to tell us a story now. She sits on a stool, takes a deep breath and simply tells us the essential truth integral to the narrative:

"The butler did it. Bye-ee!" And she leaves.

That would not be very satisfying, would it? No. Why not? Because there are no knowledge gaps. There is no subtext required so there is no work for us in the audience to do. No knowledge gaps means there is no story for us to build. We get a type of 'truth' from knowing whodunnit, but we do not get any meaning. There is truth in the words and their existence, but when we read a story we don't remember the words. We remember the meaning. A storification that gives us the sagely life lesson that crime does not pay is much more important to us than knowledge of who actually committed the crime. Meaning, not truth, is what's important, and that requires storification, and storification requires us as receivers to fill knowledge gaps and derive the ultimate meaning for ourselves.

A story is a puzzle made from knowledge gaps. The gaps are filled by the cultural knowledge and experience of the receiver. When the gaps are filled by the receiver a complete narrative in mind forms up into meaning that is guided by the author but created by the receiver.

The obvious example is a moral message in a children's story. In *Little Red Riding Hood*, the framing has us orientated to a progression whereby a wolf sets a trap for a young girl and plans to eat her. The characters make decisions that cause outcomes that have us leave the story feeling that children should not talk to strangers. The story has made sense and carried meaning over and above the narrative events. That is storification.

When an Ugly Duckling struggles to find a sense of belonging in the world and we leave the story with thoughts about what is right and wrong in the real world in areas like racism, exclusion, tribalism, ethnicity — that is storification.

However, it is happening in small and medium as well as large and epic. When someone tells you a joke, the narrative leads to a surprising outcome. The creation of that unexpected end-state in mind is the job of the receiver. This is storification. For example:

> Two fish in a tank. One says to the other: "Do you know how to drive this thing?"

What you just did in your mind is storification. It was a function of your cultural knowledge of the two meanings of the word 'tank'.

Your mind jumped instantly to the initial framing — two fish in an aquarium. The characters indulged their dialogue and now you have to make this narration into causal logic. When your sense-making mind pattern-matched 'driving' against a different type of tank and came up with an image of two fish in a military tank, that was storification. If you laugh when you hear a joke, that is proof of storification.

In drama, storification is our understanding of life and how it should be led as a result of our interpretation of a character's decisions and the outcomes those decisions harvested. Thus, when we watch *Spongebob Squarepants* and later in our real world we save someone's life through the Heimlich manoeuvre, it is storification that gave us the narrative memory that let us do that using skills we did not even realise we had.

Application

What does this mean to you as a writer? Well, it means that understanding the storifications you are going to deliver is the secret to unlocking the ultimate power in your story idea. Your audience must do the important work, so understanding where you want them to arrive through their own thought processes is essential in order that you can work back from there and design your character actions and the framing to coerce them on to that mental pathway.

As we discussed earlier, knowing the ending is not half as important as understanding the ultimate power in your story. For that, writers need to know the storification that arrives as a function of the framing and characters. Remember, the thinking is not so much:

        Beginning → Middle → End

More:

        Framing → Character Actions/Decisions → Storification

Delivering storification is your aim as a writer. How do we use the storification to drive the story development process?

2.6.2 Using the Storification

As a writer, before you can write the body of the story, you ideally need to get a clear handle on how it will storify. What is the meaning that will emerge in the mind of the receiver from the slippery fiction you construct? The characters take action, narrative logic emerges and the receiver derives meaning. Once you get far enough into developing your story that you understand the meaning that will emerge for the receiver, you can work back to construct the journey your readers will go on that will ensure they ultimately discover that meaning for themselves.

If you wish to deliver the meaning 'crime does not pay', certain story elements are instantly suggested. We need a crime that ends up causing the criminal to fail and to drop down the ladder of life, rather than fulfilling their plan to use crime to succeed and climb up the ladder of life. So, we need a criminal. We need a plan for a crime that, if it all goes as he wishes, will deliver the criminal a better quality of life. We need a morally good person working against that criminal achieving fulfilment. We need that good person to end up benefiting from their selfless actions towards a better society. We need the criminal to end up behind bars or dead. All this needs to happen through the decisions the characters make and — importantly — those decisions must involve dilemma and personal risk in order that the audience becomes firstly, uncertain about who will win out and secondly, engaged with the potential for different outcomes. OK. There is our story framework. Now we create the story using knowledge gaps in the telling. Subterfuge, trickery, misdirection, privilege and revelation, character plans, realisations and peripeteia, conflict and jeopardy. The decisions the character make will *demonstrate*, through the outcomes they reap, that crime does not pay.

In *Little Red Riding Hood*, the moral message — that children should not talk to strangers — is the starting point for the author; the meaning that they would like the receiver to end up with in mind.

That will be the storification. OK. In that case, logically, I can derive two key characters from the storification. I'm going to need a child who should not talk to a stranger. I'm going to need a stranger, and he must be bad if the child should not speak to him, and the child should suffer because of her decision to talk to a stranger if that storification is to be delivered. OK. There is a story spine right there.

As the author, I <u>start</u> from this point — my storification — however, I will organise my narration so my reader can <u>end up</u> there. I abstract away from the reliable meaning that will ultimately be demonstrated through character actions. I begin with a little girl helping mummy. They are baking cakes. The girl will take the cakes to her grandmother at her house in the woods. OK. So now we know the aim — Little Red's character plan is the framing and the audience is orientated. A helpful child visiting Grandma. Now, it would not be a story if her ambitions were simply fulfilled without incident, so we need a 'why now?' to make this particular visit to Grandma difficult for her. Enter the wolf, and let's put this character's aims in opposition to the girl. The girl is lovely and trusting, so speaks openly to the wolf, and we fear for her as she fails to read his motivation as we can. Aha! Excellent. Now we naturally have a **knowledge gap** emerging between our understanding of the wolf's motivation and Little Red's naïve lack of understanding; she does not recognise his motive. There is the story power, right there, now we understand the motivation of the bad guy and we can see every likelihood, given Little Red's naivety, that the unfolding narrative will pay off in the bad guy's favour. We project forwards and we fear he will go up the ladder of life at the cost of the good little girl. This is the power of the story so let's make sure we work it. Focus on it. It's a gap between Little Red Riding Hood's understanding of the wolf's motivation and our understanding of the wolf's motivation. Open that gap up and keep it open. In which case, let's have Little Red Riding Hood trust him. She takes his advice. She stops to pick flowers, as the wolf runs ahead to set a trap for her at Grandma's house. He does unspeakable things to Grandma, eats her, dresses in her clothes, and lays in wait for Little Red Riding Hood. Now the wolf has a plan too, which we know about and Little Red Riding Hood does not.

Their plans are the framing knowledge gaps that have orientated the audience. We have developed the characters around conflicting motivations so we have knowledge gaps that grip. We have a plan that is going wrong for the little girl, and a conflicting plan that is going very smoothly for the bad guy. We have a girl who does not know what we know — that the wolf cannot be trusted, that her plan is going wrong and we have a wolf lying in wait. Little Red Riding Hood is in mortal danger. As soon as these gaps are in place, we have grip and engagement. There is not a four-year-old on Earth who could walk away from this story now. And the author knows this. We also have a knowledge gap through the subterfuge of the wolf, and because it is in privilege presentation (we know what Little Red Riding Hood does not) it is causing excellent suspense. The author keeps this suspense open for as long as possible. Little Red Riding Hood arrives at the cottage, she addresses the wolf, they exchange their pleasantries ('what big eyes you have, Grandma...') all designed to keep that knowledge gap open — we know what she does not — prolong that grip and ramp up the suspense to unbearable levels. Then the wolf strikes, and we get the unexpected outcome: he eats the little girl. And appears to have won. Completely. Wow. That's quite a twist — two dead, a child and a granny, and the bad guy wins all. Nobody would have seen that coming. These are the consequences of Little Red's actions. She made decisions that led to outcomes. Pretty sobering stuff for our four-year-old.

We in the audience now understand everything that happened. It is a complete narrative that makes sense. We see meaning in that taking these actions (trusting a stranger) leads to these consequences (death of small child). We gain a meaning from what we have experienced: that children should not talk to strangers. This is not a mantra that is stated in the story, but it was the intention of the author to deliver it and I think we can be pretty sure that the implications of the child's actions (that is, the storification) hits any youngster firmly between the eyes. The roots have gone down into the mind of the receiver. Storification has taken place if this meaning has been communicated through the actions and behaviours of the characters; specifically, **the decisions made by the protagonist and the outcomes of these decisions**. It storifies into meaning in mind. A life lesson has been taught and learned. We instinctively analyse the narrative progression and look for where it went wrong and what should have happened. We do this in order to arm ourselves against the negative outcome of the narrative progression should we ever find ourselves running a narrative like this in real life. If Little Red had not trusted that stranger she would have been fine. There is the lesson — the prevention of this narrative logic playing out. Don't talk to strangers.

For the receiver, framing led to character actions led to conflict led to decisions led to outcomes led to storification.

This progression is — in broad terms — one very strong method for writers to manage the power in their story.

A writer needs to:

- Understand the storification.
- Derive appropriate characters and their motivations to deliver this storification.
- Ensure that the aims and motivations of characters are blocked.
- Identify and craft knowledge gaps to ensure the receiver must provide subtext. The more the better.
- Ensure the character journey *demonstrates* (show don't tell) the meaning you wish to deliver through the **decisions and choices they make**. The actions they take reap the consequences and what we in the audience feel about those consequences causes storification.

I introduce that bullet list with the words, 'in broad terms' because this is not a rule book, but these are certainly sensible considerations in the development of your story. Some or all of them will almost certainly be present in your story. The craft of an author is managed through understanding these kinds of dynamics and relationships within your story.

You might be reading all this and thinking, 'Well, that's nonsense. I just start writing from the beginning and I work through 'til I get to the end. I then do a couple of editing passes — rewriting and refining the story from the front to the back until it's finished.'

I have some sympathy with this thinking, however I would invite you to think again about what is actually going on with this process.

What really happens is that you write instinctively from the front to the back. It's creative and enjoyable. When you get to the end, you realise things didn't go quite as you expected, but it's still really good. You now know where your story goes (you will see this as your ending) and you rewrite in order to drive towards and support that ending. This process *does* work, but only because you will have instinctively included a storification. It will be there in your inspiration. You are a natural storyteller, which is why you write, and you will have delivered at least something of that storification even though you never knew it had a label. You thought you had discovered your ending, but the true power of that ending is in the storification that powers it, and when you understand that you will do much better (particularly on stories that are less inspired than your early works). You will optimise your story to perfection using your inspiration, your storification and your head. This knowledge will help you to avoid writing stories that do not really work as well as you had hoped, and deliver every story to its absolute highest potential, because you will know where that potential lies.

We transform the characters' logical progression in the narrative into a script (memory) that is based on what it means. It is the storification dynamic that causes us to lay down narrative memories; the lessons we take from understanding character actions and the outcomes they reaped. They learned — and we learned — from their actions. Now, you might say 'well, look not all stories have some important outcome or epic subtext that teaches some life lesson or whatever.'

That is certainly true, however that is not the point. The mental process of storification is triggered by filling in gaps. Storification takes place for any and every narrative progression, whether it is some epic life event or some slapstick comedy in *Spongebob Squarepants*. The mental process is a reflex response to a knowledge gap. It is unconscious, instinctive and automatic and is triggered into storification by the filling of knowledge gaps and the completion of a sense-making narrative even if the meaning is not truthful (like Santa Claus) or deeply meaningful (like the two fish in a tank joke).

Sure, the stories that win all the major awards have worthy, ideological subtext that teaches a lesson about life and how it should be led, but all narratives *that storify* carry the power to grip an audience, and all narratives that storify do so because of the dynamics in the knowledge transfer irrespective of the 'importance' of the ultimate meaning.

Knowledge gaps trigger storification because it is a natural reflex that has been built in to human survival down the millennia of evolution. It is the way we learn the truly important lessons in life and lay down useful long-term, narrative memories that can benefit us. Writers use that evolutionary reflex to trigger engagement. If the story does deliver life lessons and 'value' at that level, then it is more satisfying to the receiving mind, but it does not have to. Any knowledge gap will trigger the same reflex. It is not until the conscious mind evaluates it and reuses it that the receiver decides whether it is important or not. So as a writer, triggering the reflex with knowledge gaps is story power. That's all you need to do to generate engagement.

Our analysis of *The Big Sleep* (coming soon) proves the point. The logic of the detective story does not make sense, but the story was still able to become a classic because despite its logical flaws, it storifies very strongly.

Let us go through the storification gaps now to clarify what storification is in knowledge gap terms. We will then build further on these principles to take us into more depth with the story development process.

2.6.3   Knowledge gaps through character growth

Character growth is the most common of all the storification dynamics. When someone changes and learns and grows as a result of the decisions they make and the consequences those decisions reap, it is a clear demonstration of how a narrative progression causes life meaning to us in the audience.

Most stories are the narration of a character's literal or metaphoric 'journey', through which they will almost certainly end up a different person from who they were at the outset. Someone somewhere is likely to have changed as a result of story events and this is of visceral interest to your audience because the changes they suffer or benefit from will be a result of the cause/effect chain that emerges from the choices they make. The consequences of choices made educate us as we build and understand the logical narrative sequence the characters generate through their actions. Once the narrative sequence is complete in our mind, it is a narrative memory made from the knowledge that *these* actions in response to *these* narrative events cause *these* outcomes for the character, and through storification we relate this narrative progression to how it might apply in our own lives and we lay it down as a memory.

2.6.3.1 What is character growth?

Character growth is a change in the fortunes of a character across the course of their story experience. Their quality of life will become 'better' or 'worse' (character growth can be either positive or negative change) in some subjective sense that we in the audience can appreciate.

In a simplistic sense, this can be gains or losses of any sort. If a character finds a bag of money or gets hit by a car or gets married or falls down some stairs — these are all versions of character growth — a change in personal values, fortunes or quality of life. However, these do not carry the emotional power we want in a story, because it is not an outcome of a narrative that carries *meaning*. If someone gets a bag of money their fortunes have changed to the positive but it is not *meaningful* character growth because no difficult choices were made and there was no learning and growth in the process that caused them to end up with the money. As we said earlier, we do not cry when we see someone cry. We have to know why they are crying before we can emotionally empathise. It is the same with character growth. We do not feel the power of storification when someone gains or loses. We feel the power of storification when we know why someone gains or loses. It is meaningful when someone changes and learns and grows, and that learning and growth leads to gains and losses. Character growth is about decisions under pressure leading to consequences.

Let's take a look at two character growth examples, one with meaning and one without. In an early sequence in *Back to the Future*, Marty McFly sees a Toyota pickup truck on its way to be delivered and expresses his strong desire to own one. 'Some day, Jennifer. Some day...' From this we understand that Marty will feel a sense of fulfilment in life if he ever owns a Toyota pickup like that one. By the end of the story, he does indeed own one; however, it's bought for him by his dad, so for all that it is symbolic of Marty's journey through the story, it was his father, George, who made difficult choices under pressure, and Marty getting a pickup truck was the outcome of George's life choices. This is indirect, secondary character growth.

True character growth involves a change in a person's knowledge, values and quality of life *as a result of the decisions they make under pressure*. George McFly's personal understanding of life and how it should be lived is changed through his story experiences; his *very character* is an outcome of the choices he made under pressure of conflict. He takes on his daemons. He changes and he learns and he grows, from weak and unassertive to a strong, decisive adult. This is the story's character growth, and it is this storification that resonates so strongly with us and which gives *Back to the Future* its ultimate appeal. George — and by association his entire family — climbed up the ladder of life as a result of the decisions he made under pressure.

From my story analysis perspective, because *Back to the Future* shows the same family in 'before and after' versions of 1985, it does have a rather handy habit of being a control experiment for itself, so let's dig a little deeper into the impact of George's personal growth to see how it sits at the core of the story. What changes across the course of the telling due to George's arc of change and growth?
At the beginning of the story (1985 version #1):

- George is weak and unassertive. He is subservient to his boss, Biff.
- Lorraine drinks Vodka at the dining table.
- Lorraine looks sadly on George; she appears to regret the choice of partner she made.
- Marty doubts his music ability. He's demonstrating a lack of confidence (learned from his father).
- Marty's sister, Linda, complains that she can't get a boyfriend.
- Marty's brother, Dave, flips burgers for a living.

- The family lives in rather dark, run-down, humble conditions.

By the end of the story (1985 version #2):

- George is strong, confident and fulfilled (his first book is published).
- George has proven the characters' repeated mantra: 'If you put your mind to it, you can accomplish anything.'
- Biff is subservient and now works for George. (His choices mean he has gone down the ladder of life. His fortunes have changed to the negative.)
- Lorraine is positive, fit, healthy and slim.
- Lorraine and George are radiant; actively loving and in a happy partnership.
- Linda has too many boyfriends to easily manage.
- Dave is in a suit, working in a professional capacity.
- The family lives in relative prestige and well-lit opulence.

Ironically, it is only Marty who has not really changed and grown. He has benefited from his journey, of course, and he has grown, but his character growth is more symbolic; a side-effect of George's true growth. Marty's' personal growth is not demonstrated. He never sends his music off to the record company or somehow shows a growth in his own confidence although he did fulfil a personal ambition — he finally got to play in front of an audience.

Marty was unable to overcome Biff, who beat him up and had his henchmen lock him in the boot of a car, leaving George to fight on alone. Indeed, Marty's final meaningful action as a sequence protagonist in the second version of 1985 is to fail to get back in time to save Doc Brown from being shot. In a story in which most people would consider Marty to be the protagonist, he is one character who basically stays the same throughout and ultimately he makes personal losses that are rescued by George.

Marty's main role is as a 'proxy' for us in the audience. He leads us through the events — we see the world through his eyes and react and understand events as he does. In story theory terms, there is only one true character growth that defines the story and takes all the other characters up or down the ladder of life with him, and that is the arc of George McFly.

The Kingpin Moment
From a writer's perspective it is worth reiterating that pretty much everything in the entire story of *Back to the Future* builds up to — or is an outcome of — the moment when George McFly makes a fist for the first time in his life. It was in this moment that his character grew.

Everything before that single punch — that moment of character growth — is in service of it. Everything after that single punch is a consequence of it. The writers recognised that this moment of character growth defines the power of the entire story. Once they discovered that, it became the pivot for the story. It is what I call the kingpin moment. The moment when the storification dynamic is activated. Stories are often about a life lesson for a participant — perhaps the audience. They address the question: How should a person lead their life? The story is about those characters demonstrating how to handle a life situation. As the writer, once you know what that situation and lesson are, it becomes a great deal easier to deliver your story to its best effect.

Although the storification will not always be character growth, and it may not happen with such clarity in a single scene like it does for George, it should be possible to analyse most good stories in these terms. To find the storification; to identify the kingpin moment(s) that make the storification(s) happen. It is through these mechanisms that a story resonates in all of us. As a writer, we can use this to work everything back and forwards from these critical elements in order to ensure the story's power is harnessed and delivered.

A character takes action under pressure in pursuit of fulfilment. The actions lead to outcomes. The outcomes demonstrate to us in the audience a lesson about how a person should lead their life.

In terms of character growth as a knowledge gap, a set of values can be measured at the start and will be seen to have symbolically or actually changed across the course of the story, depicting a clear path of growth in at least one character. The gap is between the quality of life and life values at the beginning compared to those at the end.

This is, incidentally, why stories often fail to deliver a successful sequel. The protagonist has made their defining journey of growth, and once they have achieved fulfilment (whatever that means for them) there is no further personal journey they can satisfactorily take in this story. Any subsequent plotlines are most likely going to struggle to resonate. *Back to the Future* handled this by moving on to the next generation for the sequel, 30 years into the future, when Marty and Jennifer's children are struggling on the lower levels of the journey towards their own fulfilment.

This said, the character growth does not have to be as obvious as *Back to the Future*. A good novel may take 500 pages and shift its protagonist from a position of delusion to one of belief. Indeed, an ironic story may take its protagonist back to where they started or a tragic story can take a protagonist on a downward spiral into worse circumstances or death.

Even in tragic circumstances, the story power is there because the storification is there. The principle remains the same. At least one character will experience a change in their quality of life *as a result of the decisions they make under pressure*. When a character has a negative or tragic outcome it is likely that the events of the story will still shine a light on what the character should have done, so the learning is still there, but the growth is negative. Do not shun this possibility in your stories. Negative character growth is just as powerful as the positive version, if not more so. Some of the most appreciated and powerful stories are essentially tragedies — *Citizen Kane, Romeo and Juliet, Oedipus Rex, Breaking Bad, Game of Thrones, Butch and Sundance, Thelma and Louise...* the list is endless. Stories that have a winner also have a loser, and their loss is character growth that brings power and grip to the story. George McFly has a positive character growth journey, but we understand it relative to Biff's negative decline.

2.6.3.2 What to do When Characters Must Not Grow

Character growth often defines the story to a point of completion beyond which there can be no more story. However, when story creators have a character who must feature in an episode every week or throughout an unending film franchise, such as a James Bond film, a television series like *Only Fools and Horses* (written by John Sullivan), a Jack Reacher novel (written by Lee Child) or a superhero series, character growth becomes a problem. Once a character has grown, their story is complete, and they end up in a different place mentally and emotionally, from which it is difficult to begin the next episode, because a character who has grown is fundamentally changed by their experience. In episodic stories, this often cannot be allowed to happen. If the Coyote achieves fulfilment and finally gets to catch and eat the Roadrunner, the character growth arc for both is an end to it. We are done. It would be quite some episode, but it could never be allowed to happen. However, as I have said, character growth is also almost inevitable in a fine story. It is the most powerful story dynamic and is the most common of the storifications. So what does a series creator do when the character must **not** be allowed to change and grow?

Three tips:

- Ensure that one of the secondary or dependent characters does the growing. This could, of course, include the negative growth of the bad guy and the positive growth of the community or society (as found in James Bond and Jack Reacher).

- Use other types of storifications to deliver the story's main power.

- Use the early episode(s) to have the main character grow into the protagonist that will take the series forwards. In *Breaking Bad*, Walter White begins as a meek and downtrodden teacher. Through the course of the first episode he grows dramatically through the decisions he makes to become… Heisenberg. The brutal and decisive criminal mastermind. Use the early episodes as the opportunity to have your main character do their growing.

Jack Reacher is an interesting case in point. Lee Child has written dozens of Jack Reacher books now, the structure of which allows for not only character growth to make each individual story compelling but also for Reacher to end up back where he started in order to reset the character correctly for the next episode. Here is how Lee Child explained his 'next' book to me (bearing in mind this conversation was in 2009):

> Reacher is a loner. His past as a war veteran means he struggles to settle and to find the kind of fulfilment that most find through love, family and community. Reacher begins the story as a thoughtful soul, travelling alone around the USA, searching for himself. He wanders into a town on some pretext — say, to visit the gravestone of an admired jazz musician. However, the town has secrets and Reacher gets drawn in. An elderly lady is being bullied and Reacher protects her. (That's the story in a sentence.) So, logically, the first question we have to ask is obvious, isn't it? What does she need protecting from? Next there is this mysterious establishment just outside of town, and that is at the root of

the problem. So, the question is, what is the establishment? OK, so I made it an ex-military establishment, and it turns out it is nine-tenths underground. It's enormous in comparison to the proportion on the surface. What is it for? What is the problem it is causing? Who is inside and what are they doing? Clearly, from interrogating the premise, we can see that at a key point in the story, Jack Reacher is going to have to go inside this secretive establishment and pit himself against the unwelcoming, overwhelming and intimidating odds that will be stacked against him when he does.

I don't really plan too much beyond this process. I start writing by instinct and, although I generally have an idea for the main events, the detailed story and possibilities just kind of open up for me as I go along. (Our conversation is in full in *The Story Book*, 2010.)

Now, having read many of the Reacher books, the detail will build suspense through adding relentless pressure on Jack Reacher. A drugs gang will be involved. They have paid off the corrupt mayor. Contract gangsters try to intimidate the lady. The Police, the FBI and then the military hierarchy all become implicated, they all want to stop Jack from finding out what is going on, but Reacher takes them all on. At the same time, he meets a girl. Falls in love. By the end of the roller-coaster adventure Reacher has saved the old lady, held the authorities to account, meted out fearsome justice to the bad guys, cleaned up the corrupt police force and government and moved in with a wonderful woman. He is a hero of the town, a protector of morality, a pillar of the community... he has a life, a home, a girlfriend, the keys to the city. Through his actions and his decisions under pressure, his character has grown and better values have been brought to himself and to this troubled town. However, his girlfriend wakes up the next day to find he has gone. Wandering off into the sunrise. He is alone again. Troubled but soulful. Off to the next town. His character has grown, so we got the storification power that brought, but the underlying issues from the past continue to trouble his soul. These issues undermine all that growth and take him in a circle back to the beginning. In leaving, he has wiped out all that character growth. It defined a wonderful story, but now he is reset, so is able to do it all again next time. He arrives at the next town the same man who arrived in the last one, and we can go around again. Another wonderful, winning story begins. (By the way, I made up this story progression by myself for exemplification purposes. Lee Child is far, far cleverer than this! Do see my full conversation with Lee in *The Story Book* and you can, of course, read the book that emerged: *61 Hours*, by Lee Child, 2010).

Ironic Growth
Reacher is an example of an ironic arc; a happy ending for the community is tinged with the sadness of Reacher's unresolved underlying trauma from his wartime experiences. This is often the trademark of a powerful story. Happiness infused with sadness, or tragedy with an ironic positive shining through.

Ironic growth occurs where values that change to the positive in one context are balanced out by the negative arcs in another. In *I am Legend* (2007, Directed by Francis Lawrence), Robert Neville (Will Smith) achieves his aim — to find an antidote to the disease that is turning all humanity into murderous mutants — but in order to get the antidote off Manhattan Island so it can save humanity, he must give his own life; a choice he makes. Whilst Neville suffered a negative character growth, humanity benefited — a positive growth. This dynamic also features in the bible. Jesus died to save us all. He died. But he saved us all. Positive for humanity. Negative for Jesus. As it was in the beginning for Jesus, so it is in the end for Will Smith. I feel sure at least one of them would approve of the comparison.

Character growth can be a measure of either a character who knows they have grown and uses or appreciates their growth, or it can be a function of audience learning and understanding. This brings us to...

2.6.4 Knowledge gaps through vicarious learning

Often in stories, the character growth arc is evident to the audience but not necessarily or overtly achieved by the character. We in the audience learn from the story even if the character does not.

Little Red Riding Hood does not demonstrate her learning and growth. The story is a sagely warning to all of us not to talk to strangers, but there is no ongoing event that shows that she has learned her lesson or to map out for children how they should behave under given circumstances. We learn vicariously through the experience of the little girl, but we do not see if she went on to change her behaviour and be more careful next time. This is not a problem; it is a storification that characterises a more subtle dynamic, whereby the receiver of the story is left to think deeply about the implications, rather than have them made clear through exposition in the climax and resolution of the story.

This interesting dynamic is at the centre of the greatness of *Citizen Kane*. We set off on Kane's life story, from his beginnings as a child playing in the snow; his upbringing by a bank; his inheritance of tens of millions; his use of that money to become a political force, taking on the establishment on behalf of the common man; his growing influence and global power; his increasing frustration with people who refuse to accept his attempts to help them, because they see him as having an agenda.

He starts off sincerely trying to do good things, however, his power takes him to a point of excess that is not morally correct. For example, his second wife is a singer. She lacks confidence, so he builds a concert hall in her name and gives her top billing. He sees this as a kind and generous act, but she is embarrassed and tries to reject his magnanimity because she knows she is not good enough to merit the scale of stage he has forcibly made available to her. It is a function of his money and power, not her talent. Having done so much for her, he feels insulted by her rejection.

At the end of his life Kane appears unfulfilled and in the final scene we get the answer to the key question upon which the entire story is based: What is the significance of his final utterance: the word, 'Rosebud'? It was the name of his sledge, a childhood toy, and a symbolic recognition of the time when he was happiest. When he was poor, powerless and had only the simplest of pleasures. He dies evidently longing for those simpler times. We in the audience have had journalists, Kane's family and friends describe every detail of his life, actions and decisions. However, they never found out the meaning of the word 'Rosebud'. Only we in the audience see the paint burn off his sledge, and we see the sledge is called Rosebud. The journalists and everyone else in the story world go back to their lives and never find out what that word referred to, and we are left with this simple knowledge to which we add our own thoughts and provide the subtext that defines the story. It is not for me to decide what you might think from having all this knowledge, but you may learn, for example, that power corrupts. Or that in politics, populism inevitably grows into authoritarianism. Perhaps you learn that simple pleasures are more valuable than all the riches that money can buy.

When a story has such a progression, some learning takes place which potentially impacts the mindset of the receiver. Perhaps the learning is more direct — if you take these actions in these circumstances, these will be your outcomes. We learn vicariously from the experiences of the characters.

Education
All education is, of course, a knowledge gap being filled and a form of personal growth for the individual gaining that knowledge. This is why a documentary is still a story, because it involves knowledge gaps in the telling. *The Story of Steam Power* or *The Story of Medicine,* or *The Story of World War II* is not a character journey, but there is a gap for the audience between what they know of steam power, medicine or World War II before the narration and what they know about it afterwards, so it is a valid story.

Even if the story is science fiction or fantasy, the knowledge that is imparted — even that which is not true in the real world — is still knowledge that is taken on board by the receiver. For example, we know that it takes 1.21 gigawatts of electricity to power time travel and we know that to get to college at Hogwarts, you must catch a train from platform 9¾ at London's King's Cross station. It is not true but it is knowledge and it is as 'valid' as any other reliable meaning in story terms.

At the more insidious end, it is also possible to persuade people your agenda and opinions are worthy purely by ensuring they have narrative logic. Every narrative is a potential memory, so the meaning that is delivered can be angled for personal gain. Just as we were convinced of the veracity of the Santa Claus story, so we can be convinced of other meaning through our lives. Governments have long recognised the power of the storyteller, and they often make sure they have influence or even control over the media that their ideology allows. Using stories and media to adjust the minds of the receivers to a way of thinking is called cultural hegemony. We have seen how a fictional narrative can affect the mind just as effectively as a real-world experience and it is in this area of vicarious learning and education that lie possibilities for political coercion.

So, stories can educate us by giving us knowledge we did not have, either directly or through learning vicariously from the outcomes reached by characters through the decisions they make.

2.6.5 Knowledge gaps through surpassing aim

One of the secrets to a powerful storification is for it to dawn on the receiver suddenly. It does not have to — a slow-burner is also perfectly valid — but when a storification does arrive suddenly, it tends to have a stronger impact and work well. The reason for this appears to be that a receiver has invested all this time in a story, painstakingly piecing it all together, projecting forwards and predicting the complete picture… when all of a sudden a twist in the tail throws the whole narrative into a new final configuration. The mind rushes to figure it all out; that is, to construct the new causal logic so it makes sense. When it does come together, the memory is made with defences down and without too much thinking going on, and bang! It gets laid down more readily because the conscious mind does not have time to organise it against considered thought before it becomes part of the mindset. It is an automatic, unconscious process that we cannot prevent. This is why stories that have a twist are so powerful. The twist delivers a high impact on our mind; an impact we like very much because it feels like exciting new learning.

One of the best ways of introducing a relatively quick storification is by using a knowledge gap through surpassing aim.

How does it work?
With a key question dynamic, the protagonist sets out with a clear and stated aim. We in the audience know what they want and although we are keen to find out if they get it or not, it does render the ending a little predictable. So, when they reach the point at which they can achieve their goal, there is an opportunity for expectations to be twisted. For example, let us say the protagonist's experiences have changed their values. They have learned and grown, and they make an unexpected decision. They forgo the rewards we thought they wanted, even though they are now within their grasp, for some alternative outcome.

An example of this is found in *Rain Man* (1988, directed by Barry Levinson). When Charlie Babbitt (Tom Cruise) finds out that his father has died, he returns home to cash in on his inheritance, only to find that his father's fortune has been left to his autistic brother, Raymond. Motivated by his hunger for the money and confident that he can manipulate Raymond, Charlie takes Raymond out of the institution in which he lives in order to take him back to Los Angeles and get the cash out of him. However, on the road trip back to LA, he bonds with his brother. And when he reaches the point where he could secure the money he realises that he does not want it if that means losing his brother or doing him down. He has found something profoundly more valuable. He feels protective and loving towards his brother and that has overwhelmed the cynical and money-driven side of Charlie's personality. He has changed and grown and found a fine surpassing aim.

Note how this works on the key question dynamic. The key question is privilege knowledge that sets a very clear aim which orientates the audience to the direction of the story, but it can also be seen as on-the-nose writing that is making the story predictable. However, it greatly increases the power of the story if the key question turns out not to be the end-game at climax because it is overwhelmed by an unexpected surpassing aim, delivering a twist to a finer resolution and character growth.

In *It's a Wonderful Life* (1946, directed by Frank Capra). George Bailey's (James Stewart) clear and stated aim is to travel the world and make a million dollars. By the end of the film, he has failed to achieve either. He's never left his home town and he is still skint. However, he realises he is, "The richest man in Bedford Falls," because he has a wonderful wife and kids, and he is loved and respected by the community he now values and of which he feels proud to be a part. He did not achieve his aim, but his learning through his actions meant he achieved something *more* than the value he measured in dollars as a younger man.

In *A Christmas Carol* (Charles Dickens, 1843) Scrooge sets out to minimise the negative impact of Christmas on his business and finances. He ends up achieving something far beyond financial gains because he gets in touch with his humanity.

In *Back to the Future* Marty McFly's aim is to get back to 1985. He achieves his aim, but when he gets there he realises with some surprise — as do we in the audience — that he has also achieved a surpassing aim. In his battle to get back to 1985 he managed to improve his father's strength of character and, as a knock-on effect of that, the intervening 30 years have been characterised by a strong father, bringing a vastly improved quality of life for his entire family across the breadth of George's life.

As a knowledge gap, a surpassing aim is the gap between the expectation set for the audience with regard to what fulfilment means to a character and a different set of aims and values that turn out to define their fulfilment at the end of the story event.

2.6.6 Knowledge gaps through moral argument

There are some who claim a moral argument to be the definition of story. I would not go that far, but there is no doubt that this is another storification category which turns out to show up regularly in the list of the most highly-rated stories. It is also true to say that if you can identify the morality at the heart of your story idea, it is easy to use that to drive out everything you need to tell your story to good effect. Developing the moral argument is a method you can use — like any other storification — to guide the creative process. To prove the point, I will shortly use this dynamic to cynically design a story based on the moral argument.

The reason it works so well is that the morality in a story idea is directly connected to meaning in mind; that is, to the ultimate meaning you will generate in the mind of your receiver. The end-game concerned with getting the audience to nod and say, "Yes, life is like that." The moral argument implicitly addresses the question: How should a person lead their life?

For that reason, section 3.4 — Story and the moral argument is devoted to morality, ethics, story themes, moral conflict, character definitions through morality and how to drive a story design using the moral argument. For the moment, note that it is a very important knowledge gap. A gap between what an audience (and/or a character) knows about a moral issue at the beginning of a narration and what they know about it by the end. A critical storification dynamic.

2.6.7 Knowledge gaps through metaphor and allegory

In terms of my definition of story and the work encapsulated by this book, a metaphor is effectively another word for a story. While metaphor has long been associated with a psychological process, story has somehow been more linked to the text and confused with the narration. I argue in this book that a story uses precisely the same mental dynamics and reflexes as a metaphor.

A writer is not working with words. When we read a story, we do not remember the words.
A writer is not delivering a narration. That is simply the information stream.
A writer is crafting meaning into the mind of the receiver. That is, ultimately, their job. Where does that meaning come from? The writer is creating knowledge gaps and coaxing the receiver to fill those gaps and create meaning in mind for themselves. The receiver has to interpret the information stream into a representation and from that build the meaning, so everything they are given is material for a metaphoric leap to meaning. An invitation to fill a gap.

What is a metaphor?
In moment-by-moment writing, a metaphor links two disparate objects or concepts by evoking the qualities of the one over the characteristics of the other. Shakespeare, for example has Romeo use metaphor to explain his feelings about Juliet: "But soft! What light through yonder window breaks? It is the East, and Juliet, the sun!"

The two components of metaphor are known as the **tenor** (the original concept or object, in our case, young Juliet) and the **vehicle** (the quality or concept overlaid on the tenor to impart it with meaning — in this case, the rising sun). The overall effect is to provide a single metaphor: Juliet's appearance at the window characterised as the miraculous wonder of the rising sun in the form of a human face.

There is an implicit knowledge gap between the tenor and the vehicle. A gap filled by knowledge of the vehicle's characteristics drawn from the receiver's personal history and experience. By recognising how much we have loved the breath-taking glory of a sunrise we understand the impact the appearance of Juliet has on Romeo. The thoughts and feelings created in mind implicitly include evocations which rely on the receiver's history and experience to generate not only the knowledge that fills the gap but also to add together the sum of the parts (the tenor and the vehicle) to complete the metaphor. We like it, because we did it for ourselves.

If you think about it, every story works like this. Every story can be seen as a metaphor. There are the depicted events and, in our minds, there is how we build those into logical meaning in mind by relating them to our lives and existing knowledge. Every metaphor (and therefore every story) is a knowledge gap between a tenor (the information in the real world) and the vehicle (the knowledge we bring from our own lives to overlay on the tenor and give it human meaning). In the sense of everything I am presenting in this book, a metaphor is story-in-miniature, and a story is a metaphor writ large. Indeed, they implicitly overlap into one — a metaphor comprises the entire story is called an **allegory**.

A writer must think along the right lines to deliver a story. The writer does not give meaning. The receiver makes meaning, and they do so for themselves after the narration is received. It is that meaning, that memory and how it *feels* which they desire. The best writers are the ones who create the conditions for subtext.

One way to ensure your writing is compelling is to abstract tenor material wherever it is found, and to do this through the creation of vehicle material. This is a surprisingly easy method for generating knowledge gaps (and therefore interesting story) because just about everything in a narrative is — or could be — a metaphor.

For example, if you are writing a story about brutal authoritarianism it is one thing to have an army beating up people in the street. However, it is possible to present the same human dynamics between, say, ants being bullied by grasshoppers (*A Bugs Life*, 1998), a hapless, incompetent tramp hilariously getting into trouble with the police (*Modern Times*, 1936), or a group of children trying to establish their hierarchies of power without adults (William Golding's *Lord of the Flies*, 1954). Instantly the metaphorical nature of your approach introduces fascinating gaps between the behaviour of the insects/comedian/children and the way our society works in our real lives. 'Yes, life is like that'; and: 'Yes, this is how a person should lead their life'. Messages that are delivered in the meaning, not the narration.

This same principle can be applied to the smallest of objects or events too. If you have a character who dies, you don't have to show a body on the floor. Think of ways to intimate what has happened instead so that your receiver can derive the meaning for themselves. Have an unanswered phone ringing in an empty room. An empty pair of shoes. A grim worker digging a hole in the ground... Perhaps the power we need is in empathising with those who must live on without the loved one, so imagine how much more powerful and meaningful it is if someone has died and we see another person call their number, and hear the pithy voicemail message... We are now empathising and connecting so much more through the gap between vehicle and tenor than we would through seeing a cadaver on a slab.

The author Steve Askham was obliged to drive enormous distances on his travels and wanted to communicate to his readers that: 'the roads are bumpy and unmade throughout South America.' OK, that makes us think, but the way he put it was infinitely superior: 'You need strong teeth to drive in Brazil.'

This is one of the keys to fine, prosaic writing. When you abstract away from simple, on-the-nose exposition and deliver just about everything in metaphor you are turning every sentence into a form of story. Or, to put in another way, *do not deliver knowledge, deliver a knowledge gap.* Look at every sentence in this way. The more you abstract into metaphor, the more work your receiver has to do and the more they will appreciate your writing.

2.6.8 Knowledge gaps through recognition and allusion

Like every type of storification, recognition and allusion make for deep and surprisingly powerful knowledge gaps, but this is a really good one. One which is largely unknown as a story device. It is worth gaining an understanding of recognition and allusion.

Think about what is involved in a baby's recognition of a mother's face. That face quickly becomes associated with warm feelings of safety, security, love, warmth, nourishment and contentment.

This form of pattern-matching transfers readily to every aspect of our lives. When we see something we recognise as being a snapshot from a life narrative that we know is positive for us, we like it. It's as simple as that. If you show me a son, a football, a motorbike, a pub garden in the sunshine or, indeed, my mother's face, I pattern-match what it is against a complete narrative in my mind (what it does) and feel warm, positive thoughts (what it means). Equally, when we see something we recognise as part of a *negative* life narrative we use that knowledge to avoid involvement with the negative outcome and we might make efforts to prevent that narrative progression from playing out, or deploy alternative narratives to mitigate against them.

This transfers to our mental experience of stories. If we see characters connected into a narrative progression we recognise, we feel empowered by that knowledge. Even if the narrative progression is negative it still resonates because knowledge is power. In evolutionary terms this kind of recognition could be potentially life changing, which is why I am emphasising that it resonates so strongly. Every time we make an association of this type, there is a knowledge gap through that recognition. A gap we try to fill by projecting forwards along the progression the narrative is likely to take, predicting the possible outcomes for our characters and hoping they take the actions we can see in the subtext will embrace the positive potential and avoid the negative.

The French classic, *Amélie* (2001, director Jean-Pierre Jeunet) is a film which has almost no conflict. It gains its power to grip primarily from knowledge gaps through recognition and allusion. The audience are acknowledged by the narrator and by the lead character Amélie (Audrey Tautou) together breaking the fourth wall with the clever narration and Amélie's meaningful looks to the audience as she connects with us over many moments of shared recognition and allusion. For example, characters throughout the story declare their pet loves and hates and we relate to them; clingy swim shorts; dimples on fingers when one has been in the bath too long; polishing the floor with cloths under your feet; the way it sets your teeth on edge when people crack their knuckles; a guilty joy when the bull gores the matador; athletes who cry; looking around in the cinema at the faces watching the film; skiffing stones across a pond; people who have a funny laugh; deferring one's pleasures; and many more. Indeed, the entire story sits on our own love of teasing ourselves with the prospect of upcoming joy. *Amélie* plays a long, romantic game of delaying the outcome of a narrative progression. Postponing ones pleasures is a feeling we all play with, and Amélie's story is simply one long exercise in delicious delay. Recognition and allusion provide the primary story power for *Amélie*.

The Danny Boyle film *Yesterday* (2019) is another story that finds its excellent basis in cultural allusion. Jack Malik (Himesh Patel) is a struggling musician. He is knocked off his bicycle at precisely the time the world experiences a global black-out. When he comes round he slowly realises that he is the only person on Earth who remembers The Beatles. He sets about bringing all their wonderful songs to the world and, slowly but surely, he builds himself into a global phenomenon as he gets the credit as the finest songwriter the world has ever seen. Throughout his adventure, we in the audience have privilege knowledge with regard to the impact The Beatles and their music had on the world, we are onside with all the references Malik makes and we are laughing every time someone else is lacking knowledge of Beatle magic. For example, Ed Sheeran (playing himself) helps Malik to 'improve' his song 'Hey Jude' by changing the words to 'Hey Dude'. This is a story that gets its main storification power from knowledge gaps through cultural allusion.

In 1955, when Marty McFly plays the song, *Johnny B Goode* (Berry, Chess Records, 1958) three years before Chuck Berry has written it, those of us in the audience with appropriate cultural knowledge will understand a reference that Marty's 1955 audience will not. This is a song that will one day become a classic, however at the time Marty plays it no living person has ever heard it before. This is a privilege knowledge gap between us in the audience (onside with Marty) and the 1955 characters. We may also recognise the suggestion that Marty's actions in 1955 are implicitly responsible for originating the entire rock and roll phenomenon (this is the storification for that scene). As the narrative unfolds, we are pattern-matching Marty playing this song against our knowledge that it has a role in the invention of rock and roll.

Bob Gale pointed out to me that although this scene is not a logical or necessary sequence in any of the wider plotlines and is entirely conflict free in itself (and breaks lots of the rules of the Hollywood formula) it is, in his experience, the most recognised and remembered scene in the whole film, and the one most often mentioned by people when they meet him. I argue that it is powerful and memorable because the scene storifies so strongly within itself and in doing so it demonstrates the power of a knowledge gap through recognition and cultural allusion.

The same form of gap is also in play in the sequences in which Marty takes a box cart from some boys and turns it into a skateboard (the invention of the skateboard) and when Marty dresses up like a spaceman calling himself Darth Vader and plays Van Halen to George in order to convince him to ask Lorraine out on a date (using cultural tropes from the 1980s to gain advantage in the 1950s).

Another version of this type of gap can be created through recognition of occurrences within the story itself as opposed to our cultural knowledge external to the story world. For example, when Biff and George reprise their scene in 1955 whereby the bully, Biff, raps George on the head and demands to know when he will do his homework for him, the audience *recognises* that this behaviour is a repeat of an interaction we have already viewed in earlier scenes, whilst Biff and George are not aware of the allusion.

A Note on Genre
Recognition and allusion are why genre is so important to us. As soon as you have the genre criteria in your mind, you are setting a context that places your head in an appropriate receptive state. As writers, we can use this. We only need present a glimpse of a potential context and/or narrative and we can rely on the receiver to do rest of the work.

2.6.8.1 Allusion to Lifecycles

Within the context of recognition and cultural allusion, one of the major gap types that an audience simply adores is through a narrative that encompasses an entire cycle of life or a major period that defines a life. It is quite amazing how powerful such stories are. This type of gap locks on to the kind of mental dynamic we have spoken about a few times to do with the expression: 'Life is like that.' When a story resonates with life truth, whether tragic or positive, we feel empowered by it. We learn things about life that we cannot — or would not like to — experience readily in our real lives, such as suffering or dying. We are drawn to such subject matter; it preys on our minds and yet we avoid it in the real world. This is why death is a very common feature in stories. It is something we are keen to avoid in our actual lives, but also something we are anxious to understand. Stories give us understanding of things we fear. Stories give us knowledge without exposure to risk. Seeing a character go through an undesirable experience brings us **catharsis**. The intense, deep feelings involved with a close encounter with suffering coupled with the relief that it is not us who is suffering, albeit with a harsh realisation that one day that will be us.

We look on at the tragedy of others and we get a deep and visceral feeling from catharsis; one we dislike but which brings us knowledge and meaning of death and suffering. This is why we slow down to peer at a car crash. Stories are the most powerful way we can 'safely' experience these feelings and gain this type of knowledge. An entire cycle of life is important knowledge — basic understanding of death and the meaning of life.

Stories that show us a cycle of life are some of the most highly rated. *The Shawshank Redemption* (Frank Darabont, 1994); *The Lion King* (Roger Allers and Rob Minkoff, 1994); *Romeo and Juliet* (William Shakespeare, 1594)); *Citizen Kane* (Orson Welles, 1941)*;* *Harry Potter* (JK Rowling, 1997-2007); *Oedipus Rex* (Sophocles, ~429BC) and many, many more. For quick and simple examples of stories that use this lifecycle dynamic to gain their main story power, look up the short film *The Maker* (Christopher Kezelos 2011) or my own short, *Bella* (Baboulene, 2020). The latter two have no dialogue, no conflict, no bad guy — the power comes from the lifecycle dynamic present in cultural allusion.

In simple terms, we love stories that demonstrate to us that 'Yes, life is like that.' Or 'Yes, that is how a person should lead their life.'

2.6.9   Knowledge gaps through peripeteia

The peripeteia is a reversal, or twist, through which the audience is set up to expect the story to veer off in a new direction towards an unexpected outcome. It is the third component in the Aristotle principles which I shall discuss in depth shortly, so more details to come in the dedicated section 3.3.

And that is the lot! The Primary Colours of Story through framing, characters and storification. Now let's take a look at how they might be used.

Section 3 - Common Story Dynamics

Without humans there are no stories. Without stories people do not know how to function in the civilisations they have created.

Section two presented the primary colours of story (at least, the ones that are useful to a writer) in the form of a set of knowledge gaps. It is practically impossible to create a good story without using these knowledge gaps. In order to help make knowledge gaps relevant to you and applicable to your stories, in this section I shall use a knowledge gap perspective to map out a few of the more common ways compelling stories are created; namely, through conflict, the Hollywood formula, Aristotle's principles and the moral argument. I have chosen these because, although they are somewhat formulaic, they do work, they are useful to know about and they each exemplify the Holy Trinity: framing, character and storification. The Hollywood formula is built on structuralist principles — that is everything *except* the gaps — and is fundamentally a tool for **framing** a story. Aristotle came up with a wonderful progression that is a fundamentally a tool of **character** dynamics. A moral argument is based on the lessons in the outcomes of choices and is fundamentally a tool of **storification**. I will represent each of these approaches from the perspective of their implicit knowledge gaps.

These dynamics are common, however it is difficult to know whether they are a genuinely brilliant way to shape a story idea or if they have been forced so many times that they have become *de facto* standards. In the case of the Hollywood formula there is a great deal of evidence for the latter. The business side of the film industry locked on to the control they got from the formula and forced writers to use it. Over the last 100 years, it has become so locked into the DNA of both the writers and the audiences that Hollywood has become hamstrung into doing almost nothing else. More on this shortly, for the moment, just remember that although these models are well worth knowing about, there are no rules, and my hope is that writers will recognise the freedom that is facilitated by a knowledge gap approach. Knowledge gaps remove the strictures of the models I will describe and bring potential for entirely new and perhaps previously unseen story progressions. The point is that all stories use knowledge gaps in the same way as all art uses the primary colours. So start from anywhere, go where your mind takes you and throw your story paint around! If there are gaps, there is power. It is as simple as that.

Actually, I do have a rule. It goes like this: If YOU like it, do it. If YOU like it, it's right. If YOU like it, someone else somewhere will like it too, so keep the courage of your artistic convictions, keep true to yourself and go for it. That's the only way to satisfy your heart, and if your work resonates with a small percentage of the population you have a market. Be true to yourself, and you will write the perfect story.

If you want to override your heart with, for example, commercial considerations – fine. No problem. Fair enough. Analyse and make changes but write it from the heart *first*. Rewrite from the head if you feel a need. As the saying goes, there is no such thing as a writer, only a re-writer.

Write from the heart. Rewrite from the head.

We will go into this further when we look at the story development process in section 4. For the moment, let's get stuck into the story fundamentals, beginning with some good old conflict.

3.1 Conflict in Stories

If you want to have brilliant doctors in the world, you must have challenging diseases. If you want a brilliant protagonist in your story you must have breath-taking forces of antagonism.

No two ways about it, conflict is up front and centre for Hollywood. Indeed, story gurus down the years have hammered home the rule that you cannot have a story without conflict. However, this is not true. There are plenty of fine stories out there with little or no conflict. The story of how two lovers meet could include action, romance, character, intrigue, suspense and form a drama without conflict. The French film, *Amélie* (2001) is precisely this. The story of a couple finding love. It works. A glorious, beautiful, full length, highly rated film story with no bad guy and essentially no conflict. *La La Land* (2016, director Damien Chazelle) largely fulfils this same brief with little or no conflict, at least until the final sequences. Raymond Carver's story *Why Don't You Dance?* (Carver, 2003) is a story with no conflict and although it is a short story it is the basis for the Hollywood feature, *Everything Must Go* (directed by Dan Rush in 2011). The film of *Mary Poppins* (1964, directed by Robert Stevens) has minimal overarching conflict and no antagonist and yet the characters develop and drama is present. In fact, *Mary Poppins* is an excellent example. I will explain where *Mary Poppins* gets what little conflict it does have in a moment. I have made a film myself entitled *Bella* (Directed by Craig Hinde, 2020) which has no conflict, no dialogue, no bad guy… and I think it's brilliant. The story development process for *Bella* and blogposts on where it gets its power to grip are on my website at www.baboulene.com or my company website at www.dreamengine.co.uk.

All this aside, the vast majority of the finest stories have conflict and they have it in spades. It is no coincidence that, in every conflict, there is an implicit gap in the question: Who will win out? The rock or the hard place? The problems associated with conflict tend to be that most writers do not understand the true definition of conflict, as distinct from 'a really difficult challenge', so they fail to use and set conflict up in compelling ways. Often when writers come to me with a story they love, but which has a nagging problem they cannot pin down, the issues are with the conflicts.

Let's face it: You're lovely, aren't you?
Many of the writers I work with do not like the dark side of their own stories. Indeed, they do not like the dark side of themselves. Writers are often pacifists. They write because they are artistic, thoughtful and lovely and would much prefer to express themselves in writing; either because they find face-to-face confrontation difficult or because they want to express themselves very precisely and without interruption. Writing things down achieves this. There is a belief that most stories are autobiographical, even if we are not conscious of it, and this loveliness of writers is the source of a common problem. Writers give their good guys all the power and resources they need to get on in life... and they hamstring their bad guys. Their stories comprise unbalanced or poorly formed conflicts in which the forces of good slam the bad guy to oblivion at the first opportunity. The writer might gain a great deal of relief from this, but it is not great story! Often my job is to convince some lovely person that they have a dark spot deep in their heart; there is a bastard in there somewhere and we must find a way to let it out to express itself! It can be quite a journey...

More often than we realise, it is the dark side that gives life to the story. The negative forces are the reason the story exists and the reason we need a good guy at all, so look at it like this: If you do not empower your bad guy, the good guy cannot show how heroic they can be. The good guy can only be as strong as the forces of antagonism demand, so building the bad side is, necessarily, building the wonder and brilliance of your story. By situating the goodness as a function of the badness, most people can find a way to get in touch with their inner-evil-self. Antagonism is the food of protagonism.

Without diseases there are no doctors. The nastier the disease the more admirable the doctor who cures it.

What conflict is not

Conflict is defined, for our purposes, as the placing of two sets of aims in opposition to each other. Commonly, this places the aims of the good guy in opposition to the bad guy, but, as we shall see, there are several other places to find conflict. Before we talk about what conflict is, let's have a few words on what conflict *is not*.

Writers often confuse 'conflict' with a 'really tough challenge' and it's very important to understand the distinction. If we offer a mountaineer the challenge of climbing a mountain we are obliged to warn them of the dangers: "Gotta be honest — people have died up there. It's freezing, there's no oxygen, conditions are awful. The whole climb is a nightmare. You sure you wanna do this?"

And being a mountaineer they rub their hands together in delight and say, "Ooo, yes please! That'd be great!"

Yes, there are dangers but there is no dilemma in the decision. Our mountaineer will feel thoroughly fulfilled by the experience and, let's be honest, we are not particularly interested in watching him climb the mountain, right?! It's not great story because it's not meaningful conflict. It is not pleasant to admit it to our mountaineer, but it is not until something goes wrong that we become interested in his journey. We watch downhill skiing not to see who wins but for the thrill we get from watching a high-speed accident.

Climbing the mountain is a challenge, but it is not meaningful conflict. Why not? Because there is no choice of evils. No dilemma. He may be a mountaineer but he's not a fool. If it's too dangerous, he'll leave it a couple of weeks whilst the weather clears up. When he does go, he will mitigate any risk with his experience and a ton of safety equipment. In short, he is removing the knowledge gaps, which means there is not enough *story* for us to be interested. It is our job as the author to make him unsafe. We are the God of this story, so how about we make his decision to climb a little less easy:

'The mountaineer risks death on the mountain because the weather is atrocious, conditions are impossible and he will almost certainly die. No sensible mountaineer would climb at this time. However, if he does not climb the mountain... his climbing partner and best friend, stranded near the summit and with a broken leg, will certainly die.'

Ah. Right. Previously, the risks were low and he could sensibly enjoy his hobby. Now there is risk, a knowledge gap ('Will he rescue his buddy? Or will he die as well?') and *a difficult choice*. Now we will learn something of the true character of our mountaineer. Will he risk his own life to save his partner? Hmmm. Do we think he will go? Yes, of course he will. He is never going to leave his friend to die. Ah. Right. So it is still too easy to make a decision. He will risk his life for his friend, so, as writer and as the God of this story world, we add more to the other side of the conflict equation to make it even more difficult for him. Let's add that he has a solemn pact with his climbing partner that each will leave the other to die and save themselves if one becomes a life-threatening liability. They agreed it in advance — better only one of them dies rather than both of them. Hmm. It adds something, but he'll still choose to go save his friend. So, round we go again and we add more to make things harder still. Let's add a wife, who shakes as she harangues our mountaineer: "Right! I've had enough! I can't stand it anymore. You have nine kids who need a father. If you set one foot on that mountain, I'm off!"

"Yes, but my best buddy is dying up there! I can save him."

"Better he dies up there than both of you — you agreed that yourselves. Listen, it's simple. If you go, I *promise* you will never see these kids again. You're a father now! You have a responsibility to your kids to stop risking your life."

Now it's getting tasty... it's getting to be a difficult choice. Will he risk his own life and the wellbeing of his wife and children to go back up there? But his friend is dying. He is pretty sure he can save his friend and get back down. Should he not at least try?

Now both options have a cost, both have a benefit and he has to make a choice **now** because the clock is ticking down on his friend. Risk his own life or let his buddy die. Go save him... but risk death, divorce and never seeing his kids again. It is this dilemma of the conflicts that makes it interesting. The cost is what drives the story, not the benefit. Yeah, yeah we are all happy when someone wins out and does well in life, but it is not a patch to how interested we get when someone faces difficulties. Now we really light up. Rubbing our hands and salivating at the prospect of pain and suffering. We do not like to admit it — we do not even like it in ourselves — but it is there in us all, and it means story is generally built on the dark side. Conflict is not about the benefit. It is about the cost. It is the cost that turns a challenge into a meaningful conflict which has us in the audience leaning in with sordid interest at the delicious awfulness of the situation. We want to see people in difficulty making choices we will learn from. We do not want trouble for ourselves but we can learn through watching others struggle, and whether we like to admit it or not, we get something out of it. It is hard to find catharsis in life, so we like it when we get it through story.

We find out who a person truly is when they must make a *decision under pressure*. Now we're interested. Now we're going to learn something about life. Why? Because now the conflict is meaningful. The decisions and choices our mountaineer makes will have serious implications — *whichever choice he makes*. Note that as the writer we are the architects of the story and what we are crafting is the difficulty for the character. It is our job to box him in; to give him pain and dilemma that we can watch and enjoy with a side order of schadenfreude as he is forced to make the decisions that make the story gripping.

To return to a previous example, the conflict faced by George McFly through the kingpin moment of *Back to the Future* is meaningful. He must stand his ground against the feared bully, Biff (and risk getting six bells kicked out of him) <u>or</u> he must run away, as we know he desperately wants to (and leave Lorraine to be abused in the car by Biff). There is a choice of evils. Each choice has a cost.

Conflict is dilemma and choice, not the scale of a challenge. If your character's conflict is not a difficult choice, it is your job to load more factors on the easy side to balance it up, like I did to annoy a mountaineer. You will not be able to do this on every occasion, but thinking along these lines will always, always improve your characters and your story, even if you cannot manage to turn every conflict into a kingpin beauty.

3.1.1 Where can conflict be found?

Normally, when we think about antagonism we think about a bad guy, but this is just one type of conflict. Classically, there are six: person versus self; person versus another person; person versus society; person versus machine; person versus nature; and person versus fate.

I have reduced this down to four levels of conflict based on the level of influence the character has on the outcome. Let's start from the outside, and work our way in, and we will use *Back to the Future* to exemplify them so that you can see how these different levels of conflict work together in a single story, like different size cogs turning together in a story engine.

3.1.1.1 External conflict

Events that are out of the character's control generate external conflict. Person versus fate would be a fine example. Weather events, accidents, acts of God, Mother Nature, illness, coincidental actions of random third parties. Anything that causes conflict and there is nothing that the protagonist can do about it, such as the cataclysmic weather event that opens (and causes) the story in *The Day After Tomorrow* (director Roland Emmerich, 2004) or the aeroplane crash that opens (and causes) the story in *Castaway* (director Robert Zemeckis, 2000).

In *Back to the Future*, Marty McFly is driving fast, trying to escape from being shot by terrorists chasing him in a campervan. He does not realise that once his vehicle hits 88 miles-per-hour he will travel through time. He does not expect or intend to go back in time, but he does, and this unintended event generates the conflict that causes the story of *Back to the Future*.

Once he is in 1955, Marty rescues his father from a car accident. In doing so he steps into the car's path and the accident happens to Marty instead of his future father. This accident is the external conflict that defines the stories major subplot.

3.1.1.2 Institutional conflict

Institutional conflict is delivered by rules and regulations. Person versus machine and person versus society would be good examples. The police and justice system, the authorities and institutions, school and college, hospital, bookmakers, traffic wardens, doctors, soldiers — any entity which delivers a 'faceless' rule-base and over which the protagonist has limited influence or control. I don't know if you have ever tried to change the mind of a police officer with regard to the rules they are obliged to apply but it can be very tricky indeed.

Institutional conflict also includes the rules of the story world. In a sci-fi story, for example, the rules of that world must be made clear and must be obeyed. *Back to the Future* falls into this category, so there are institutional rules with which Marty goes into conflict. We get to understand that it takes 1.21 gigawatts of power, channelled into a flux capacitor doing a speed of 88 miles-per-hour to make time travel happen. This rule of the story world underpins institutional conflicts at the root of events in *Back to the Future*.

In a drama set in the real world, rules apply both in the sense of society but also nature. In the film *Juno*, our eponymous hero is in conflict with the rules of pregnancy and childbirth, over which she has only limited options and influence. Not just the medical regulations or the abortion clinic rules, or the laws of the land regarding underage sex, but the natural rules of the story world — pregnancy happens from having sex; pregnancy is a ticking clock that will turn into a baby; pregnancy is a process that is difficult to change and influence; pregnancy is the basis for the conflicts in the story of *Juno*.

3.1.1.3 Relationship conflict

The most common conflicts in stories down the millennia are relationship conflicts — conflicts that are person versus another person. In general, conflict occurs when two or more people have aims that are mutually exclusive. Two characters want the same thing and only one can possibly win out: a classic story conflict. Both Olaf and Sven want the same carrot. Only one can win out.

In *Back to the Future*, both George and Biff want to be Lorraine's romantic partner. Only one can win out. Such conflicts allow for more influence and control for the protagonist, who has a fifty-percent stake in any relationship conflict and can use that to coerce, cheat, deceive, convince, misinform, encourage — whatever it takes to swing the outcome towards their benefit.

Do I need a bad guy?
In relationship conflict terms, most writers assume there must be a 'bad guy' in a story, but this is not the case, and having a character who dresses in black, twirls their moustache, cackles and does evil may lead to weak stories. That sounds like a glib comment, but many, many stories are written with basic, one-dimensional bad guys and it's a shame, because the potential of the story is often not realised if the dark side is not fully drawn. As I said earlier, it is critical to the dimension and worth of your 'good guy' that they are given convincing and dimensional forces of antagonism to prove themselves against. Focus on the dark side and build that antagonism as beautifully as you can, because it is that which makes your story fly. Your good guy can only be as heroic as the dark side demands.

In *Back to the Future* we cannot call Biff a bad guy simply because he finds Lorraine attractive and wants to court her. We can empathise entirely with someone being attracted to another person. And the authors give us additional reasons to empathise and understand Biff's actions by having Lorraine state that she wants 'a strong man. A man who can protect the woman he loves.' Well, guess what, they don't come any stronger than Biff, and if you want protection, he's qualified. Sure, he gets power and status in life through his physical superiority, but that's life, right?! The law of the jungle. Survival of the fittest. It's a valid part of a human life and he has the attributes. His approach is understandable. We can empathise with him even if we do not agree with him.

In *Breaking Bad*, Walter White sets out with honourable intent. He is dying of cancer and wants to provide for his family after his death. Of course, we support this aim. When he kills a brutal drug dealer this might be unethical, but we still support him, because our morals allow for a good man like him to get rid of a low-life who is bad for society anyway. We can excuse Walt's actions and still feel OK about ourselves. Walter White is an excellent example of a bad guy crafted beautifully to ensure we empathise and relate and *feel* for him. An excellent example of how a bad guy is the major power in making a story wonderful.

Much of the time, in the finest stories, our forces of antagonism are created from our disagreement with a person's moral stance, even though their motivation is understandable. Our differences amount to nothing more than differing opinions. Looking at relationship conflicts through a moral lens tends to bring us more sophisticated stories, some of which do not have a bad guy at all, just a conflict of moral positions. *Juno* is a fine example. You probably have a view on pregnancy and abortion. Your pro-life/pro-choice stance will be the polar opposite to perfectly decent people with integrity and good reasons for their opposing view. They are not 'bad', but they are in conflict with you. In such dynamics lies the opportunity to create compelling story without a 'bad guy'. The story of Juno has no bad guy. (We will look deeply at this example in section 3.4 — Story and the Moral Argument.)

3.1.1.4 Internal conflict

Internal conflict — person versus self — is the least well-explored form of conflict and yet is often at the root of the finest stories. Many children's stories, for example, have no bad guy. If you are targeting five-year-olds, you cannot have out-and-out evil, psychological torture and blood up the walls, so writers must come up with smarter ways to bring conflict and antagonism to their stories, and internal conflict is often the answer.

For example, what little conflict there is in *Mary Poppins* comes from the father's misguided approach to bringing up children. The 'bad guy' is a totally benign and loving father who wants the best for his family. Mr. Banks is a city banker who is ruled by his work. He is stressed and devoted to his job, and as a result he is a tense and serious chap. He's forgotten how to live in the here-and-now, enjoy his life and play with his children whilst they are young. He is in conflict with his own up-tightedness. Mary Poppins, Gawd bless 'er, shows us the right way to be. She gets control and discipline but within a context of fun and happiness.

At climax, the behaviour of his spirited children puts the father under pressure to explain himself to the grey suits at work. He is put under pressure to demonstrate his commitment to work or lose his precious job in the bank. He makes his decision, casts off his banker's mantle and goes off with his kids to dance and sing with a street full of chimney sweeps. They all live happily ever after. Brilliant. He was never really a bad guy, he was a **misguided** good guy, but he represented the antagonistic need of the story perfectly. He had internal conflict which pressured him into a choice... do right by the bank and his work or do right by his home and family. He initially makes the wrong choice... and the story is about how he overcame his internal conflict; how he changed and grew and came around to the right choice. Excellent character growth and learning took him to a new level of understanding of how a person should lead their life and the story was complete.

In *Toy Story*, there is no bad guy. The principal antagonism comes from the internal conflicts of both Woody and Buzz. Woody is **jealous**. He is the leader of the toys and Andy's favourite toy. The arrival of the impressive, gadget-packed Buzz Lightyear threatens Woody's status and he actively sets about removing Buzz from the community. We think of Woody as the protagonist and the 'good guy', but through his internal conflict, he is the antagonist and is trying to rid his world of Buzz. This is a terrific example of the kind of well-crafted 'bad guy' I was discussing earlier. We can fully appreciate Woody's actions. They are understandable. We don't approve, but nobody would ever point at Woody and call him a bad guy. He's struggling with jealousy and we *empathise*. Perfect antagonism through character.

Buzz is also struggling with internal conflict. He is **deluded**. He thinks he is a real space ranger and acts accordingly. Much of the conflict in the story comes from Buzz's delusion. So, both Woody and Buzz are the good guys and the protagonists, but both are also the source of the story's antagonism. The story is, if you think about it, principally about Woody's jealousy. Children relate readily to this dynamic, of course. It is precisely the kind of character growth we all have to go through in growing up and fitting in with other people. Woody and Buzz's problems will not resolve whilst they continue to be self-absorbed and squabble, but the moment they begin to work together, they get positive outcomes and ultimately, once they are cooperating fully, they win out. Buzz is devastated to find out he is not a space ranger. He is merely a toy, but he changes and grows and learns the value of a toy in the world. He learns to value himself for who he is. Woody is put under pressure to overcome his jealousy and work with his rival, Buzz. He does so, and as soon as they start to work together, they get the outcomes that represent a happy ending and they learn to love and appreciate each other. This is terrific character growth and, like all the best stories, their growth is applied to the conflicts that are holding them back in life, and that learning takes them to the positive, successful outcome. Wonderful.

Many of the finest stories have a player with an internal conflict they must overcome in order to move forwards in life. The protagonist has inner conflict. Perhaps he is frightened, riddled with guilt, or racked by self-doubt, naivety, insecurity, phobia. when the decisions a protagonist has to make throws them directly into conflict with their inner drives, there is a story.

As ever, *Back to the Future* is a fine example. George McFly is a coward. He avoids confrontation at any cost. He knows what he should do, but he does not have the courage of his convictions. The story is fundamentally designed around placing pressure on George McFly's moral weakness. Everything in the entire story — every character and every event — builds relentlessly to the kingpin moment when George McFly is cornered into facing his own internal conflict.

George McFly is the bad guy. He is the one providing the critical antagonism that drives the main story power of *Back to the Future*. Just like Mr. Banks, Woody and Buzz, Juno and many, many others, George's internal conflict is making him the principal antagonist for the whole story.

3.1.2 Meaningful conflict

It matters not which level your conflict is on, it is greatly improved if it is **meaningful**. Meaningful conflict is not just a challenge. It is not simply an obstacle or a problem in the way of a character ambition. The conflicts that really deliver story power and take it to the next level do so because they place a character on the horns of a dilemma and force them to make a choice or take a decision under pressure. That choice or decision is difficult, because the author has made sure it is. They have painstakingly crafted the framing and character actions to ensure the character is trapped into that deliciously horrible position.

George McFly was crafted into just such a dilemma, so let us run through the principal subplot, but this time examining the conflicts in detail.

Marty disrupted the meeting of his future mother, Lorraine, and future father, George, in 1955 and Lorraine became infatuated with Marty instead of George. Marty makes a plan with George to cause Lorraine to dislike Marty and fall for George. She expressed her desire for a strong man, so the plan is that Marty will take her to the *Enchantment Under the Sea Dance* and make inappropriate sexual advances towards her in the car. He knows how prudish his mum is in 1985, so is sure she will be horrified at his behaviour. At precisely 9.00pm, George will emerge from the dance, catch Marty abusing Lorraine in the car, drag Marty off her and pretend-beat him up. Lorraine will be so impressed by the strength of her knight in shining armour that she will fall in love with George, who will take her into the dance where they will kiss on the dancefloor and history will be back on track.

Marty and George role-play their plan. We in the audience know precisely how things are supposed to go.

On the night of the dance, George emerges from the dance at 9.00pm. He sees a struggle going on in the car. He strides over to play his part in the charade. However, when he opens the door, all ready to say his lines... to his horror, Biff has contrived to be in the car instead of Marty and is making genuinely inappropriate sexual advances to Lorraine.

George faces a choice of evils. He must stand his ground against the feared bully (and get six bells kicked out of him) <u>or</u> he must run away, as he always does when faced with conflict (and leave Lorraine to be abused in the car by Biff).

The key point to note here is that George McFly has a dilemma. He will either give in to that pressure he feels to run away as usual (and suffer the consequences) or risk his personal safety and stand up for what he believes in (and suffer the consequences).

At this kingpin moment, the authors have framed and crafted the story beautifully. They have boxed George in so that there is no escape. He must face his own daemons and make his difficult choice. *A choice under pressure of conflict.* This is a major part of the craft of story creation: when you find a situation in which your character wants something, it is your job to introduce new characters, events, objects or conflicts that force them into difficult decisions. A choice of evils. A rock and a hard place. The horns of dilemma. The tougher their choice the better your story and the more powerful the storification.

Now the chips are down, George has a decision under pressure of conflict... and now we will find out who he truly is. George cannot let Lorraine suffer at the hands of Biff, so he makes a fist for the first time in his life and stands his ground. In this moment, under this pressure and with nobody else to pass the buck to, he discovers inner strength. He does have the courage of his convictions and he changes and he grows before our very eyes. We see the fruits of this growth as he punches Biff out with a single punch. We then see how this self-discovery — this personal growth — characterises and improves his life from that moment onwards. Why is this so significant? Because it is *meaningful* conflict.

In standing up to Biff, George did not only solve a problem. He did not just rise to a challenge. He took action under the pressure of conflict... and in doing so he challenged his internal fears. He took a huge personal risk and it worked out. The outcome was positive, so he learned and he changed and he grew as a person and we in the audience understood a lesson about life and how it should be led. We understood that to lead a fulfilling life, a person must have the courage of their convictions. Yes, that is how a person should lead their life.

Most of the finest stories carry this kind of storification, and most of them get it from placing the protagonist into a meaningful conflict that forces them to make a difficult decision under pressure.

Think about the basis of the original *Star Wars* (Directed by George Lucas, 1977). Luke Skywalker has a problem with stormtroopers. They come over the horizon at him hundreds at a time. Each wave that he wipes out is followed by another. It's relentless. However as we sit there in the cinema enjoying the show, there is no number of stormtroopers that could really make us feel anxious about his prospects. Yes, the battles are spectacular and go very nicely with the popcorn and Coke; and yes, these stormtroopers can be tricky devils, but, well… deep down, we know who is going to win, right?! So, the writer (George Lucas) made things more difficult. He turned this really big challenge into a meaningful conflict by turning into a difficult decision under pressure.

How? Well, it took only **one** stormtrooper to arrive to give Luke a difficult choice. One stormtrooper who wants to kill him… but that one stormtrooper is Darth Vader. And that one stormtrooper is also Luke's father.

Ah.

Now Luke has a proper dilemma. He can take on Darth Vader (and risk murdering his own father) or he can lay down his weapon and try to connect with his father (and risk being killed in cold blood by the Lord of the Dark Side). Now we are gripping the seat. Now our popcorn is forgotten. What's he going to do?

This is a meaningful conflict — one the writer has taken a lot of time to frame and craft into place — and it makes for powerful story. Luke has a deliciously horrible choice to make under pressure of conflict. The choice he makes and the outcomes he reaps mean we will learn about Luke and his true character, and we will learn about life and how it should be led.

Other stories have the same dynamic but it is less focussed on one kingpin moment. As a story, *Juno* is one huge meaningful conflict. The entire story is a moral dilemma. Juno can have the baby (and lose her own youth to motherhood), or she can terminate the baby (and live with the feelings murdering her own baby). Again, the writer, (Diablo Cody) crafts the framing and character so that we understand she definitely does not want either of these options... but the baby is coming and she has increasing pressure to choose.

It is also interesting to note how the conflicts are ramped up one on top of the other in *Back to the Future*. We think of a story as a linear sequence of events, but a fine story has a vertical dimension created by making conflicts dependent on one another. This also reflects the story structure that builds storification upon character upon framing. *Back to the Future* is a series of nested, interdependent conflicts:

The external conflict that frames the entire story (can Marty get back to 1985? How will he do it?) cranks down onto the institutional conflict (can Marty get history back on track before he leaves to go back to 1985 so he can exist in future?) cranks down on the relationship conflict (can George overcome Biff and win the hand of Lorraine?) cranks down on George's internal conflict (can George overcome his cowardice and stand up for what is right in the face of his nemesis, Biff?).

So as the story progresses, the conflicts all ramp up the pressure and build, one upon the other. Each is dependent upon the resolution of the next until it is all wound up as tightly as it can be... on poor George McFly and his internal conflict, an impossible choice and a decision under pressure.

Once George makes his choice, in that kingpin moment, the positive outcome breaks his internal conflict. George's character has grown.

He does now have the courage of his convictions, and all the other conflicts, wound down tightly on top of this one, can now be resolved. Once he has resolved his inner conflict, he now has the courage of his convictions so he can defeat Biff. That means he can win Lorraine's hand. That means history is back on track. That means Marty will be born, so he can now hit the bolt of lightning. That means he can time-travel back to 1985. We arrive back in 1985 to see that everything has changed now that the family and world of George McFly has been characterised in the intervening years by a strong man instead of a weak one, and that gives George's character growth huge meaning in our minds (storification) as we consider what we have witnessed in George's journey.

As you absorb stories in the coming months, try to figure out what it is, in terms of meaningful conflict, that happens to the protagonist that brings the story its power to grip and engage you. If it is a highly rated story, I would bet it will have a choice of evils leading to a storification along these lines.

There is also more on this topic, and some further examples of conflict architectures, in *The Story Book*.

3.2 The Hollywood Formula

The fabled Hollywood formula came into being right alongside the emergence of cinema itself. The first films arrived with the 20th century, and things developed very quickly from there. According to David Bordwell, by 1917 what he called 'classical Hollywood cinema' was already established, a component of which was 'canonical story format'. A set of structural imperatives which he describes as being at the core of 'classical Hollywood narrative'. In summary, they were given as follows:
- Introduction of setting and characters
- Setting of protagonist goal(s)

- Actions to achieve goals complicated by obstacles and conflict
- Climax and resolution.

(From Bordwell, 1985b, pp.34,35)

The key point to note is that these principles were developed across a period of around 15 years (say, 1902-1917) within a film industry lacking some extremely important foundation blocks, such as integrated sound and sophisticated editing. The lack of sound meant no dialogue, of course, and the lack of sophisticated editing meant options such as close-ups and the subtlety and nuance of facial expressions were not available to the storyteller. In those early days the focus, literally and metaphorically, was very strongly placed upon action and spectacle. That focus on action rather than character is reflected in the rash of story development guidance for writers which was established in this same time period. A period that **completed** more than 10 years before integrated sound became established in the mid-1930s! The focus on spectacle never left the frame from then until now and it is upon these principles, *from over 100 years ago and on flawed premises*, that contemporary scriptwriting manuals are based.

Now, before I get ranty, I will stop there. Suffice to say that if this area interests you a deep investigation of the history and progression of film storytelling and the guidance that ran alongside it is in my academic work — *Story in Mind* (2019). I shall take a deep breath, calm myself, and jump forward to today.

The outcome of those foundational imperatives is that narrative theory and 'guru' advice has been passed down from generation to generation across 120 years, and the bias towards action and spectacle that originated in the flaws in that guidance have been perpetuated to today. Each progression – for example, in technology — for the last century has been used far more in the progression of spectacle and action than it has in the development of character and nuance, and the structure of existing highly-rated stories has underpinned any new guidance for writers — a very good reason why the same rules endlessly perpetuate to the next generation of writers.

Does the story have a protagonist by page 3? Does it have a clear setting, story world and period by page 10? Is there an inciting incident on page 27 which sets the protagonist aim and raises a key question in the mind of the audience? Is there a mid-act turning point on page 60? And so on. The business side loves all this, because the story can be 'measured' against these tick-box criteria and a presumption of 'goodness' and popularity can be made against the score to decide if the story is good enough or not. When an analyst looks for structures, they will find them, count them, and on this basis give the story a green light or 'pass on it'.

These analysts do not find knowledge gaps, of course, because the gaps are between the structures. Knowledge gaps are precisely the bit that is not there — the constitutive absence — the holes that define the presence of the net. The most important elements of story are not the visible components the analysts are looking for. At best, their approach establishes something of the framing. However, overall it misses all the knowledge gaps in every category and completely misses storification.

In my seminars, I use the following analogy: Every genius that has ever lived had a skeleton. There is a 100% correlation between the presence of genius and the presence of a skeleton. It is not unreasonable to assume, therefore, that the skeleton is something to do with the substance of genius. And if that wasn't proof enough, there is further evidence, because if you remove the skeleton from a genius they suddenly don't seem half so clever any more. So, it is obvious: To understand genius, we must understand skeletons.

Using this logic, story theory has devoted itself to an ever more forensic investigation of the structures in the text of existing stories in order to discover the secrets and substance of story. Now, you and I know that the secret to genius is not in the skeleton, it is in the mind. It is equally true to say that the substance of a story is not found in the structure of the text, it is in the mind of the author and the mind of the receiver.

A story is a psychological interaction between an author and a receiver. One head to another. The structures in the media that carry the narration between them is merely facilitating the communication. It is not of primary concern to understand the structures in the text that composes the narration. A telephone wire facilitates a conversation, but the wire does not bring any meaning.

This said, the emergence of more flexible and agile production channels, such as Netflix and Amazon, are moving us on from these established tropes. Ironically, because Netflix *et al* are working on much lower budgets they are reducing out the spectacle and effects and working much harder on compelling characters. And this is leading to stronger stories and enormously popular series.

I find it interesting that a majority of the finest films are stories from novels first and became films later. A novelist is unrestricted and simply writes a fine story. The film specialists then adapt it for the film medium. This is the correct model. Storytellers are storytellers. They should not even think about medium while they are writing. I advise scriptwriters to develop their stories without using scriptwriting software or any other medium-specific formatting or consideration. Just write the story, using a pen or a word processor, your head and heart and imagination and creativity and inspiration, then adapt it for specific delivery media or budget considerations later. Bob Gale said to me: "The best way to get a movie made is to write a novel." I believe this is very good advice.

The main point for this book and for all writers is that we are storytellers. We should not have to think about structure at all. For a writer, the structures in existing texts are not useful, because a writer does not start from there. A writer starts with an idea — a story seed — and needs to use their creative inspiration to develop that, not a pre-set structure from somebody else.

The psychology defines the genius, and the psychology defines the story, so while it is worth understanding the Hollywood formula it is not necessary or wise for you to adopt it as your template. Your story will definitely have structure once it is finished and knowing the Hollywood formula can help you to read that structure after you have written your story. That understanding can be helpful — retrospectively — in problem resolution. However, thinking about structure *before* you write your story is restrictive, limiting, reductive and makes for predictable story that is not from the heart. The most important and defining components of every story are the storifications, and these are the most ethereal of all. They are an outcome of framing, character and knowledge gaps and are the least amenable to structural imperatives.

Turning points and the key question
Anyway, where were we? Ah. Yes. The Hollywood formula. These days the focus of the Hollywood formula is centred on conflict, turning points (addressed shortly) and the key question dynamic. If you remember, an inciting incident raises a key question in the mind of the audience. The key question is held open across the long haul of act II during which the answer to this key question is thrown into doubt by the forces of antagonism ranged against the ambitions of the protagonist. The key question is finally answered at the climax of the story.

The Hollywood formula uses the key question to generate a classical three-act model. (Each act is *still* based on delivering the 'canonical story format' from 1917.)

- **ACT I — 'Setting of protagonist goals'**
  All the information that the audience requires so that the inciting incident raises the correct key question in the mind of the audience and sets the protagonist on his journey.

- **ACT II — 'Complications through obstacles and conflict'**

The battles and conflicts between the forces of protagonism and antagonism that throw the likely answers to the key question into doubt.

- **ACT III — 'Climax and resolution'**
  Act III is the ultimate battle which answers the key question. This is followed by the resolution, which shows how the world has changed following the decisions of the protagonist and the outcomes those decisions reap.

Back to the Future is very tightly structured in line with the Hollywood formula. A fine example of how it can work. Act I takes more than 30 minutes. It is quite surprising to think that Marty spends close to one-third of the story in 1985 before the inciting incident hits, which is the moment he accidentally goes back to 1955. Everything before the inciting incident ensures that the correct question is raised in the mind of the audience. We know that he did not intend to go back in time and he makes it clear once he has arrived that he does not want to be there so the key question is raised: Will Marty get back to 1985? How will he do it?

Act II is the battle between the forces of protagonism and the forces of antagonism surrounding this key question. Essentially, creating and addressing the conflicts we listed earlier, and piling them up on the soul of poor George.

For the Hollywood formula, the climactic battle that will answer the key question is the entry point to act III. Will Marty get back to 1985? How will he do it? As he heads off to channel the power of a bolt of lightning into the flux capacitor and make his journey back to 1985, this is the beginning of act III. There is no way back from this — it is all or nothing. The key question is then answered through the climactic action: Yes, he will make it back to 1985, and he will do it by harnessing a bolt of lightning.

The remainder of act III is then the resolution material, showing us what 1985 looks like now Marty has fought and won his battles. 1985 is very different, of course, because the intervening 30 years were characterised by a strong, confident father figure, not a weak, subservient one.

> **Note**: This traditional progression, based on the key question, ignores the most important moment – the storification. When George makes a fist and he changes and grows, this is the storification and this defines the ultimate power in the story. It is from this kingpin scene that the conflict logjam is broken and all the conflicts resolve. However, this is the Hollywood formula, so Marty is depicted as the protagonist and the storification moment goes unnoticed. This is because in the Hollywood formula, turning points are king. George's kingpin moment of storification is the most important dynamic in *Back to the Future*. It does at least make it onto the card in the Hollywood formula, but only as a turning point in the life of Marty McFly.

3.2.1 Turning Points

While I do not agree with a story being driven so determinedly by turning points, they are well worth knowing about. The major boundaries between acts in the Hollywood formula — and, indeed, between other story events — are defined by turning points in the character's lives. A turning point has a rather unique position in a story because:

- **A turning point is a measurable element of the creative process.** Turning points are generated through the conflict in a story event.

- **A turning point is a measurable element of structure.** Turning points can be clinically identified, pointed at and evaluated through analysing the structure of a completed story or story event.

Under the rules of the Hollywood formula, when desirable *creative* elements come together appropriately they deliver a turning point which is 'visible' from the *structural* viewpoint. While this is not something that should drive a writer's development process, this can be very useful when *analysing* a story or when trying to resolve story problems, because if an event structured using the Hollywood formula is failing to please us, testing for a turning point can often provide clues that tell us why.

Turning points define the presence of a change in the protagonist's emotional position and that generally happens through conflict. You almost certainly do not have *effective* conflict if it does not generate a turning point, so this next bit is worth understanding.

A turning point
occurs when the protagonist's emotional 'charge' switches across the course of an event (scene/act/sequence/story...)

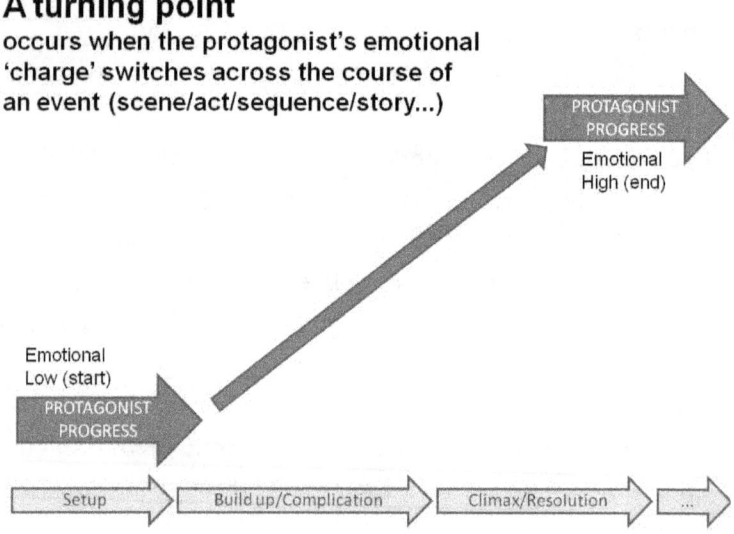

Figure 11: A turning point

We should be able to take any given event in a story and 'measure' the change in the values at stake for the protagonist across the course of that event. This can tell us if the event has a turning point.

For a story event to have value in the context of the Hollywood formula, it needs to have 'turned'.

For the Hollywood formula, this is all about the necessary and inevitable conflict. For the turning point to occur, the following elements need to be present:

- A protagonist with a protagonist aim for the event.
- An antagonist (or forces of antagonism) set in direct opposition to the aims of the protagonist.
- The two go head to head.
- One wins and the other loses.

Put simply, a turning point occurs when things get significantly better or worse for a protagonist across the course of a conflict event.

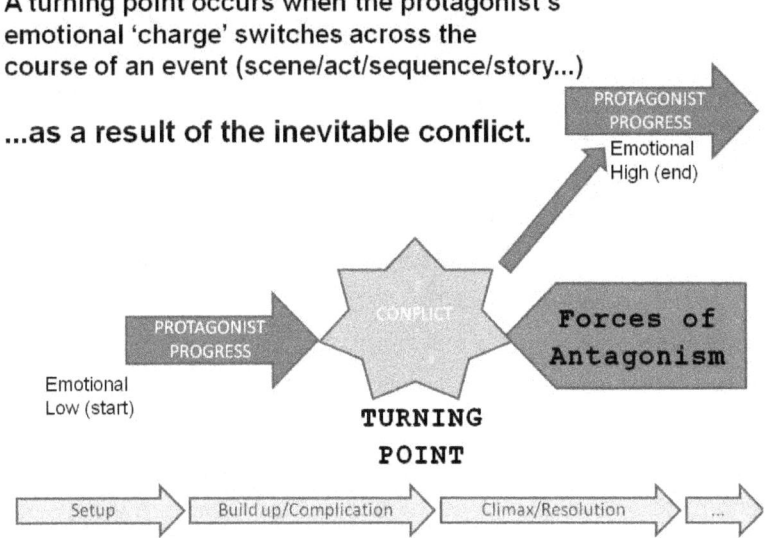

Figure 12: Turning point dynamics

For example?

Let's take a good old fairy tale. A dragon moves into the cave in the hills above a village. Every day he flies down to toast and eat a couple of villagers. A brave knight steps up. He girds his loins, takes up his sword and while his mum desperately tries to stop him, he announced that he is going up into the hills to teach the dragon right from wrong. This is the act I setup that raises a key question in the mind of the audience.

The knight heads off up into the hills. The dragon looks out of the cave and thinks: 'Hmmm. I've met one of these before. Crunchy on the outside but with a soft centre. Yummy!'

The knight takes on huge odds and they go into conflict... The knight uses a concealed portable fire extinguisher but it runs out too soon. He's going to need some fancy footwork now... But then the dragon's pilot light goes out, and the odds swing back in favour of the knight. Then the dragon sweeps the knight's sword away, and traps him up against the wall. It's all over now.. The dragon opens his mouth wide around the head of the knight... and his false teeth fall out, dropping to sit in a circle round the feet of the knight, like a pair of discarded knickers, and the dragon's long nose droops pathetically. Things have once more swung towards the knight... All of this is the act II conflict which throws the likely outcome into doubt.

In the climactic battle, the knight wins! Hoorah! The dragon is vanquished. The knight drags the beast back to the village and slaps it victoriously on the barbeque. The village is saved! The king rewards the knight with a castle, the hand of a princess (sometimes an entire princess) and a shed full of gold. This is the act III climax and resolution. The knight's fortunes have changed across the course of the telling because of the decisions he made under pressure of conflict. He has moved from an emotional low at the beginning to a relative high at the end, as has the entire village. The dragon has moved from an emotional high at the beginning to an emotional deadness at the end. A moral message is delivered. If you sacrifice yourself bravely for the benefit of society you will do better than if you are self-centred and just look after number one.

Back to the Future has dozens of examples of this structure. When George stands on the brink of his kingpin decision, he is in a difficult place at an emotional low. The plan he and Marty made to trick Lorraine into finding George attractive has gone wrong because the giant bully, Biff is in the driving seat next to Lorraine instead of Marty. Lorraine is in danger at Biff's hands, so George makes a fist for the first time in his life and they go into conflict. Eventually, he overcomès the bully and wins the girl. He ends the scene on an emotional high through his decisions and actions under pressure of conflict. George's emotional 'charge' has gone from a terrible low at the point he opened the car door to hugely positive across the course of the scene, so the scene has turned. Let's document and measure that.

From a formulaic structural viewpoint, it is likely that the scene is a winner if it has:

1) **A protagonist with a protagonist aim for the event.**
   At the scene level, the protagonist is George. His aim is to defeat the bully and get the girl.

2) **An antagonist (or forces of antagonism) set in direct opposition to the aims of the protagonist.**
   The antagonism in the scene comes from Biff. Both he and George want Lorraine's hand, so the conflict is inevitable and only one can win out.

3) **The two go head to head.**
   The conflict engages directly and effectively as George and Biff fight.

4) **One wins and the other loses.**
   George knocks Biff out with a terrific haybaler of a punch. George wins and moves emotionally from negative to positive. Biff loses and moves from positive to negative.

5) **A character's values and quality of life move strongly to the positive or negative relative to their starting positions in the story event.**

   The scene's resolution shows the way the world has changed. George leads the adoring Lorraine on to the dancefloor where they kiss for the first time. Through his proactive decisions within the scene, we in the audience comprehend the meaning in the narration we have absorbed. George has transitioned from a weak and single loser to a proud winner with a girlfriend and a future.

This measurable transition in the protagonist's fortunes, achieved through the actions he takes under pressure of conflict, indicates that a turning point is present, and the scene has turned. Biff and Lorraine's fortunes have also changed significantly across the course of the scene, so the scene evidently 'turns' in more ways than one.

This is a classic, definitive Hollywood formula scene progression. In *The Story Book* I go through the whole of *Back to the Future* in these terms, detailing the turning points at the beat, scene, sequence, act and story event levels so if you are interested in further analysis here, do please refer to *The Story Book*.

3.2.2   Note on turning points

The example depicts a switch from an emotional low to an emotional high; a switch in life values for the protagonist from negative to positive, however things can equally move to the negative and the scene will still turn. Indeed, the shift only has to be 'relative'. A turning point can represent a shift in protagonist fortunes from positive to dramatically more positive; or from negative to extremely negative. There simply needs to be a relative and appreciable shift in values, achieved through a character's decisions and actions under pressure of conflict for a scene to turn.

Romeo and Juliet journey from positive (falling in love and planning their future) to negative (both dead). A tragic outcome tempered only by the idea in the mind of most audience members that at least they are now together and will be so forever.

In *I am Legend* Dr. Robert Neville's journey has a dual 'happy/sad' outcome. He moves from positive to negative in his personal life (he sacrifices himself and dies for his cause) but through this action, humanity journeys from negative (being wiped out) to positive (Neville's cure saves humanity).

A progression to the negative that is counterbalanced out by a second progression to the positive is known as an 'ironic' arc. This is often the design for a tragedy.

All these stories show clear turning points, driven into place by the actions of the characters under pressure of conflict, and therefore give us the early clues that they are likely to be viable and compelling stories. It is also worth noting that this exact same model is applied at the scene, sequence and act level, as well as the major turning points that define the entire story.

3.2.3   The Hollywood formula — major turning points

We also need to talk about the mid-act turning point. This is a relatively new concept (credited to Syd Field in the 1960s) which led to the classical three-act structure actually having four acts.

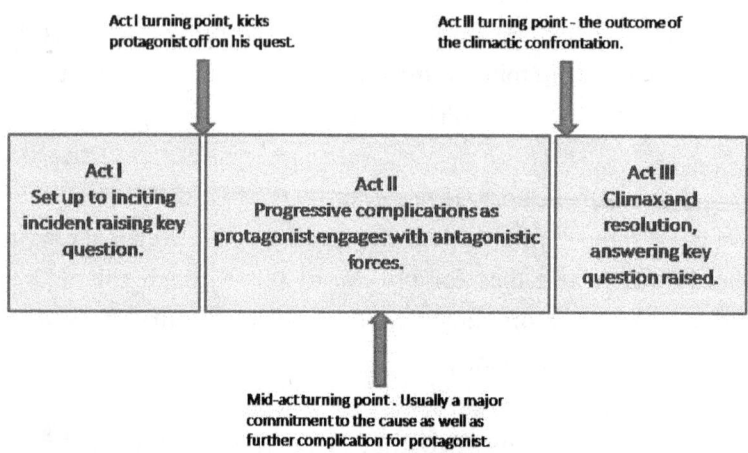

Figure 13: The major turning points

There are usually three main turning points in the plot of a classically structured Hollywood film story, as shown above. The first one is, more often than not, also the inciting incident that raises the key question (but does not have to be). The key feature that distinguishes an Act I turning point from the others is that it should set the protagonist off on their quest, and we should understand their story-wide purpose and see their direction change as they set about fulfilling it.

In the common case for the Hollywood formula, the Act I turning point is a 'call to action' for our hero. It is designed to propel the protagonist in a wholly unexpected direction and define their goal (perhaps more clearly than the inciting incident alone) and might refine or help to clarify the key question raised.

In *Toy Story* (director John Lasseter, 1995) the inciting incident and act I turning point are not the same event. The inciting incident occurs when Woody finds Buzz Lightyear in his place on Andy's bed. Woody's reaction on meeting Buzz raises the key question: will Buzz replace Woody as leader of the toys and Andy's favourite toy? However, this is not enough to frame the story, because we do not know what they are going to do. The second part comes some twelve minutes later when Woody hatches a plan to 'lose' Buzz down behind the chest of drawers. This simple plan will solve everything. However, when he executes his plan, it goes wrong. He accidentally knocks Buzz out of the window. The other toys see this happen and lose trust in Woody. They think he's a murderer. His attempt at fixing his first problem has had the opposite effect and multiplied his problems (his fortunes have gone from bad to much worse). He is now no longer Andy's favourite toy, he is no longer the respected leader of the toys, he has no friends and stands accused of murder. This turning point sets Woody off in a new direction, and with a quest: To find and save Buzz Lightyear in order to restore trust and regain the respect he needs to be the leader.

The Cohen Brothers' film, *No Country for Old Men* (directed by Ethan and Joel Coen, 2007) is similar. There are two time-separated events that comprise the entire Act I turning point and inciting incident, but in this case, the two things must be taken in combination in order to get all the necessary information across.

Llewelyn Moss (Josh Brolin) stumbles across the carnage of a drugs deal-turned-shoot-out in the remote desert of West Texas. Everyone is dead but for a dying Mexican, stuck in the driver's seat of a car, who begs Moss for water. Moss leaves him to die because he finds two million dollars of drugs money. He gets clean away with the cash, leaving no link to himself whatsoever. This is surely a turning point in his life — his fortunes have changed dramatically — but there is no key question raised yet. Although such a sum of money is surely 'life changing', his story has yet to be given its direction. As he lies in bed in the middle of the night, he feels guilty that he left the Mexican to die. He returns to the scene of the shoot-out to give the man water... and his car is discovered by police. This is the real turning point. His identity is now known and the chase is on from both the police and the psychopathic and relentless bad guy, Anton Chigurh (played by Javier Bardem) who will hunt him without mercy to get the drug lords their money back. Now Moss's fortunes have gone massively to the negative, his direction is changed and the key question is raised: Can Moss outrun the police, and Chigurh, and get away with the money? Both events — the discovery of the cash and the return to help the Mexican — are needed before the full inciting incident/turning point job is done, and we in the audience are orientated to the widest arcs of the story.

The mid-act turning point

A full-length story tends to meander during the long haul of act II. Hence, a Hollywood story generally has a mid-act turning point, which divides act II into two. If you think about it, a mid-act turning point is also a natural requirement if three acts are going to deliver a happy ending. The turning point at the climax of act I will have sent fortunes downwards and the dynamic for the major turning point at climax must go from an all-time low at the entry to act III to a high point for the story to end on a positive.

That's confusing... Hold on, I'll draw a picture... There.

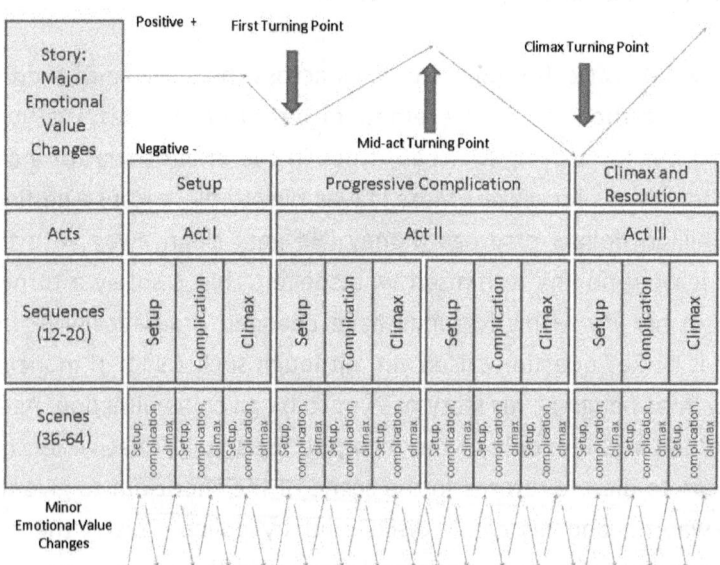

Figure 14: Classic shape for a Hollywood roller-coaster

As you can see in the line of arrows representing the 'Story: Major Emotional Value Changes', act II begins from an emotional low (as a result of the first turning point that defines the climax to act I when the protagonist's world is thrown out of balance and their quest is defined by the key question). However, the whole of act II also needs to *end* on an emotional low if act III is to end high and deliver a happy ending. In between, it is therefore logical to arc fortunes high by the centre of act II in order to be able to drop back to the necessary second low at the end of act II in order to have a happy ending as an outcome of act III.

Figure 14 depicts the structure of *Back to the Future*, showing the major emotional swings for the protagonist. This is a classic Hollywood formula structure with a happy ending. Following the 'top line' arrows in the illustration, Marty's emotional position begins flat in his normal school day, but takes a big negative hit when he gets sent back in time at the end of act I. It rises gradually as he finds Doc Brown and gets a plan together for how to return to 1985, but his fortunes take a massive hit at the mid-act turning point when he realises he has interfered with future events; his parents are not going to meet and, even if he can return to 1985, he will not exist when he gets there. He is going to die. Things continue to slide to an all-time emotional low as the clock clicks down and, time and again, Marty's attempts to reunite his parents fall on stony ground. That is, until the moment his dad finally makes a fist and wins the fight with Biff. From here, all the problems resolve and his emotional position swings to the positive, again and again, to finish at an all-time high.

There are two circumstances when this kind of structural understanding is very handy. Firstly, and most importantly, when you are writing a scene/sequence/chapter or even an entire story and something is bugging you about it. Knowing how to analyse the structure of your story can be hugely beneficial, so this understanding can be an effective tool for story analysis and problem resolution. You know something is not right, but you cannot put your finger on it, so analyse your story event for conflict, emotional charge and turning points and you may well get clues as to what is bothering you. Additionally, as I said earlier, almost all stories have a key question. The only thing that changes is how obvious it is. So, if you have a problem with your story or story event, checking the key question and turning point dynamics that come with it can be very revealing and might just be the key to understanding what is wrong. Of course, you might not choose to address these problems by bringing your story into line with the formulaic imperatives, but if they help provide you with some means of identifying why you have doubts about a story event, then fine. Sometimes it can be handy.

Secondly, in the life of a fully professional writer, churning out stories at the rate of one every year, sometimes it helps to have options. When the muse is failing to show up, when inspiration is hard to find but you really need to keep cracking along, it is very easy to use these criteria to cynically cobble a basic event together and label it up in the step outline (which I will explain in depth shortly) so that you can continue to make solid progress and keep your writing momentum.

Overall, my view is that it is useful to know about the Hollywood formula, understand it, and use it when it can be useful and that is when you have an early draft and are in analysis mode. Once a story is written and you are in editing/polishing mode, it can be a useful tool in problem solving and analysis. The Hollywood formula is not a dirty word but keep it under control and locked in your writer's toolbox for those occasions when it might prove useful. Life is much more fun as a creative and your stories will have more zing and originality if you allow your story to emerge from your natural organic ability, imagination and personality. Good story is not about structure, it's about knowledge gaps, so start from anywhere and go wherever the muse takes you. Your story can be utterly without structure as far as your imagination takes it forwards. As long as there are knowledge gaps, there is story power, so just go for it and let the structure take care of itself in your wake.
Primarily, note that the Hollywood formula, by focussing so firmly on the key question, can miss critical character dynamics that hold the

keys to the real power of the story. As ever, *Back to the Future* provides the perfect example: The Hollywood formula is entirely centred on Marty McFly and his time-travel adventure, when the real power of the story is George McFly's character growth.

If you don't like yourself very much, a deeper investigation of the history and progression of classical Hollywood cinema and the development of formulaic storytelling is in my academic work: *Story in Mind: A Constructivists Narratology* (2019). An in-depth analysis of the structure of Back to the Future can be found in *The Story Book* (2010), from which some of the above illustrations are taken.

3.3   Aristotle's Principles

When it comes to existing story design my favourite is undoubtedly Aristotle's principles. Reading his work was mind-blowing, because I was effectively in communication with a man in the same business as me but some 2,350 years ago, on a subject that is essentially unchanged to this day, and his arguments are as relevant and valid as anyone else's in the contemporary discussion. Indeed, I feel his principles are undervalued because they define a clear progression that is a function of characters and their behaviours, which means they complement and inform story content rather than reflect the plot in a narrative structure like everybody else has since.

I also find it surprising that although they do still teach forms of Aristotle in film schools, his principles are often not rendered clearly and they are not appreciated for the power they can bring to modern story-telling. I believe that this is because most analysts equate Aristotle's harmatia with the inciting incident, which is not necessarily the case. They ignore the anagnorisis, or 'realisation' as not relevant to today's storytelling, which is a big miss, as we shall see. They also associate the peripeteia solely with the inevitable death of the protagonist in Greek tragedy and therefore irrelevant to stories that are not tragic, and from there it becomes an academic discussion of what Aristotle means when he uses the word 'catharsis' which, while fascinating, is not helpful for the writer trying to power up a story idea.

In each case it is a shame, because a contemporary reading of Aristotle can be of great value to a writer. It is also interesting from my perspective that each of his three basic facets firstly, implicitly embodies a knowledge gap, and secondly, each sits in one of the three areas of my own theory: Framing (author's role) Character (character's role) and Storification (receiver's role), so Aristotle is a fine fit for my approach. Let's go through his principles and demonstrate how and when these elements can be used to fine effect in contemporary storytelling.

Once again, let's use the kingpin scene of *Back to the Future*; the scene in which Marty and George plan to make George appear strong in order to make him attractive to Lorraine. In the plan, George will handily turn up at just the right time to catch Marty making inappropriate sexual advances to Lorraine. George will pretend to beat Marty up. Lorraine will be full of admiration for her knight in shining armour and will fall in love with George.

Aristotle's principles comprise three elements: the harmatia, anagnorisis and peripeteia.

1. **The harmatia**
   Translates as a 'mistake' or 'error' which throws the protagonist's world out of balance, raising questions in the mind of the audience: 'what is going to happen?' 'How will this be fixed?'

   In our scene from *Back to the Future*, the harmatia occurs when George and Marty's plan goes wrong. George arrives at the car, ready to play his role in the charade to make him look strong. He rips the car door open and says his line:
   'Hey you! Get your damn hands off her.'

But it is not Marty in the car playing his part. It is the dreaded bully, Biff, making genuinely inappropriate sexual advances towards Lorraine. The plan they made has gone wrong and George's world is thrown out of balance.

Note how the harmatia is separate from the inciting incident and key question for this story event. The inciting incident is the deployment of the plan, and the key question is: Will the plan work? Will Marty and George successfully trick Lorraine into thinking George is a strong man? The harmatia is different. It identifies the moment the world is thrown out of balance when the plan goes wrong. For me, this is much more important because is attached to a character interaction. The inciting incident/key question is attached to the **plot** (what happens – they make a plan) whereas the harmatia is attached to the **character** — what are the implications for George's life and prospects when the plan goes wrong and his world is thrown out of balance.

2. **The anagnorisis** ('realisation')
   Is the moment in a narrative when the full awful truth of the situation is fully appreciated by the protagonist. Things are much, much worse than they originally thought. In Aristotle's time, when the anagnorisis hit, matters had already gone irretrievably wrong. Anagnorisis generally occurred too late to allow remedial action in a Greek tragedy, and despite the protagonist's desperate scramble to rescue the situation, the anagnorisis is the realisation that it is all too little too late.

   Incidentally, for me the realisation is the trigger for empathy because it generates a deep response in terms of the way the audience *feels*. If the protagonist is still alive and kicking but suffering (or tragedy in Aristotle's time) is now inevitable, this engenders a deep and visceral response in the onlooking audience. A pit of dread in the stomach. Death is coming for the protagonist in the story world, and we feel it too; we feel something we do not get to feel in our normal lives.

Empathy accompanies the realisation. As discussed earlier, we do not cry when we see someone else crying. Anagnorisis is the moment we deeply understand why someone has every right to feel desperate. Now we empathise and feel that emotion too. Empathy leads to catharsis when tragedy then comes calling and death befalls the hapless victim of life. Now our feeling of empathy for the person suffering the realisation turns to catharsis as our own soul reacts to the proximity we are feeling to death and suffering. As close as we generally get before we are on that slide ourselves. It is a deep and powerful sensation — almost beyond feelings. A visit to the cliff edge of life and a moment of clear vision into the abyss — the valley of death.

When we relate the protagonist's situation to our own mortality, this is catharsis. We all know that life is ultimately a tragic story for each and every one of us. Catharsis is the embodied, instinctive *realisation* of that truth but it comes with a feeling of relief that today is not that day for us; we are looking on as that moment arrives for somebody else so we are as close to feeling death as we can get whilst being safe at the same time. It is very difficult to describe — hence the endless academic discussions — but it is also something we automatically understand. That pit in your stomach as you feel trepidation deep within the fibre of your being.

This is why I feel realisation is so undervalued by writers and by story theory, and why it is a wonderful thing to lock on to and understand as a writer. In particular, note how a 'realisation' happens for the audience member, not just for the protagonist. Shakespeare's *Romeo and Juliet* is a classic tragedy in Aristotle's terms, however it is the audience that has the anagnorisis — the realisation that the series of events will lead to Romeo and Juliet's deaths if nobody within the story does something about it. And nobody does. This is a complete tragedy — and Romeo and Juliet *never* find out the truth of what happened. I would argue that an audience realisation, when coupled with the catharsis of a beautifully tragic peripeteia, is perhaps the most powerful dynamic in story. In this day and age, most stories do not deliver the full realisation/peripeteia tragic pairing, preferring the peripeteia to be a twist to an unexpected happy ending, so the power of Aristotle is reduced, as we get the deep empathy but lesser catharsis.

George McFly's anagnorisis comes when he 'realises' that he has a stark choice: stand and fight his giant nemesis, Biff (and get six bells beaten out of him) or turn and run away as he usually would (leaving Lorraine to be abused by Biff in the car). George's anagnorisis is a choice of evils. And he has to choose one of them. He gets that pit in his stomach as he faces life, and we feel for him.

There may be more than one realisation in a story (in *Back to the Future* there are 27) and the power of a realisation is something that is not valued highly enough in modern story theory. Look for realisations; they are a hard-hitting knowledge gap (for there to be a realisation there must have been knowledge missing), so build to that gap; hold it open and value it. It is a moment of strong engagement as it causes audience engagement. Plus, of course, if you have a realisation you have the potential for an entire Aristotlean progression. Finding the realisation can help you find a spine for an event. Indeed, in pure Aristotle terms, a true anagnorisis **must** be causally linked to a peripeteia.

3. **The peripeteia** ('reversal')
   Is best seen as a twist in the tale. As a story event approaches its climax the audience has generally been given strong expectations as to what will happen, and the outlook generally will not be looking good for the protagonist. The peripeteia is the

twist in expectation for the audience, specifically in the context of the realisation (anagnorisis).

In our example, the expectation set by the realisation is that George will either get beaten up by the bully or he will run away and leave Lorraine to suffer. Neither is a good outcome. The peripeteia twist is a third way we did not see coming. George chooses to stand his ground and then — big twist — he wins the fight. This brings the audience the modern-day version of a peripeteia (that is, the Hollywood outcome is rarely tragic): the audience gets what they want (a win for their hero), but not in the way they expected.

These are the words I use to explain the common contemporary path through the climax of a story event using an anagnorisis/peripeteia pair: *The audience gets what they want, but not in the way they expected.*

We wanted George to get it together with Lorraine and for Marty to exist in the future. We got what we wanted but we did not expect that it would be through George finding a strong and assertive inner self that even he did not know was there. This connecting with his inner soul is the power of anagnorisis, empathy, catharsis and the finest stories.

Hopefully you can see that in a tragic tale, anagnorisis causes us to empathise and the tragic peripeteia — the consequent suffering and death of the protagonist — causes us to feel catharsis. These feelings are rarely experienced in life, so gaining those insights into our soul from a story is a rare and wonderful thing. The maximum power of a story. Do not be avoidant of tragedy in your stories. It can take your audience to places they will rarely get to go.

As discussed earlier, in *Back to the Future*, the writers made enormous effort to corner George into a choice of evils, but now look at what they did in crafting their story in the context of his realisation. The anagnorisis and peripeteia pair could only work if all the necessary elements of *all* the characters, their motivations and situation were crafted painstakingly into place. We in the audience had to be *prepared*. George had to be shown to be a coward to convince us that running away from a girl being raped would be a realistic possibility in our minds. If you think about it, that takes some doing, right?! So, the writers showed us not just his fear of Biff and what happens when the two of them share a scene (Biff bullies George every time, and George avoids the confrontation every time to make the point beyond doubt) but George also runs away from the most trivial of confrontations. He even says out loud in the early sequences in 1985: "I'm sorry son. I'm just not very good at confrontations."

From this we know that he continues to be a chicken from his school days into middle age. It becomes embedded into our accepted understanding of who George is, and therefore sets up the possibility of an unexpected twist when he stands his ground. Once you, as the writer, know the outcome for a character, you can work back to craft an appropriate framing and supporting characters in order to ensure the conditions exist for your protagonist to arc effectively to their finale.

In this sense, when you find a realisation or the potential for a possible twist in expectation, this is a great opportunity. It is part of your craft to work backwards and forwards through the rest of your story to make the most of these wonderful moments. If your character's jaw suddenly hits the floor because they realise some truth about their situation this may well be an anagnorisis (or could be turned into one). Work backwards to embed a harmatia. Take if forwards and craft in a peripeteia. You can be sure that these dynamics will deliver powerful story.

Oedipus Rex

If you fancy a real Greek tragedy, read the story of Oedipus. Written by Sophocles around 430 BC and originally called *Oedipus Rex* or *Oedipus the King*. This is a proper tragedy. I absolutely love it, but it is not exactly cheerful! (the fact that I love it demonstrates that a tragic outcome is, secretly, something we like to experience, even if we equally talk about how dreadful it was. When I say, 'give them what they want', tragedy is something they want.)

When Oedipus was born, an Oracle prophesied to his parents that their son will murder his father (King Laius) and sleep with his mother (Queen Jocasta). To defeat the prophesy, the king and queen leave Oedipus in the mountains so there will be no connection between them and the prophesy cannot play out. This is the harmatia for Oedipus; his world is thrown out of balance as his parents leave him to a fate unknown. However, Oedipus is found and adopted by a couple who bring him up as their own. He survives and becomes a man.

Many years later, when travelling one day, Oedipus gets into a fight with a man. He wins the battle and as the man was of high standing, he also wins the man's status… King. He also wins his queen. Great luck for a poor man travelling randomly. Oedipus's anagnorisis comes much later when he realises that the man he fought and killed whilst travelling was his father and therefore the queen he gained through that killing — a woman with whom he has been sharing a bed since — is his mother. The prophesies have all come true. The truth hits Oedipus hard (anagnorisis). He rushes to get to his queen before she finds out the awful truth, but he is too late. She found out what happened and has hanged herself (peripeteia). Oedipus — in trying to do the right thing at every turn — has murdered his father, slept with his mother and she's now hanging dead from the ceiling. So Oedipus spikes his own eyes out with needles. Ahh, they don't write 'em like that anymore. (The full story is readily available to read for free on the internet.)

If you watch *Back to the Future* again, see how much Aristotle you can find — particularly anagnorisis/peripeteia pairings. Whether by accident or design, they occur time after time. To help you along, I'll give you one more example.

in *Back to the Future*, at the moment when Marty McFly is accidentally sent back in time to 1955, he sees Doc Brown attacked by terrorists and mown down in a hail of gunfire. This is harmatia; Marty's world is thrown out of balance. In act III, when Marty returns to 1985, he deliberately comes back ten minutes early to prevent this tragic event, however his plan is thrown off when he comes back in a different part of town and now he has to get all that way across town to save Doc. This is his anagnorisis — his pit-in-the-stomach realisation that he has messed up disastrously. His journey across town eats up the ten minutes. He arrives just in time to see Doc Brown mown down again... and now Doc is dead. The audience is sharing the horror of this realisation and are as sure as Marty that there is no way back from this tragic outcome. There's no escaping the tragic truth. Marty could have come back the day before or a week before, but he messed up. And Doc is dead. The peripeteia (reversal or twist in expectation) comes as Marty cradles Doc's head and mourns his death... and Doc sits up. He's alive! He did read the warning Marty tried to give him in 1955 after all and is wearing a bullet-proof vest. What seemed impossible is now the outcome. Doc is alive. A perfect example of a modern Aristotle progression.

We knew *what* was most likely to happen. We didn't know *how* it was going to happen. We got what we wanted, but not in the way we expected.

Incidentally, the *Frozen* trailer is also based on a perfect modern Aristotle progression. See if you can pick it out. To give you a clue, the anagnorisis (Olaf's realisation) is very clear. Start from there and work backwards to harmatia and forwards to peripeteia twist.

3.4 Story and the Moral Argument

There is usually a clear morality at the heart of a good story. As children, one of the first joyful experiences of story is when we recognise the moral message. We storify for ourselves and feel terrific satisfaction. As we grow older, we think our stories become more sophisticated and the moral message is a vestige from childhood. Nothing could be further from the truth. The wrapping gets more complex, but an underlying moral basis is surprisingly persistent.

A children's story is generally based on the conflict between bad guys driven by self-interest and goodies fighting for the wider good of society. Returning to our dragon living in the hills terrorising a village and eating villagers, we have a self-serving/society-negative bad guy dragon. A brave knight steps up and puts himself at personal risk. (He is a selfless/society-serving good guy.) The knight takes on huge odds and we fear for him... but he wins out. The dragon is vanquished and society rewards the knight with a kingdom, a castle, the hand of a princess (in fact, an entire princess...) and a shed full of gold. This basic pattern to the stories we receive is how we are encouraged, from the very beginning of our storied lives, towards good moral behaviour. The message is clear and oft-repeated: You will gain more by serving the society that supports you than you will by being selfish.

Little Red Riding Hood, her grandmother and her mother are villagers. The wolf is a dragon. The Woodcutter is the knight. The moral lesson is taught: Small children should not talk to strangers. The three little pigs are villagers. The wolf is a dragon. The third pig is a brave knight. The moral lesson is taught: Do a proper job or suffer the consequences.

The cosmos is a village. Thanos is a dragon. The Avengers are the brave knight. The moral message is taught: Good people must stand together to defeat evil.

Marty McFly and his family are villagers. Biff is a dragon. George is a reluctant (but surprisingly) brave knight. The moral message is taught: You must have the courage of your convictions to lead a fulfilling life.

If you consider all the superheroes, every detective, James Bond, Harry Potter, Star Wars... these are relatively simple to see in the context of a basic morality. A clear bad guy serving their own best interest at a cost to society. Socially conscious good guys giving of themselves to do right by wider society and getting rewarded by society for their altruism. Many stories are essentially a moral lesson about how the best way to serve ourselves is to serve the society we ultimately rely upon.

There are narrative theorists out there who go so far as to *define* story as a moral argument. I would not go quite that far, as there are plenty of stories that do not fit. However, it is true to say that the finest stories do have a moral argument at their roots. For some stories it is up front and centre and for others it is dialled back, but it is quite surprising just how common it is. Most importantly, from a writer's perspective, it is very useful indeed to identify and understand the morality at play in your story, so in this section I will explain what morality is from a writer's perspective, then show how understanding the morality in your story can be used as a wonderful tool to help you to:

- Create relevant, well-motivated characters.
- Define the core conflicts and spine of the story.
- Unify your story around a clear theme.
- Define the subtext that gives your story its ultimate meaning and life truth (that is, give it its storification).

As you will see, if there is a moral argument that is clearly central to your story, you can choose to use it to drive in excellent story elements and as a basis for your story design.

3.4.1 What is morality?

For story purposes, morality asserts a subjective value on behaviour. The story presses our mental buttons and coaxes us to think in polarised terms about what is 'right and wrong'; 'good and bad'. 'Good' moral behaviour is socially positive and 'bad' (immoral) behaviour will harm oneself or another person. I put these terms in quotes because they are subjective, and the space this subjectivity leaves for passionate opinion is where the story potential lives.

On this good/bad basis, there is a clear morality at the heart of most stories. The main emotional pressure comes from the fear that the bad (immoral) side looks like it is going to win. The society that supports us is breaking down. Social order is in jeopardy. We feel unsafe. Other stories provide a more complex and nuanced presentation. They still have their basis in morality, but with lots more subtlety. In *Three Billboards Outside Ebbing, Missouri* (directed by Martin McDonagh, 2017) the moral argument concerns where the line lies in the extent to which a member of the public can or should hold the police to account. Of course, we must be able to do so (we have seen what happens in countries where the police run the state), but at what point do we have to back off and say, 'Well, police are generally good people and I'm sure they tried their best. Some crimes cannot be solved,' and move on with our lives? How do we legislate for that? Who polices the police?

Notice how every character in *Three Billboards* is defined by their moral stance in terms of police accountability. All the conflict is generated through the way each character actively represents — and fights for — a different (that is, a conflicting) moral stance. The subtext we take away with us having experienced this story is a moral lesson about how those who have suffered a crime should behave and be treated when they are angry, emotional, vengeful and desperately wanting justice. Notice how the whole story becomes greater than the sum of its parts because the morality spills out from the story and into the truth of our real lives and feelings about our justice system. Everything — every character, every event, the whole story and its subtext — is threaded through with the moral question regarding how we give the police power and yet, at the same time, hold them accountable. This unifies the story and gives it authority and cohesion. *Three Billboards* is a very good story, and I argue that this is, to a great extent, a function of how the moral argument is used to craft characters around what I call the moral maypole. Each individual's moral stance links them to everybody else around the moral maypole and naturally forces them into difficulties with each other as soon as the dance begins. It is interesting that the clear 'bad guy' (the original rapist and murderer) does not appear in the movie. The crime took place before the film begins and it is all about Mildred and how justice works.

Every character in *Three Billboards* **is defined by their moral stance** in terms of police accountability. Mildred's (Frances McDormand) daughter was raped and murdered. She is seeking justice and we completely understand that the fuss she is causing by putting up the billboards and calling out the police chief, Willoughby (Woody Harrelson) is justified. It is an unorthodox way to go about it, but we understand. Mildred's cause is greatly enhanced in our minds as we get to know a police officer on the case — Dixon (Sam Rockwell) who appears to be everything that society fears may lurk within the police force. A violent man, parading his power and abusing the privileges his badge gives him. His moral position is that the police should be free to do as they see fit. They should mete out justice as they see fit and be untouchable. He goes too far, by a long way, and is 'bad', but note how he changes across the course of the telling. He undergoes moral learning and we appreciate that. We know what is right and what is wrong, however, we feel entirely justified in throwing our support behind Mildred in her campaign against the Police. Things become difficult for us, however, as we realise over time that Chief Willoughby is a decent man, doing his best. He also wants justice to be done, and he also wants Dixon to understand that the privilege that is afforded a police officer comes with responsibility. We begin to see that police officers are human beings, facing huge challenges, and they have human frailties like everyone else in society. It is not always easy for a police force that is stretched. The moral argument begins to swing round. Notice how **all the conflict is generated through these differing moral stances**.

As the story enters its climax, Mildred is working unofficially with Dixon. He has been suspended from duty (because of his immoral behaviour, not befitting an officer) and is hoping to regain some credibility through working on the case as a vigilante outside the force (a morally questionable decision...). He convinces Mildred that he has found the rapist who murdered her daughter. They decide to take the law into their own hands and, driven more by the hope that they are right than the integrity of the evidence before them, they set out to take decisive action. If the police will not provide justice they will do it for themselves. However, on the long drive to hunt down the man and mete out justice, the emotional frenzy reduces. Mildred realises (anagnorisis) that this is not right. Gradually, Mildred and Dixon look at themselves and what they are doing. They cool down. They back out of the plan. And they go home. And that is it. The peripeteia is that nothing happens. Mildred has changed. She has grown. She is accepting that the process of justice must be allowed to take its course and that although our agencies must be accountable, emotionally-driven vigilante action is not right. In this moment, as cinema-goers, we feel a little let down, because in the movies — in that Hollywood DNA encoding to which we are so attached — they were driving towards a big exciting climax to the story. The ultimate battle (with the dragon) that will decide everything. Well, they were, but the conflicts were inside themselves, and that was where the battle was won. In this film, a component of the peripeteia is that it actually twists this element of the audience expectation of a Hollywood film as well as the expectation set by Mildred's motivation and anger within the story.

Here they are simply backing out of violent retribution and 'doing the right thing'. Many people are disappointed by *Three Billboards* for the anticlimactic ending, but it is in this moment that the storification hits, and this same audience finds it satisfying when they think about it and talk about it the next day. It is one of those stories whereby perhaps you tell people the next day that you didn't like it much, but as you explain what happened you realise that you got far more out of it than you thought you did at the time. The reason is because the <u>story</u> continues to develop in your mind in subtext after the end of the <u>narration</u>. It continues to storify and you come to understand the true depth of the storification over time.

The subtext we leave the story with is a moral lesson. When a story has a moral argument, the outcome in storification is a lesson in life and how it should be led. A story of this nature normally delivers one of two moral imperatives. You own the story in your head and think to yourself:

> 'Yes, this is how a person should lead their life.'
> Or
> 'Yes, life is like that.'

Design
Note how the morality under question led the author to derive characters that represented the different moral stances. The different moral stances naturally generated the conflicts, and these conflicts, in turn, defined a form of key question: which moral stance will the protagonist eventually adopt? The protagonist makes their choice and must live or die by their decision. This provides the climax for the story and, of course, the all-important storification, which is the moral argument being embedded into the mindset of the audience through understanding the characters' actions, their decisions made under pressure of conflict, the outcomes those decisions harvested and their own consequent moral learning and growth.

Now we begin to see how empowering it is to know the morality in your story as you start to develop it. Just take a moment to think about being the author of *Three Billboards* (Martin McDonagh). Imagine being armed from the start with this understanding of the moral argument with which you are working. Understanding the morality that defines your story goes a long way in informing the characters — the characters *have* to represent *these* contrasting stances to deliver on *this* morality. Each character's moral stance is in conflict with another's so it drives the contents of the events and the arcs of the story. Morality can be used to map out the way the story *has to be* and brings it immediate cohesion, unity and power. This is why it is so wonderful for you to understand the morality in your story. You can use the moral argument effectively as a story generator (something we will do in section 4). Threading the morality into every character and event gives a story its **theme**.

3.4.2 Story theme

When people think of a story theme, they tend to identify with some topic from the content. High school, friendship, time-travel, childhood, romance, and so on. These are not the 'theme'. The theme of the story is an expression of the morality threaded through the narration.

Everything — every character, every event, the whole story and its subtext — is threaded through with the moral argument and this unifies the story and gives it authority and cohesion. Once you understand the morality in your story idea, it begins to write itself in these terms.

Let's use this to build a story. Take a real-world moral issue. Say, the moral argument surrounding teenage pregnancy. As an author, your job is to use characters and events to storify the issues in the argument. You set up your moral maypole, then give a ribbon representing a moral stance for each character. One is pro-life, one is pro-abortion, one is driven by religious imperatives, another by the father's responsibilities, one with the legal perspective, pro-adoption, babies-as-commodities, the rights of the unborn child, the rights of the pregnant child's parents... then begin the dance.

The film *Juno* (2007, Dir. Jason Reitman) is a story in this space. If these are the moral imperatives at play in a story discussing teenage pregnancy, then what characters do we need to deliver them? Well, we need a teenager who gets pregnant. We need a father of the baby — say, another teenager. We need a character representing pro-choice and abortion. Another representing pro-life and the rights of the unborn child. When Juno decides that adoption is the best idea, we need prospective adoptive parents, who come with their motivation and moral perspective. They bring with them a legal representative, so the societal ethics come into play, and so on.

Note that there is no bad guy in *Juno*. The conflicts come from the different stance each character adopts around the moral issue. All the characters are driven and opinionated, but their agenda and motivation is understandable. The story comes from the multiple viewpoints of what is right and wrong in this moral argument and the writer (Diablo Cody) shows this through characters that are driven and motivated by their passion for their chosen viewpoint. The 'truth' of this story — the meaning that will emerge through storification — is going to come from Juno herself (played by Ellen Page). She is there in the middle having to make a decision — a life-changing, difficult and grown-up decision — in her young judgement and at the centre of this dizzying array of adult opinions. She spends the majority of the story uncertain as to what direction to take, but in the end, her growth is one of finally taking charge of her own situation. She is only a teenager, but the baby is in her womb and, ultimately, she has to live with her decision. She stops listening to others, takes responsibility and makes her choice (which turns out to be a peripeteia twist we did not see as an option).

Look at the story design. A moral argument wrapped in Aristotle.

- Juno becomes pregnant (harmatia — her world is thrown out of balance).

- Her *realisation* (anagnorisis) is that she is on the horns of a moral dilemma. A deliciously horrible choice of evils. She must either have the baby (and lose her youth to motherhood far too early) or have an abortion (and murder her own baby). A meaningful conflict forcing a decision under pressure and highlighting to the audience the moral argument under discussion.

- She makes her decision, which is a clever, unexpected 'third way' out of the conflict (peripeteia): the twist in expectation is that she will not take either choice. She finds a couple, Vanessa and Mark, (Jennifer Garner and Jason Bateman) who cannot have a child. They will adopt the child so Juno does not have to be a mum or murder a baby. Perfect.

This is all far too smooth and easy for a decent storyteller to allow, so the writer (Diablo Cody) asks: How can I box Juno back in again and make life much more difficult for her?

- New Harmatia: (World thrown out of balance) Vanessa and Mark split up. Juno now has no couple to whom she can adopt the baby out.

- Realisation: It's too late. The clock is ticking and other choices are no longer available. Juno is going to have a baby whether she likes it or not, and she cannot adopt it out to the couple any more. We cannot see a way out of this for poor Juno. She didn't want to become a mum, but we cannot see any other outcome now.

- Peripeteia: Juno takes charge and finds a 'third way'. It's the modern age. A woman does not have to be in a couple to adopt a baby. Juno adopts the baby out to Vanessa. She will be a single mum, but so what?! She was always the main earner and she is the one who wants to be a parent. She splits with Mark but still takes Juno's baby into a privileged and loving life. Everybody wins.

We wanted Juno to be happy. We wanted the baby to be happy. We wanted Vanessa to have a child. We got what we wanted, but not in the way we expected.

Despite the 'funkiness' of this film — the unusual music and the impossibly brilliant teenage dialogue — we learn life lessons from the story and emerge from it with a clear understanding of how difficult the issues are and the ethical choices that must be made by the authorities. The morality-as-theme is not only central to every character and every event but also a terrific example of how you can use morality in defining the characters, conflicts and events of your story.

A quick word on ethics
There are many and varied moral stances that can be taken on the issue of, say, teenage pregnancy. Your personal morality on an issue is subjective and may differ vastly from others who are still valid human beings with every right to their view. However, in society we have to choose a single specific 'applied' morality to become the law and it is the job of those who run the society to decide what moral stance is adopted to define this society. So, for example, the law might say that a pregnant girl can have an abortion only if she is under 18 or has been raped, and under no other circumstances. A lawyer defending a case might personally feel this law is wrong (their personal **moral** viewpoint might differ profoundly from the law asserted by society), but **ethically** their profession requires that they uphold the law as it stands irrespective of their personal views. They will defend and apply the law, even though they disagree with it. Ethics is 'applied morality', and if society is to work, only one viewpoint is deployed as law. I mention this because these areas,

where there are ethical disagreements on moral issues, are fertile ground for stories.

For example, the same ethics that sit beneath *Three Billboards*, to do with accountability within the justice system, also sit beneath *The Shawshank Redemption*, *The Big Sleep*, *Murder on the Orient Express* and many other fine stories. The authors have characters whose personal morality is at odds with the law, and yet they feel so strongly their morality is better for the people who are suffering that they break the law and go ahead with their own morally superior agenda. (Or is it..?) If you can find a moral dilemma you will always have story potential.

There are many other forms of expression around 'how a person should lead their life' which are not specifically moralistic or which do not involve ethics but which can work in the same way, as interesting spaces for story development, such as 'karma will get you' or 'love will win the day', 'crime doesn't pay', or 'smile and the world smiles with you'. These kinds of things can trigger possibilities for meaty stories which are not necessarily 'arguments'. Whatever you can find to pin down the theme of your story will help you, and I will show you how shortly in section 4 on story development.

The dark side
The immoral side of the argument is of course at least half the story. In the same way that your hero can only be as heroic as the bad side demands of them, so, as we said earlier, make sure you focus on those parts of the moral argument that you do not necessarily agree with yourself. Empower the characters that represent opposing moral standpoints. Give them resources and power, and make sure they are well motivated and strongly represent their point of view. As we said earlier, in fine stories, the bad guy's actions and moral stance should be understandable. We should empathise even if we do not agree with them. In *Three Billboards*, the antagonism that delivers the story comes from the actions of Mildred on one side, and the police on the other. Mildred crosses a line and breaks the

law — the law she is trying to hold to account. Both sides of the argument behave with justification, and yet both sides behave immorally and both sides break the law. As with many of the finest stories they are all 'good' people but with different personal issues and moral perspectives. You could say, they are simply at different stages on their journey to complete understanding of the morality that underpins the justice system. When they understand it, their character has grown and this is the storification dynamic we can take away with us.

Writer Vince Gilligan said of his approach to *Breaking Bad* that he wanted to see how far an audience would go in continuing to support a protagonist who is behaving immorally. Walter White's actions are immoral and illegal, but at the same time, he is trying to gain money to provide for his family after his upcoming death, and this is understandable. We empathise. As Walter becomes involved in the brutal underground world of the drug lords, he starts to mete out justice according to his own moral judgement. We support him on his journey, because those who are suffering his 'justice' are criminals. Those taking the drugs were doing it anyway, and the drugs Walter makes are pure, so what he is doing is kind-of-sort-of better isn't it?! It's amazing how we can be persuaded to support someone who is, after all, a criminal and keep rooting for him long after he becomes a murderous drugs lord himself!

Note how, as Walter's immorality begins to pay him, the story is generally crafted to shine a light on the good that is losing. The innocent who are harmed. Excellent, masterful storytelling. Get your audience firmly stuck on the horns of a moral dilemma and you have a winner. (That is, get your protagonist into positions where they have to make awful, morally difficult decisions.)

Most of the kings and queens in *Game of Thrones* (and, indeed, in history) would say that the beheadings and the wars and the murders committed in their name were necessary to build and maintain a peaceful society. Are they being morally excellent and sacrificing themselves for a greater good, or are they simply self-interested? By the end of *Game of Thrones*, this is the big question. Is the leader a benign 'good person' charged with the tough job of meting out necessary execution, or a power-crazed nutter getting a taste for killing?

Often in the finest stories, the good guy becomes immoral themselves — even in their own terms — in order to overcome the bad guy and assert the appropriate morality (bring the world back into balance) by the end. In *Back to the Future*, George McFly has to beat up the bully, Biff in order to assert a morality that disapproves of beating people up. In *The Shawshank Redemption*, Andy Dufresne (Tim Robbins) has to break the law — he is responsible for a murder and breaks out of prison — in order to assert good moral justice over the criminals in charge of the law. In *Three Billboards*, Mildred is the victim of crime, but ends up committing crimes in the pursuit of justice. Juno behaves immorally in the context of teenage pregnancy. In having underage sex she hurts herself and those around her.

Allowing the protagonist to be immoral in order for them to progress is a powerful dynamic for a writer, as the protagonist finds themselves not only fighting the forces of antagonism, but also fighting their allies who can no longer support the course they are taking once they cross a moral line. Walter White breaks the law in order to provide for his family after his death. However, when his family finds out what he is doing, they oppose his actions. His wife, Skyler does not want his drugs money and wants nothing to do with him or his illegal activities. He has now alienated the very person he was trying to help in the first place. Now what does he do? Back down? Stop trying to help her?!

It is also interesting to note that, as an audience, we apparently have little appetite for immoral outcomes to our stories. For all the Machiavellian directors strutting around Hollywood telling us how alternative they are, and authors who like to shock us, flamboyant actors and the extreme characters they create, nobody ever writes a story where undiluted immorality wins out. It would be possible to create a perfectly 'structured' story in which, say, a paedophile gets what they would consider to be a winning outcome from a classroom of two-year-olds, and it would be a story. I can barely bring myself to write those words and I cannot imagine anybody would watch it. As a society, we reject stories that depict moral outcomes we consider unacceptable.

Isn't that interesting? And doesn't that make life difficult for us as story creators? As we said earlier, every audience knows essentially what is going to happen before they take their seat in the cinema or pick up the book. The good guy will win. The bad guy will get their come-uppance. How are we supposed to weave an intriguing tale or lead our audience a dance when our outcomes are so predictable? This is where the peripeteia is so important. We must put our characters into a place where the feared outcome — the immoral outcome — appears to be inevitable. Then find a way to twist out of that predicament and into the outcome we do want. Give the audience what they want but not in the way they expected.

Understand the moral issues under discussion in your story and you will have one of the secrets to story cohesion and the power to grip and engage. Does that morality imbue every sequence? Is every character in your story motivated by a moral stance in the moral argument your story presents? Are your conflicts driven by the differing moral positions between the characters? Does your protagonist become immoral (that is, hurt themselves or others) in the actions they take to achieve their aims?

If the answer is yes, your story will have beautiful, complex, dimensional beauty of the type that characterises some of the most highly rated stories.

3.5 A Story Theory Exercise

Before we move on, here is a small exercise for you. Watch the film *The Post* (Spielberg, 2017). It is a fine, highly-rated story, with clear turning points. Identify the following story dynamics, and you will have a complete understanding of how this story works.

> What is the morality under discussion in this story?
> What is the inciting incident?
> What is the key question or questions?
> Are the key questions answered at climax?
> Identify some turning points.
> Which is the kingpin scene causing storification?
> Is there a meaningful conflict at the heart of the story?
> Whose character grows through the kingpin scene?
> Is it possible that the storification causes a receiver to think about the moral issue in society today?

The answers are coming right after this and take us to the beginning of the next section (3.6 - Knowledge Gaps Through Comedy, below), so if you wish to watch the film before you peek at the answers you will need to fuzz your eyes up as you skip through to section 3.6.

3.5.1 Exercise answers

This section delivers answers to the story theory questions posed at the end of the previous section, regarding the story dynamics integral to the film story *The Post*.

What is the morality under discussion in this story?
The Post addresses the issue of press freedom. The newspapers receive government classified information. Should the government be able to gag the press and prevent publication of confidential information in the interests of national security, or should the press be free to expose government activities and publish as they see fit for the public interest?

The story builds characters around this moral argument. The government and legal advisors on one side, the newspapers and journalistic integrity on the other. It places the owner of the newspaper, Kay Graham (Meryl Streep) into an impossible position in the middle, forcing her, ultimately, to make a difficult moral choice.

What are the inciting incident and key question?
The inciting incident is the arrival of secret government information at the newspaper. The key question is raised: Will the editor Ben Bradlee (Tom Hanks) and the owner Kay Graham risk going out of business and going to jail to publish a story they know should be told (because it exposes government deceptions) even though they also know if the government get their way, the story will unquestionably put them out of business and they will go to prison?

Are the key questions answered at climax?
Yes, they are. Kay makes her choice. The paper publishes and although the government reacts aggressively, dozens of other regional papers in the US publish the story too, showing solidarity for freedom of the press and making it basically impossible for the government to stop them.

Identify some turning points
There are many to choose from, but perhaps the stand-out is when *The Post* journalist Ben Bagdikian (Bob Odenkirk) brings a paper bag in to Ben Bradlee, containing... dozens of other regional papers that have come out in solidarity for press freedom. Their competition have published the story too, because the cause is one they support, and their fortunes change dramatically. I have chosen this turning point because it is unusual. We in the audience are already feeling positive, because Kay made her difficult choice to publish, but we are still anxious to see that she gets the outcome we hope for and this moment turns the story from the positive to the even-more-positive.

I will use another example of a turning point to introduce the kingpin scene, coming next.

Which is the kingpin scene?

Around two-thirds of the way through the film, the presses are ready to roll. Kay and Bradlee have made the difficult choice to do what is morally right but they are taking significant personal risks. They will stand up for the freedom of the press and go to print having decided that their story is different enough from the *New York Times* and is therefore not subject to the government injunction. However, *The Post's* legal guys have dug up some new information. The source of *The Post's* information is the same as that of the *New York Times*. *The Post* is therefore subject to the same existing injunction that has slapped down the *New York Times*. Kay and Ben will go to prison if they are found guilty of breaching the injunction. This moment is a very stark turning point to the negative and it heralds the arrival of the kingpin scene. Kay has a stark choice of evils. Does she go to print anyway, standing by her principles of press freedom but risk her newspaper being shut down and she and Bradlee getting sent to prison for breaching the injunction? Or does she obey the law. Keep the newspaper safe, keep the investors on board, keep her staff in work and keep herself out of prison… but abandon her principles? Can she truly keep her own integrity and keep this job if she is not true to these principles? But at the same time, can she see her business go down and all her beloved staff lose their jobs over this one story? It is still wrong to break the law, whatever your principles…

This is meaningful conflict. The writers hold us at this moment, hanging beautifully on Kay's moral dilemma. Remember I stressed the importance of a 'realisation'? That applies double when the realisation is with the audience. Hold them there. Milk it. Let the audience truly appreciate the situation. This is powerful story.

Whose character grows through the kingpin scene?

Kay has to make a decision under pressure. She has no choice but to make a choice. She chooses her principles over the law of the land. She gives the order to publish and be damned. Her character grows through this process. She inherited the newspaper and has been a nervous, uncertain manager so far, but we see her become certain of herself now that her internal conflict is broken. She's made her choice, so now the decisions that follow become clear and the story accelerates. She may as well be hanged for a sheep as a lamb, so she goes forwards with clear ambition and determination. She changes and she grows, and the story will now resolve as a result of this difficult moral choice.

This is the ideal in a story. The character changes and learns and grows *as a result of* the decision they make under pressure. They then apply that learning — the grown character drives the story forwards as a direct result of their learning and growth.

Is there a meaningful conflict at the heart of the story?
Yes. As we have seen, Kay's choice is a meaningful conflict because it is a dilemma. A choice of evils. Save yourself (a self-centred option) or stick with your principles (a socially-conscious, society-benefitting option).

As you watch the film, notice how the characters are crafted throughout the first two-thirds of the story to create the precise conditions required to make that kingpin scene a difficult dilemma. We have characters who unequivocally represent the journalist's side of the story (Bradlee, in particular). Fritz Beebe (Tracey Letts) who represents the corporate and financial side of running a newspaper. Robert McNamara (Bruce Greenwood) as the defence secretary, bringing us the inside track on the government's position. Last but not least, we have Kay Graham, who the writers are boxing in and who must make the ultimate decision. For this to be a meaningful dilemma notice how she is portrayed as from a background other than journalism (she was not from journalism; she inherited *The Washington Post* from her husband when he died).

It is interesting how a political thriller like *The Post* can be so similar in underlying storification dynamics to a sci-fi action adventure story like *Back to the Future* and Meryl Streep's Kay Graham can be so similar to George McFly!

Does the storification make one think about today's society?
Of course, storification is individual to each receiver, but I think we can safely say that in today's world of social media, fake news and trust in politics, this story jumps out of the confines of the story world and makes us think about the role and integrity of the media today.

3.6 Knowledge Gaps Through Comedy

Humour is highly subjective, of course, and my rule of thumb is to avoid any attempt to formalise or 'measure' humour. My first two published books were humorous works, and I can assure you from my time in research that formal theories of humour not only suck all the fun out of laughing, but also do not really cut it. One person's hilarity is another's offence, and it is impossible to set down any guidelines except one: 'If it's funny enough, it's good enough.' And that is basically it. There is no objective side to it.

I do make a distinction between short pieces of comedy (sketch shows and gags, for example) and stories of longer duration. If you are writing a longer work, it is extremely hard to sustain an audience without any story design. I recommend efforts are made to ensure the humour is couched within a story that does have the kind of structure and principles detailed in this book. If you can do this, you will find yourself with a work of great value. Production companies and publishers are short on comedy and will welcome it with open arms. The reason comedy often fails is not because the humour is weak, but the story that frames the humour is weak. If you take a classic full-length comedy, such as *Airplane!* (1980, directed by Jim

Abrahams, David Zucker and Jerry Zucker) it may appear zany and unstructured, but it is not. Beneath the bonkers, there is a very rigid, classically structured Hollywood formula story.

Ex-fighter pilot Ted Striker (Robert Hays) was traumatised by his experiences as a pilot flying in the war. He is forced to face his fears and board a commercial flight in order to get close to his flight-attendant girlfriend, Elaine (Julie Hagerty) to try to win her back. Despite his extraordinary efforts to get on the plane to see her, she is resolute that their relationship is over. During the flight, everyone who ate the chicken meal gets unwell, including the pilots. The pressure builds on Ted to take over and pilot the aeroplane, despite his fears, flashbacks and trauma. The key questions that frame the story are clear: Will Ted land the plane and save all the passengers? And in subplot: Will Ted win back the love of Elaine? I am sure you can see the character growth in Ted overcoming his fear to successfully land the aeroplane. You can possibly also see his anagnorisis (realisation) that he has no choice but to face his daemons and fly the plane or give in to his fears and let the plane crash. Now, think about that plot summary. What you see is a very strong dramatic premise, a character growth driving the story progression through mental trauma. A story resolution based on Ted's learning and growth. Not a great deal of humour in there, right?! This is, I believe, a very good reason why the film is one of the greats. Of course, the humour is top quality, however, full length comedy needs strong story if it is to sustain interest across two hours.

The full length works of Charlie Chaplin have an episodic structure; unusual for a feature film. For example, *Modern Times* (1936, directed by Charles Chaplin) is effectively seven stand-alone sequences that combine to answer a story-wide key question presented on an inter-title card in the opening shot: Is work the root of happiness? A fascinating subject, embracing serious social questions and political rhetoric. Chaplin's tramp character sets off in search of work and this pursuit is the framing for each of the comedy set pieces. Each episode begins with him going to a new job, raising the question: Will he keep this job? Will it bring him happiness? The patterns in set: He gets a job; he delivers the comedy routine within the work context; he messes up hilariously and loses the job. By the end of the seven episodes he has found love, and does not have a job. He does find happiness, but in his relationship, not through getting a job. The corporate bosses, the authorities and the principles of capitalism are exposed and undermined through comedy. Indeed, Chaplin was recognised as a strong political force while he was becoming the first truly great autonomous Hollywood filmmaker (that is, he built his empire outside the studio system that owned everything and everybody else). He was anti-establishment and pro the working man, and this is evident in the character dynamics of his slapstick routines. The governments of the time were scared of his power and insidious political influence to the extent that President J. Edgar Hoover made it his personal mission to get Chaplin branded as a communist and deported from America. The story key question and the life-values 'explored' in the clever framing give the story a serious dimension and meaning hidden within slapstick comedy. *Modern Times* is a classic example of the power of storification. Chaplin himself is a masterful example of how innocent framing and abstract character actions and behaviours can create storification (meaning in the mind of the receiver) that is delivered purely through subtext.

I cannot give you any principles for writing comedy, because I do not believe it can really be taught, and, to be honest, I am rather pleased that this is the case! For what it is worth, there are two main theories of comedy, and — surprise surprise — they both embody implicit forms of knowledge gaps. I feel that knowing about these is of limited value, but I will present them for you anyway so that you can make your own mind up.

1. **Superiority Theory**. According to Bardon (2005. p.3), the superiority theory of comedy was first documented by Plato and Aristotle some 2,300 years ago. It holds that we find

humour in the recognition of the downfall or inferiority of others, and we pleasure in the implicit superiority of ourselves. Hence, many favourite comic characters are inept, incompetent or foolish, from circus clowns and court jesters through Chaplin's tramp, of course, and on to contemporary characters such as Basil Fawlty, Inspector Clouseau and Johnny English.

Many people don't like the idea that someone must look down on someone else for humour to be present. We prefer to think we are better than that. However, once you begin looking at what makes you laugh it is difficult not to recognise that there is a lot of truth in that.

However, many disagree with the superiority theory, giving examples such as puns, riddles or humorous images, in which humour exists where no superiority is involved, and philosophers, such as Francis Hutcheson, Immanuel Kant, Arthur Schopenhauer and Søren Kierkegaard encouraged us to embrace and advance the **incongruity theory**.

2. **Incongruity Theory** holds that humour is found primarily in a recognition of "an incongruity between expectation and reality [...] some sort of unusual or unexpected juxtaposition of events, objects, or ideas" (Bardon, 2005, p.6).

   For example, in the joke we told earlier: 'there are two fish in a tank. One says to the other, 'do you know how to drive this thing?' The incongruity is present in the difference between the expectation created by the first sentence (an image of two fish in an aquarium) and the ultimate meaning established by the end (an image of two fish finding themselves in charge of a military tank).

Although the incongruity is evident, Charles Gruner argues that such humour still involves superiority in the 'cleverness' of the authors as they (at least temporarily) "'defeat' their public with brilliant verbal exhibitionism" (Gruner, 1997, p.145).

Knowledge gaps in humour theories

That is basically as far as I would like to go with theories of humour and — rather conveniently for my research — both theories include an inevitable, unavoidable knowledge gap. With both incongruity and superiority, there is a gap in knowledge that signals the presence of humour: Between the 'knowing' superior and the ignorant inferior in superiority theory or between what was expected and what actually happens in the case of incongruity. In either case, a knowledge gap is implicit whereby a scenario is deliberately built in one direction and then paid-off in another. The setup creates a knowledge gap between the implied and the actual situation. The sudden pleasure of understanding that comes in the switch from one to the other, and this is the cause of the laughter.

A knowledge gap through comedy is present when there is:

a) A tangible switch from an expectation set to a new superiority dynamic, or

b) A tangible switch from an expectation to an incongruous outcome.

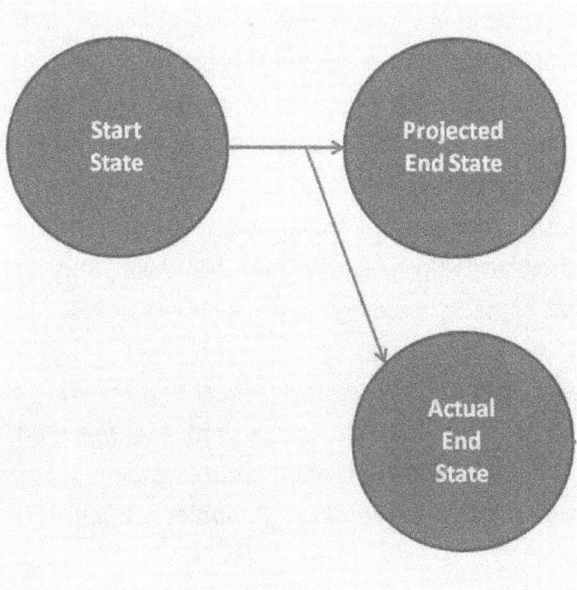

Figure 15: Humour dynamics

An example of both these dynamics is found in *Some Like it Hot* (1959, directed by Billy Wilder). Gerry and Joe (Jack Lemmon and Tony Curtis) are disguised as women, Daphne and Josephine, in order to get work in the all-female band and escape identification by the mob. When they arrive at the hotel with the other members of the band, despite being dressed as women, they are competing to impress the attractive lead singer, Sugar Kane (Marilyn Monroe). Jerry (as Daphne) offers to carry all Sugar's bags and musical equipment. This is incongruous behaviour for one woman towards another and the audience knows what Sugar does not: that Daphne is really a man trying to impress her by being chivalrous. Joe, as Josephine, sees the pointlessness of chivalry between women, thanks Jerry/Daphne warmly and loads her up with 'her' bags and musical equipment as well, asserting a superiority over Jerry in their competition for Sugar's affections. Joe links arms with Sugar and they stroll unencumbered into the hotel. It is measurable incongruity and superiority of this type which characterises knowledge gaps through comedy.

In my categorisations I have comedy as a character gap, but really comedy could be anywhere across the board and can be seen as a storification in itself. For a person to laugh they must have filled a gap that takes a setup state to a new state in mind. That new state is a narrative that has causal logic and makes sense, albeit possibly incongruously, and when it makes sense it locks in and creates a memory. That adds up to storification. However, this just serves to confirm that comedy is a weird space, all on its own.

I hope this is of interest. Personally, I feel that knowing about these theories is of limited value unless you are engaged in formal research, in which case I refer you to my academic work *Stories in Mind: A Constructivist Narratology* (Baboulene, 2019).

3.7 Unconventional Story Dynamics

> Few screenplay manuals inspire confidence. If you want proof that contemporary Hollywood is formula-ridden, look no further than Syd Field's 'Paradigm.' (Bordwell, 2006, p.27)

Syd Field is one of many 'gurus' who have refined and perpetuated the Hollywood formula, and most guidance you can get today is generally that same old canonical structuralist dogma reheated in some way. It has reached the point now — after 100 years of this — that we barely know which came first. Audiences are conditioned to expect the Hollywood formula as readily as the scriptwriters are conditioned to force stories into it. It's part of film DNA.

However, it is important to note that there are plenty of amazing stories out there which do not follow the pervasive model. Examples of award winning, highly-rated film stories that have unconventional design include *Amélie* ((Jean-Pierre Jeunet, 2001) with its almost total lack of conflict and a basis in recognition and cultural allusion (see section 2.6.8); *Pulp Fiction* (Tarantino, 1994) with its seven narrative threads; *Hugo* (Scorsese, 2011) with its hidden key question and motivation; *The Royal Tenenbaums* (Wes Anderson, 2001) — a slice of life in an unusual family; *Atonement* (Joe Wright, 2007) with the metaphysical role of the narrator and author; *Memento* (Christopher Nolan, 2000) — a story told backwards; *The Big Sleep* (Howard Hawks, 1946) which does not make sense but storifies so strongly it works; *Almost Famous* (Cameron Crowe, 2000) takes us on the 'boy to a man' journey of life-learning as Cameron Crowe gets a music journalist's job on tour with a rock band because Rolling Stone magazine did not realise he was only 15 years old; *Eternal Sunshine of the Spotless Mind* (Michel Gondry, 2004) which is, well, just wonderfully bonkers, to name but a few.

In short, no formula has ever been put forward that applies beyond a narrow range of stories that fit the rules. In the context of film, look up the short film, *The Maker* (2011, written and directed by Christopher Kezelos), or *Boy* (2012 by Prasanna Puwanarajah) which can be found through a Google search. Wonderful film stories, but which do not obey the tick-box criteria even if these criteria are softened to apply to a short film. Neither of these films even has conflict.

Novels, of course, and literature in general, can be extremely free-form and have never really been reduced to formula in the way film has. The Hemingway short: 'For Sale. Baby's Shoes. Never Worn' is a story with no conflict in the denoted meaning of the text. It does not even have any characters within the text. No existing story theory (and certainly no formula) exists that could even explain why this is a story. (The exception being the theory encapsulated in this book, of course...! All stories are made of knowledge gaps.)

So do not see these classical models as compulsory requirements or best of breed solutions. They are merely ways that structure has been used to deliver a story which has then been copied so many times it has become formalised. However, the point with any story is not the structure; it is that it only works when it delivers on storification. This is why the formulae baffle the experts. They do work sometimes, because sometimes they storify. That is the key. Structure is not the key. Delivering on storification is the key.

Generally speaking, the structural approaches to story form are based on the framing. In the same way that a cyclist cannot cycle without a bike, and an artist cannot paint a portrait without a canvas, and a coffee needs a mug and a genius needs a skeleton and the holes that define a fishing net need string to tell us where they are, so it is the framing that underpins a story, but the framing is not what brings it power and magic.

The key to story power is ultimately in the storification. This is not a rule book, and there are plenty of stories out there with low levels of storification, however all stories storify, and the finest stories storify the most. In life, storification is the process of making a narrative memory. In story, storification is the art of causing a receiver to generate a meaning for themselves in their own mind from the material you fed them in the narration. If it is done exceptionally well, using knowledge gaps, they will also lay down a memory.

The key to storification is not the structure; it is getting the receiver to fill in a knowledge gap to complete a beat/ scene/ sequence/ story, and if that completes a narrative progression that makes sense, it will storify into meaning in mind. That is all you have to do.

So start from somewhere different. See where it takes you. As long as you have knowledge gaps, you have compelling story, so trust the gaps and reject the dogma. Sure, there are limits, but these are the limits of language; far less restrictive than those on a painter, pianist or dancer. You know your story will grip if it makes sense and is made of gaps, so go wherever you like. Get there using gaps, and you cannot go wrong. All of which brings us rather nicely to the story development process.

Section 4 - Story Development

A story is not just a text that is read; it is an encrypted conversation between an author and a receiver. Understanding the coding and decoding in that conversation is the secret to fine storytelling.

Every journey begins with a first step. And every story ever made – from the simplest of cartoon strips to the most epic Greek myth – began with an idea. A seed of inspiration that is so compelling to its owner that they devote their life to turning it into a form that can be delivered to the mind of another. They develop it into a concept, a premise, a series of drafts and, ultimately, a glorious final product.

The originating idea may be tiny, but it is also critical. Never forget that the nugget that so inspired your head is also ever so likely to be the reason why it will inspire someone else in its final form. The better you understand the inspiration that got you so fired up, and the better you retain the integrity of that inspiration as you get deeper and deeper into your story, the more cohesive, authoritative and compelling the final product is likely to be. I would suggest this is one of the hardest things in story creation. We have good ideas, but they are ethereal and amorphous. Getting a firm grip on the little nugget of inspiration that gives the whole thing its beating heart is difficult, and retaining it as the spine to your story as it develops is even harder, but it's also one of the secrets to ending up with THE story that you hoped to deliver when you felt so motivated at the beginning.

The challenge, then, is to work out what inspires you and convert that into a narration that will inspire someone else. In essence, the process becomes one of combing backwards from this inspiration to find the characters that will deliver it and then forwards towards storification to see how the ultimate power is coming along and then downwards to the framing that will give the perfect spine to the whole thing. The art of story creation is in learning to understand what is in line with the spine you are trying to create and being knowledgeable enough — and strong enough — to reject what is not right.

The ultimate aim is to get a grip on your storification. Once you truly know the storification, that is when the real breakthrough has happened. You know everything you need, because everything in your story that is **not** storification is there to build towards and support the storification; or it is an outcome of the storification. Once you have this you can start the really beautiful artistic process of building a narration that will grip and intrigue a receiver by working backwards and forwards, up and down, from the power-base of storification.

When you listen to music, joyous and wonderful things happen in your mind. Emotions are triggered. One step back from that and we have a label for it. Let's say it's called *The Minute Waltz*, written by a chap called Chopin. Perhaps just the mention of the title or the name 'Chopin' is enough to evoke feelings of joy and wonder. Next step back from that, and there are more practical things. Some recording equipment. A piano. A person to play it.

This is how abstract the ultimate mind-born joy of emotional stimulation is. When we listen to *The Minute Waltz*, the artist who is responsible for your feelings — Chopin — is not there. He's been dead for centuries. The piano is gone. No recording equipment or engineers are present. These are the framing elements and characters responsible for your emotions, and yet they are not ultimately present as part of what we *feel*. This is storification of the highest order. This is what we, as writers, must evoke in our receivers through the writerly work we cause them to do through our words. We must make them feel something once we — and our words — have delivered and are gone.

As writers, we are not writing a narrative, we are generating feelings, knowledge, understanding and memories in the mind of the receiver.

This chapter is an explanation of how to work forwards and back, forwards and back to find and then generate the storification that will live on in the mind of your audience long after the narration has finished and you are gone.

4.1   Begin at the Beginning

The first thing to say is that the initial period of story development should be very free-form. It is almost impossible for me to generalise the nature of your inspiration and for the most part I should not try. Perhaps more importantly in these early stages, you should ignore me! Ignore everyone. Let yourself go! Get inside your own head and give your imagination free rein. The best advice in these early stages is: Think about it lots — work it for the inspiration. This is a lot about how you are *feeling*. Make rough notes, but do not worry about detail. *Avoid* detail. No character specifics or dialogue or iconic scenes. It is tempting to go deeper but try to resist nailing anything on. Make notes on depth and bank them — a lot of what you think may be there in some way at the end — but try your hardest to remain abstract. Why? Because you do not know if this event or gag or character or iconic moment will be relevant to the story you end up with, and the problem with going into detail is that you will fall in love with it. It will become precious and wonderful... and your story will become biased towards it. At some later point when it really really should not be in the story, you will struggle to do the right thing and murder your baby. You have invested in it, so you will force your story to find a home for it. Writing great story is hard enough without having to accommodate cuckoos from another story.

Resist going deep. Just begin to create the step outline (more on this shortly) and make notes that are enough so you can recall the thoughts you had and revisit the inspiration. Allow the story to butterfly in your mind. Let it happen. See where the muse takes you. There is no direction at this point so just go with the flow.

Stories are — and should be — very personal. Have confidence in yourself and your idea, because there is only one person you need to satisfy with this story and that is you. I get a lot of private clients who I quickly realise are really looking for reassurance rather than story theory, and for the most part, their needs are within themselves. Forget everyone else. Please yourself. You are the God of your story and your story has one job... and that is to please YOU. If this story only ever ends up pleasing you and nobody else, then it has done its job. If it happens to resonate with a percentage of the population and makes you some money, then whoop-de-do! The best chance you have of ending up with that commercial product is to capitalise on the inspiration you are feeling for yourself. If you like it, then there's a good chance it *will* resonate with other humans, so own it.

What I can tell you for sure — one of the characteristics of all the famous story creators I have met is that they have self-confidence. They write their material the way they think it should go and the world can take it or leave it. Only you can tell your story the way it should be told.

So, with the above caveat firmly stated, I will now start to tell you what to do... Seriously, how can I balance advising you to ignore others and pleasing only yourself, with being a story consultant and writing a book like this one?! Well, ultimately, whether we like it or not, stories get complicated. As the work develops, it becomes hard to see the wood for the trees and most writers find that their story drifts over time from their original inspiration, often in highly frustrating ways that they simply cannot identify and fix. Next after that, others get involved, particularly when stories get produced or published. The beating heart gets lost. One of the main reasons I believe EVERY full-length project that ever gets made should have a story consultant is because a story expert should be able to identify and protect the story's beating heart and ensure it does not get lost (or more often, trampled to death in the rush to make a film). A story consultant maintains an objective viewpoint that helps the writer to understand and then keep sight of their inspiration; identifies and documents the main strengths of the story; protects, nurtures and optimises the dynamics that makes it compelling. In the film industry, I often see my role as one of reminding people that without a story, nobody on the project has a job. Director, actor, cameraman, grip, chippy — whatever. They would all be sitting at home doing nothing... Unless there is a story to give them something to do, trillion dollar industries just disappear; and yet the story is rarely given the care and understanding it deserves.

I would also mention that most successful people are very productive. There is a good deal of pretty poor material in their overall output, however, that tends to fade into the background and get forgotten, whilst the ten percent of their output which is amazing takes them to the top of the world. History tends to forgive artists their ninety-percent. Why? Because they give us the ten percent that is golden. Delivering art on that basis takes a degree of bravery, but it works. Two points here: firstly, that level of productivity (along with not caring too much what other people think) is an indicator of a person who is more likely to be successful. Secondly, retaining that early fluidity and avoiding detail helps you to find and lock on to that golden ten percent. It also helps you to seek and destroy the poor stuff early on, speeding up your process of finding and delivering on the ten percent.

Practical guidance
Once you have let your imagination run wild, done some deep thinking, asked yourself: 'What if..? What if..? What if..?' and 'Then what..? Then what..? Then what..?', made copious notes and enjoyed some delicious moments playing with tantalising ideas in

mind, you should find a narrative progression beginning to gel in your mind. At this point, you can gradually become more pragmatic in the way you might work that inspiration.

What you are looking to get from your mental meanderings are four things that give clues to the nature of your storification:

- A character and a literal or metaphoric 'journey' for that character. What changes over time for a character?
- The motivation and ambition for that character. What is driving them? What might fulfilment mean?
- A clear conflict may offer itself, an aim for the character or a problem to solve.
- A moral dilemma or argument.
- Any form of knowledge gap.

Other good clues to powerful story are a dilemma. A realisation. A character plan. A lie, secret or subterfuge. An irony that says: 'Yes, life is like that.' None of these are compulsory — don't force anything — but if you happen to spot any of these forming up they are signs of powerful story development.

Ultimately, what we are aiming to find through these clues is a storification. Let us remind ourselves of the storification gap types that will deliver, then go through some examples of how to link your initial ideas to ultimate deliverables:

The Primary Colours of Story

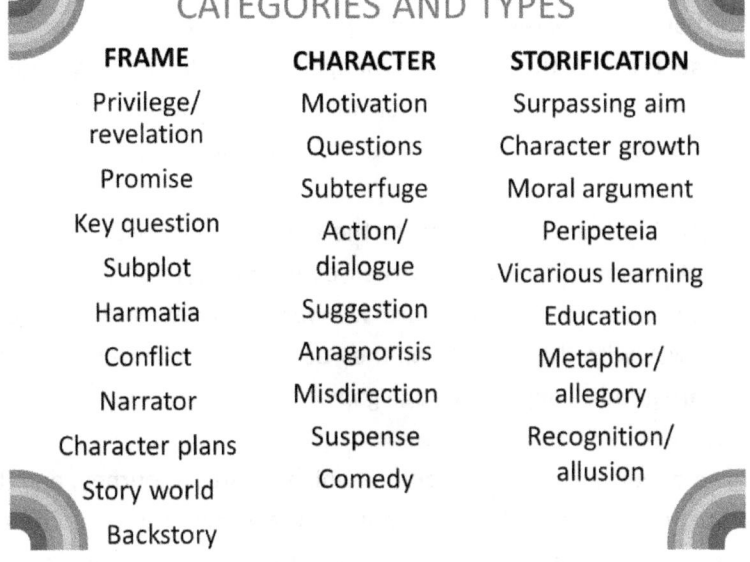

Figure 16: Storification gap types

Here are some basic thoughts and ideas for stories that might emerge from the initial inspiration. See if you can pick out how these might now step forwards, from the initial random thought, into a character and a path they might take.

1. **Did you ever think about breaking the law? I've never done it before, and if I could keep my cool, and continue my law-abiding life on the surface, I reckon I could get away with it.**

   OK. So there is clearly a character here. A normal, decent, law-abiding person. What if they consciously decided to break the law? But why would they? Just for a laugh? Could be. A bored rich person. Surely, they don't want to risk going to prison? But if they did, that would certainly be an example of 'yes, life's like that.' What if they are dying themselves? That way they wouldn't care if they got caught or died during a crime. That would empower them in a strange way. Let's say they have responsibilities they cannot live up to. They want to make lots of money from their crime to provide for their family after they die. OK. Good. Now we have a character — a good person who has a criminal secret, so there is the basic knowledge gap. Brilliant. They could keep their secret from their family too. A double life. Nice. That would be a huge, pervasive knowledge gap.

Their criminal activity takes them into conflict with the laws of the land (and probably their own morality) and brings us a character journey, because we want to know: will they get away with the crime? Will they be caught? Nice! All of these are good strong knowledge gaps.

We have a journey, a clear ambition, which creates a journey, and it generates conflict, and it is all wrapped in a knowledge gap. There are clear and powerful characters that can represent the moral positions. This looks very strong indeed. Let's move up the picture and see which of the storifications might jump out at us from here.

Surpassing aim: OK so I could see a situation where the character achieves what they wanted — they get the money to provide for their family after their death (that sounds like a key question waiting to be grabbed there, right?) then use their knowledge and experience from their crimes to do something wonderful for society or for others in their situation. They go to prison... but save a thousand lives.

I like that. However, we said they are dying so the clear outcome is an ironic ending with a negative surpassing aim. The character gains all the riches for their family... but has to sacrifice themselves to achieve that. Lose the battle, win the war. It's still a surpassing aim, even though it is a negative. That sounds very powerful, and is of course, the basis of *Breaking Bad*.

Character Growth: There is also the basis for character growth in that premise. The protagonist grows from poor to rich in the positive arc, using their criminal alter ego to generate lots of cash for the family in the long term. However, there is also a great deal that can be learned about life and how it should be lived as they become *less caring*. Someone who is not afraid to die is going to be more cavalier. If you are not scared of death you have an advantage over adversaries who are more concerned for their personal wellbeing. There could be a lovely character growth arc here from a meek, overly-cautious starting personality to someone who realises that the decisiveness that comes with a lack of fear for their own safety can take you a long way. The storification can make us all think about how overly cautious we are. How much we could benefit in our own lives from being a little more decisive and less risk-averse. There are a lot of possibilities here.

Moral Argument: There is a clear moral dilemma for someone under this kind of pressure. Should they break the law to save their own family? Well, no they should not. However, we are following a personal journey, so we empathise strongly with the difficult decisions that must be taken. The premise has a strong moral argument — yes, work hard to support your family. That is a moral positive. However, if that hard work is also criminal and society-negative, we have a moral negative and the audience will not run like this. We need to boost the other side of the argument. How about if we can get society-positive value from his unethical behaviour? In becoming a drugs lord himself, he can mete out appropriate justice to the current incumbents and make us see some positives for society in his journey and actions. A true vigilante. This line of thinking has great potential. If a man breaks the law to deliver something we would subjectively see as society-positive, we will support that, right?! But at the same time, we will worry about the implications. This is a terrific moral argument.

Vicarious Learning: Note how, as writers, it is not our responsibility to deliver an 'answer' to the moral argument. Simply presenting the argument is intriguing and engaging. We could have our protagonist's decisions under pressure deliver an outcome that demonstrates a morality on one side of the argument or the other.

On the one hand, the law is an ass. It is important that people have the strength to do what they believe is right. On the other hand, the law is there for good reasons that keep society safe. Simply presenting the moral argument creates story power and brings learning to the audience with regard to how a person should lead their life.

I rather like the teaching that comes with a person who is dying therefore becoming more decisive and sure of themselves. I have mentioned many times that the key to strong character is to have them make decisions under pressure, and a character who does not fear a negative outcome is going to make decisions. There is a clear lesson here for all of us in terms of *how a person should lead their life*.

Peripeteia: We have a clear ambition for the protagonist, and we are pretty sure now that he will be successful in achieving that (gaining the money that will provide for the family after his death). How can that outcome be a twist?

Remember, peripeteia is linked to a realisation, so let's think about a realisation for our protagonist. The main knowledge gap is that his family do not know what he is doing. He has become a major drugs lord, and his family still think he's just meek old Walter. At some point, his family finds out... and they massively disapprove. He is breaking the law and bringing dangerous bad guys to their doorstep and his family are not interested in all this drugs money. His realisation (anagnorisis) is that his efforts have been all for nothing. His wife is not grateful for his endeavours. She is angry. The aim of his entire risky and difficult programme is now nullified. Pointless. His *life* is now pointless. And, as his wife is quick to point out, they are now accessories to his crimes so even if he did get them the money, they would go to prison for him after his death and the money would all be taken away.

The peripeteia twist would therefore be that our protagonist does not give up. He continues to pursue his ambition to give his family riches after his death. His continued pursuit of money his family does not want will make him appear self-centred. He's doing it now because he just loves the life. However, he has a plan; one that he implements beautifully and it makes the money legally 'legitimate' when it arrives after his death. A wonderful, amazing and brilliant peripeteia twist in the endgame of *Breaking Bad*.

Metaphor: The question for an author is: What is the meaning I will place in the mind of my receiver? This is why all stories are metaphors. Every story is a representation of some human causal logic that has meaning, and is therefore a metaphor. The more clear that representation when the receiver does their writerly work, the more that story is appreciated.

Once we have decided not to be prescriptive about the moral argument we are becoming more metaphoric in the overarching messages. In tangible messages, the law wins and the criminal loses. The story is an allegory that says 'crime doesn't pay'. However, in the way the story is set up, it did pay, because the protagonist was going to die anyway and did get away with the money. The metaphor is strongly present in the sense of making us think about how a person should lead their life. It made us think about being more cavalier. Taking more risks and making our lives more interesting. Most of the finest stories are a metaphor for life and how it should be led.

In big picture terms, notice how there is an overlap between different storification dynamics. Each one seems to simply roll naturally into the next one. I find it very interesting that as a storification begins to emerge from a story idea, it is often a good sign that as one comes through clearly and begins to drive the story, several of the others often start to light up as well. A moral imperative drives a character growth drives a surpassing aim that brings vicarious learning... that kind of thing. You know when you are hitting the money when not just one storification shows itself — the whole board begins to light up.

2. **Wouldn't it be great if you could meet your parents when they were your age – see what they were like when they were young and see if you would bond and be friends?**

Not forgetting, at this early stage of development, we are looking for a character and a literal or metaphoric 'journey' for that character. Some rough idea of what fulfilment means in the destination of the journey. A conflict, an ambition or a problem to solve. Knowledge gaps in the delivery.

> In this premise we clearly have a character — one who meets his own parents at the same stage of life, so in fact, three clear characters. For them to meet at the same age, one or other must time travel. A literal journey. OK. So our character is, say, a teenager, and goes back in time to meet his parents when they were his age. What is the ambition? To meet same-age parents. But so what? Where is the fulfilment? Not sure. What about a problem or conflict? Not sure. Knowledge gap? Well, I guess if his identity is secret from his parents, there is a strong and pervasive knowledge gap. If that is a secret, then it would be natural for a parent who meets their future son to feel a terrific sense of attraction to them, right?! He's your kid! So, his mum will fall in love with him. Wow. There's a great conflict. You cannot get funky and romantic with your own mum! Apart from anything else, that would mean the mum would <u>not</u> fall in love with the dad. But then the kid won't be born. Aha! Nice! Now we have a problem... Get your mum to stop loving you and fall in love with your dad so you can exist in the future. THERE is the ambition, the conflict, the motivation and agenda, the journey and a huge baseline knowledge gap.

I hardly need mention that this is the basis for *Back to the Future*. Bob Gale (writer/producer of *Back to the Future*) told me that their initial premise was this:

A kid goes back in time. He meets his parents and his mother falls in love with him.

That was it. They got development funding on the basis of this and the whole story grew from this seed. In *The Story Book* I devote a whole chapter to Bob Gale stepping me through the story development process for *Back to the Future* from this starting point, so I won't repeat that here. Suffice to say, it is a process of saying, 'What if? What if? What if..? Then what? Then what? Then what?' Endlessly interrogating the idea, squeezing it for compelling possibilities. Keeping the good ones. Throwing out the less good ones. And when you get a good one, you put that stone in place and go round again. What if? Then what? At every level. From the top level story arcs through subplots, sequences, chapters, scenes, beats — it is the same process of developing the detail of the journey and driving in knowledge gaps.

Nothing is fixed. It's all just notes. Ideas and notes. And the bin. Murder your babies. Don't settle. Think again. And again and again. This is the process of story development. Your inspiration will only take you so far. After that — it's hard work.

Clearly, in the case of *Back to the Future*, the storification Gale and Zemekis decided to major on is George McFly's character growth. He is placed into a position where he must make a difficult decision under pressure. Through this, he changes and grows from a weak chicken into an assertive person, and applies that learning firstly to defeating the bully, Biff, and then to his entire life.

3. I got pregnant when I was only 15. I didn't want to be a mother but I couldn't face a termination.

Now this is a beauty, right? a character and a literal or metaphoric 'journey' for that character – it is right there. Some rough idea of what fulfilment means in the destination of the journey? Well, that is clear as well — finding a way out of the situation would represent fulfilment. Is there a conflict, an ambition or a problem to solve? Motivation and agenda? Character plans? They are all right there.

The whole thing implicitly contains a huge, defining knowledge gap through the key question: Will the teenager be forced to become a mother or terminate her baby? What will she do? This is, of course, the story of *Juno*. A character, a conflict, an ambition, a journey through pregnancy and a lovely big key question.

Naturally, the thinking moves to the storification and I can see two obvious candidates leaping to the fore. Firstly, I can see a moral argument. How should a pregnant teenager act in these circumstances? How should they look after themselves and the baby? Because they are so young the question is also raised: How should society treat a teenager who gets pregnant?

Because this is a moral argument, the characters blossom right out of the moral premise: A teenager, an unborn child, the father of the child, the girl's father, mother, siblings, the school, church, law, doctor, pro-life, pro-choice and so on all take their place around a moral maypole where their individual passion for their moral stance creates the conflicts with each other.

There is also a meaningful conflict in the choice of evils the pregnant girl has to decide between (become a teenage mum OR murder an unborn child) and a peripeteia twist in the possibility of choosing neither of them. The writer, Diablo Cody, used the possibility of adoption as a 'secret third way' to slide out of the dilemma. Juno can achieve both — not become a mum AND not have a termination. So for that to be the peripeteia we have to have a realisation (anagnorisis) that her situation becomes impossible... (the adopting couple split up, so the adoption option goes away) and then we twist back to it (she adopts the baby out to the single mother).

A moral argument causing a meaningful conflict, all wrapped in Aristotle to make it fly. This is a wonderful example of a story writing itself once everything must function in support of clear storification.

4. **What if a cat sees a mouse?**
    We are looking for a character and a literal or metaphoric 'journey' for that character. Some rough idea of what fulfilment means in the destination of the journey. A conflict, an ambition or a problem to solve. Motive and agenda. Knowledge gaps in the delivery.

    We have two characters, a cat and a mouse. A clear journey — the hunt and the chase. Fulfilment for the cat is to catch the mouse. Fulfilment for the mouse is to escape the cat and find a peaceful life. We have conflict and an obvious key question dynamic: Will the cat catch the mouse? And that delivers a lovely knowledge gap through key question. Yup. It's all there.

    Where is the storification in something as simple as this? The storification is in the cultural allusion — our recognition that 'life is like that' when cats and mice are brought together and life is reflected in the story. There is also a morality that makes us squirm a little in all stories like this. Our instinct is to side with the pursued. We want the mouse to get away. When we watch six lions cornering a water buffalo or a spider catching a fly, or a crocodile drifting unnoticed towards the drinking antelope... we want the prey to get away. However, in nature, if the prey lives, the predator does not eat and will die, so which is it to be?!

And yet, at the same time, that is not true. A part of us *wants* to see the wasp get caught in the web. The croc hit the antelope. Battle commence between the lions and the buffalo. Something deep in our nature wants to see life in action and to understand the life truth and the life-and-death narrative. It is empowering to learn about, and we get feelings of empathy and catharsis from learning about a process without suffering from it. This is a very powerful component of story. This is why giving your protagonist horribly delicious decisions to make causes such powerful stories.

In the final analysis, *Tom and Jerry* has low storification, and it is well worth noting that there are many, many stories that do not storify in grand ways. In particular, genre productions such as musicals, ballet, comedy, a sporting event, documentary, horror and so on, *may* not be relying as much on the storification dynamics for their power to entertain. The songs, dance, humour, education or relatable fear are up front and centre, and the story is only a part of the whole. This said, if you are making a genre piece, it will be infinitely better if the story is crafted strongly as well!

For another film that demonstrates a storification through cultural allusion see my own short film: *Bella* (2019). I am not sure where it will be as you read this, but my websites will be a good starting point: www.dreamengine.co.uk or www.baboulene.com. The story has no bad guy, no conflict — not even any dialogue, but still has power because of strong storification through cultural allusion. I demonstrate the entire story development process, from story seed to silver screen, on my website and in an accompanying book, entitled: *Working with a Contemporary Step Outline – the tool of choice for story development.*

4.2   The Seed Sprouts...

Of course, you will not get the premise perfect immediately. My listings above make it all seem an absolute breeze, but these examples were derived retrospectively and may have taken weeks, months or most probably years to truly find their ideal form as they originally developed.

The job in these early stages is one of capturing an essence of character and their journey. As you play with possibilities about, for example, how things might storify, you can do so fully aware that you can explore an avenue with no commitment to it. It is all very flexible, and that is how it should be. You will know when something is a keeper and equally you will know when something is best off parked for the moment or binned immediately. Just remember that it is the storification that brings ultimate power, so if you are struggling to decide which route to go, pick the most powerful storification and work back from there.

When you play with character actions, think about what fulfilment means for that character and therefore the obstacles and dilemmas that you can deliberately put in the way. This is the fun bit — imagination and creativity triggering inspiration and ideas. The knowledge gaps listed in the primary colours are inevitable. You cannot make a story without them, so working with them, using them as triggers for the imagination and considering the possibilities that arise from that is sensible work.

Each and every knowledge gap in the primary colours could potentially offer the basis to the next phase of story development, so go through them one by one. Could your character have a plan? What would that look like? Does your character have a secret? Could a juicy dilemma-based conflict be driven into place here? If some specific knowledge gap does take your fancy, try it in privilege. Then in revelation. Hide the necessary knowledge from the protagonist instead of the audience. See what that does.

Try not to think so much about *what happens*. That is plot, and it is a function of character. Try to think more about characters and their desires, motivations and ambitions. Think about what fulfilment means. Then how that journey towards fulfilment can be blocked and frustrated, and how that can lead to difficult decisions that cause storifications.

4.3   The End is the New Beginning

When you read a book, you do not remember the words.
You remember the meaning.

The process of *telling* a story is to give the narration, and the narration has a definite ending. It finishes. The media that deliver it are gone. So is the author. It is simply what it means that is left in the mind of the receiver. Ultimately, the author is not writing words; words are simply tools. The author is not narrating — that is just an information stream. The author is creating meaning in the mind of the receiver, because that is all that is left once the author and their narration are gone. THAT is the endgame as far as the author is concerned.

What is the *meaning* in your story? What is the moral argument or the life lesson you aim to deliver? What is the enlightening subtext delivered through metaphor or allegory? What is the moment of growth and learning for your protagonist in terms of their personal transformation? In what way do the audience learn something new? What is the cultural allusion that makes us think and say to ourselves: 'Yes. Life is like that' or 'Yes, that is how a person should lead their life'? What is the realisation that hits your character? How is the peripeteia which that realisation creates going to twist and surprise your audience? If you know the key question, how might that translate into a surpassing aim? What is the greater knowledge, such as the vicarious learning your story might deliver? Some or maybe just one of these is the ultimate resource for your writing, because you cannot start to tell your story properly until you know the storification. As we shall see, once you are armed with your storification, then you know the job your framing must do to orientate your audience towards the right story. Then you know what your characters must be like — how they must be motivated and what their personality must be in order to drive them into making the choices which push them towards fulfilment and generate that storification.

More often than not, the main storification hits home late in the story but it is not the ending. The storification *causes* the outcomes which drives the ending. They may or may not occur at the same time but they are separate entities. As we discussed earlier (see figure 5), It's less:

BEGINNING → MIDDLE → END

A series of events — and more:

FRAMING supports CHARACTERS take DECISIONS lead to OUTCOMES create STORIFICATION.

The ending forms out of the storification, and it is far, far more important to know your storification before you can possibly know what your ending (or beginning, or middle) can appropriately be. Thus, the story development process becomes a matter of combing up the idea to a possible storification, then taking that possibility and combing back down again to see how that works in terms of supporting it with appropriate characters and frame.

Consider the kingpin moment in *Back to the Future* when George makes a fist and goes through his character growth transformation.

The framing and character actions that go before it are defined by the need to:

a) Put Lorraine in this car and at the centre of a love triangle with George and Biff.
b) Get Marty out of the car. Render him helpless and unable to help (the authors get him locked into the boot of the band's car).
c) Put Biff in the driving seat (literally and metaphorically).
d) Put George in the position where he is put under massive pressure to make the most important decision of his entire life.

I do not mean simply putting George in the car park at 9.00pm; I mean putting everything in place to ensure we in the audience know what this *means*; that he is a weak man; that Biff terrifies him; that Lorraine is an incurable romantic looking for a 'strong man'; that Marty is motivated to live on and to save his own future. Everything has to be perfect for the kingpin moment to storify; that is, for George to go through his character growth event.

All the characters must be in these places and have these attitudes to craft this kingpin moment. This is not the 'ending', but it is the *ultimate* moment that defines the story and it shapes not only all those elements that go before but also the ending (that is, the climax and resolution are facilitated by this storification).

Of course, not all storifications are so focussed on a single moment like this. There will certainly be more than one storification and they may be spread across multiple events or the whole narration. I am using *Back to the Future* because it has a clear, singular storification event for the entire story, but there are many more at every level. The storification can always be understood and can always be used in this same way; to define what *must be* in place for the storification to fly and, when it does, to define what the outcomes are that represent the climax and resolution.

4.3.1 Storification Example

The story of *The Big Sleep*, a 1939 novel by Raymond Chandler later became what many consider to be the definitive *film noir* movie and one of the most popular films of all time according to polls and public ratings. The film was directed by Howard Hawks in 1946.

But get this. It is a story which does not make sense. And yet it is a much-loved classic. How can that possibly be? The answer is simple: For all its flaws, it storifies very strongly. I use it as a fine example of the importance of the storification. The story makes no sense, but people still love it, and the storification is the reason.

The story builds a complex web of relationships, blackmail and criminal activity, including seven murders. The plot is notoriously confusing and the outcome uncertain. One of the best-known Hollywood anecdotes concerns the film's perplexing plot. Lauren Bacall, who played Vivian Sternwood, the lead female role, recalls:

"One day, Bogie [Humphrey Bogart] came on the set and said to Howard, 'Who pushed Taylor off the pier?' Everything stopped. Hawks sent Raymond Chandler a telegram asking whether the Sternwood's chauffeur, Owen Taylor, was murdered or if it was a suicide. 'Dammit I didn't know either,' Chandler recalled." (Ebert, 2012, p.27)

The story crafts Marlowe (Humphrey Bogart) into a difficult moral position where he must make a difficult decision under pressure. In a world where crime pays, Marlowe is a detective who is uncompromising in his determination to uphold the law. However, as we approach the climax of the story, he has done his detective work and he has uncovered the bad guys, at least one of whom is a murderer. They are Carmen (Martha Vickers) and Vivian (Lauren Bacall) — the daughters in the family who employed him in the first place. Vivian is the woman he now loves. The daughters have committed crimes, however they were also victims who were retaliating to the blackmailers, so they were to some extent justified.

But they did break the law. Marlowe is placed into a choice of evils whereby either his principles (the law must be upheld at all times) or his personal morality (Carmen and Vivian broke the law for good reasons) and his heart (he has strong feelings for Vivian) must be compromised. Eventually he makes his choice: He chooses to also break the law. Marlowe colludes with the sisters (indeed, he commits murder himself) because he understands that they were being blackmailed and exploited. The letter of the law would punish Carmen and Vivian so he helps them to kill Eddie Marrs — the real bad guy — and frame him for the crimes the sisters had committed. Marlowe puts his personal morality ahead of the law and even though it made him into a criminal as well, we in the audience feel it is a good outcomes (that is, a morally justifiable, society-positive outcome) to the story. He took a decision that put his own life in danger as well as Vivian's. The outcome was positive. The family was saved and we in the audience realise that for the law to work the people who are empowered by it need to have integrity themselves. Marlowe had integrity and things became better for Vivian, Sherwood, Carmen and indeed for Marlowe himself and beyond that for society, as the true bad guys were rubbed out and Marlowe and Vivian plan to work together to help Carmen with her mental health into the future. This is why we love the story — because it storifies. We learn a life lesson from the outcomes of the choices made under pressure of conflict.

However, was Marrs really the bad guy? What on Earth happened that gave Marlowe the knowledge he needed? It's really confusing. There are, for example, 227 'question' knowledge gaps opened in *The Big Sleep*. Most are not answered. (For comparison, *Back to the Future* has 83.) The audience does not know that these, and many other framing and character gaps, will not be addressed or revisited. They use the gaps to project into the narrative logic... and the story does not make sense. However, because the storification gaps are so strong, and because there are so many knowledge gaps in total, these unresolved gaps are forgotten... at least for a while. The confusion kicks in later, when we think about it more deeply, and yes, it does lead to a sense of dissatisfaction. We ask ourselves: 'Wait a minute. That doesn't make sense, does it?' Ultimately, we think perhaps it was our own fault and we missed something. And we forgive the story — perhaps even enjoy it more — for this unorthodoxy that toys with us. I feel sure this winning overall effect was unintentional (indeed, quotes from the director, Howard Hawks, serve to prove this when he tries to explain how he thinks it works. See Ebert, R. 1997) and yet there are interesting lessons to learn, the main one being the clear message that storification gaps — which are huge and beautifully crafted in *The Big Sleep* — are the most important types of gaps. Find and deliver storification and your story will fly.

4.4 Combs and Tangles

The combing process I mentioned earlier is really rather important. As I mentioned, it is difficult to teach story theory because creating a story is not a linear process. It is not like building a Lego house, where you simply keep putting bricks on top of bricks and it gets bigger. We think it might be like this, because this is how we write our first pieces. Writers nearly always begin with short works. A 1000-word article; a short story; a college piece for English. We do well, and gain confidence. The method for these shorter works is simple. We begin at the beginning, write until the end. Read it back. Edit. Read it back. Edit. If need be, throw it all away and start again. Read it through. Rewrite. Rewrite. Rewrite until done.

Then we decide to go for it and write a full-length work — a two-hour script or a 100,000-word novel — and we set about it using the same method we used for the short piece. Start on page one with 'once upon a time…' and just write. Read it back. Rewrite. Read it back. Put it on a shelf for a few weeks. Read it back again with fresh eyes. OK. I think I know the problem now. Rewrite. Read it back. And so on.

Of course, the rewrite method becomes impossibly unwieldy for a big project and it can take a long, long time. To be honest, it *can* work, and is often the way writers achieve their first full-length work. However, a writer's first stories are often the most inspired. The writer has been working them in their mind for years and years so there is a much better chance of it emerging well-formed with the rewrite method. Most professional writers will tell you that their early works did come to life in this way, but as they sped up their process and got to understand how much reworking is needed, they adopted different strategies to prevent having to rewrite the whole thing multiple times. A professional writer will expect to go through something like six to ten drafts to get to the final manuscript. The idea of rewriting 100,000 words six to ten times is not something any normal human being would sensibly do to themselves — indeed, it is basically unsupportable as a method — so pretty soon they abandon the 'rewrite' method for something more managed.

The tool for managing your story along the whole of its length and up and down the multiple levels without having to rewrite 100,000 words ten times over is called a step outline. I thoroughly approve of the step outline and recommend you use one.

4.5 Scene Design and the Step Outline

The step outline has been around for a very long time. It goes back to the days when writers used quaint old typewriters and actual sheets of paper, and getting a final polished manuscript was even more difficult and complicated than it is today. In those days, good preparation was even more important as editing even a single page was that much more difficult.

A writer would use what are called index cards. Small, A5 size cards, each one used to represent a story event. When the creative process threw up an interesting possibility that felt like it might be a keeper, the writer would note it, in bullet point form, on the front of an index card. As they began to get some feel for *how* they might deliver that event, they would expand on that possibility in more detail on the back of the index card.

So the front of the card might say something like:

Sarah murders Robert.

Now, this murder will be an event in the story, so it needs to fit reasonably in the flow of the story's wider arcs for the big picture to hang together and for the story to make sense. A full-length story could comprise 20 or 30 of these top-level bullet-points, so as long as it fits as a logical progression at this high level, this is all we really need to know for this story event. *How* Sarah kills Robert is not important to the wider arcs, as long as it does happen. How she kills Robert is an opportunity for the writer to be creative, because how it happens will come from the writer's imagination. Let's say the writer initially thinks about Sarah hiring a contract killer. It gets the job done but this idea loses its attraction after a while. The writer feels Sarah needs to be proactive. She must actually do it herself. Why, though? She must be angry with him. Let's make him an adulterer. That is why she is angry. OK. But he's probably bigger and stronger than her. She will need to be clever about it. How about if she cuts the brake pipes on the car? Nah. Cliché. How about if she slips something into his drink? Poisons him? OK. I like that. Where does she get poison from? Let's make her a doctor so she can get the goods and have her poison him. Nah. I don't like that. She would be the primary suspect immediately and she wants to get away with this. It has to be the perfect murder. How about a botanist? She is a plant expert. She gets the poison from nature, and on the surface she seems like a harmless biologist. Nice! I'm liking the dimensions and possibilities in here. This expertise could be used elsewhere, too.

With each possibility, the writer looks at the potential for the story event to be engaging. In other words, the potential for delivery using knowledge gaps. Initially, Robert is an adulterer, and that is his secret, so we have a knowledge gap. Then I think I might have Sarah find out. Now she knows what he has been doing, but he does not know that she knows. Another intriguing knowledge gap — what is she going to do? She will kill him, that's what. I might let the audience know she is going to do that. A privilege dynamic.

And do not forget that each of these event possibilities need to be established, so we are creating new bullet points on new index cards that go chronologically in front of 'SARAH MURDERS ROBERT'. One card might say: 'ESTABLISH: ROBERT IS AN ADULTERER', another might say: 'ESTABLISH: SARAH IS A BOTANIST'.

We will develop these threads as well. Establishing that Sarah is a botanist may be a simple matter of having a scene play out while she is at work. It could be incidental. Establishing that Robert is an adulterer is likely to be an entire sequence or several scenes. For the moment, we have our index card and we are managing our story's development.

If we know Sarah has poisoned his drink, and Robert does not, then we have a fine knowledge gap and tension as we ask: Will he drink the wine? Will he discover what she's done before he takes a swig? Did he just switch glasses with her? And her dialogue is all sweetness towards him — she's talking about reconciliation and how much she loves him, when we know what she's put in his drink… There are differences in the knowledge held by different participants, so we can be sure there is audience engagement as this scene plays out. These kinds of possibility — *how* the scene is delivered — are noted on the back of the index card.

Because of these knowledge gaps, we can be certain these events will be engaging. This also builds our characters. We know Sarah is a botanist and she's smart. Ok. That has an impact on her development across the whole piece. We know Robert is unfaithful, and we are going to make him a big dude to create difficulties for Sarah in killing him, so again, this shapes his character. He's also attractive to at least two women here, so let's make him a handsome rogue. His motivation is to get women into bed. He is an unscrupulous seducer of women.

Over time, the author begins to tire of the poisoning scene. It's too slow. This is an action adventure, so we need more, well, action and adventure in the way Sarah kills Robert. Sarah knows Robert likes sex, so why don't we have her hide a knife by the bed and stab him to death during sex? Oooh! I like that! This detail goes on the back of the index card, and the author lives with it for a bit. Powerful, sexy action scene, and excellent knowledge gaps when we in the audience know the knife is there by the bed and Robert does not. But then the author watches *Basic Instinct* and *Game of Thrones* in the same week and realises it's not quite as original as he thought it was.

Having thought this through and come up with something the author finds appealing, the detail gets written in summary form — a paragraph or two at most, no dialogue or detail — on the back of the index card. The front of the card has not changed — Sarah kills Robert — but the way that scene is delivered has changed several times. This card is doing its job, but of course, the flexibility is still there to take on more new ideas or make more changes quickly and simply at any time. It's quick and painless to introduce change, so let the imagination run wild! It's all good! Indeed, at some later date, when there are 30 index cards out on the floor, this one might not work at all anymore. It is simply taken out and the author can see what the whole story looks like without it.

Front of card (what happens)

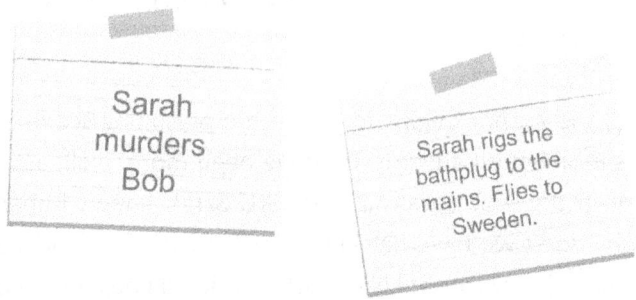

Rear of card (how it happens)

Figure 17 - Index cards capture what happens at the top level of your story

Each index card is likely to inspire or imply other story events. For example, this card implies that there is a story event in which Robert commits adultery. So, we have another character — his lover — and it implies another event in which Sarah finds out about his adultery. We don't know how, so a card goes down that simply says 'Sarah finds out about the adultery, and plans her revenge'.

The story is still fluid. The detail entirely flexible. And making changes does not carry with it a sense of dread that goes with having to integrate change in a 100,000 word fourth draft. The step outline becomes the major tool of story development, working for you at every level of the story hierarchy.

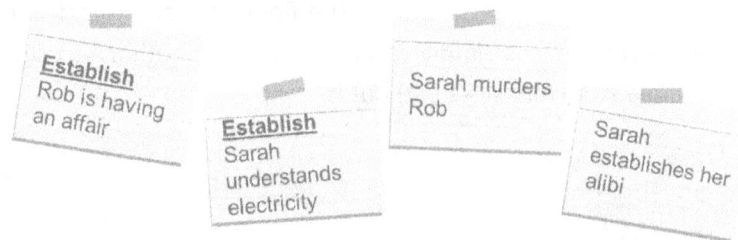

Figure 18 - Index cards build to represent entire story

If you use this method, even in software, you can tweak it for your personal preferences, but there are surprisingly few cards to map out a step outline for a story. I know these days it would be strange to get off the computer and go get some physical index cards. Indeed, most scriptwriting software has an equivalent facility for story development along these lines. However, I have done this with actual index cards and I recommend it. I printed out my step outline on hard-copy sheets (I used printer paper not index cards, but it's all the same). I wrote the plot requirement of the story event on the front of the page with a marker pen and more detail on how to deliver that requirement through character actions on the back. I laid it all out on the living room floor and there it was! My entire story mapped out in front of me! It was very helpful and a stark, refreshing contrast to the small window you have through your computer screen. Seeing it in one spread definitely inspires change and brings a view of the kinds of things the computer screen cannot give. You get a terrific feel for the key dynamics and important moments.

Once you have all your index cards, and each of them has a summary sentence on the front regarding 'what happens' and a paragraph for how it will be delivered on the back, and you have reached the point that no further changes are suggesting themselves… you are ready to write the first full draft. More on that in a moment. Before we move on, the step outline is an invaluable tool in story development and I would like to offer the following tips and suggestions in its use:

1. **Do not write dialogue or detail**

    There are two reasons for this. First and foremost, when you write dialogue and detail you fall in love with it. Your characters begin to gain a bigger presence in terms of who they are, the things they say and the interactions they have. You end up creating characters and events that you fall in love with or iconic moments that you adore. When this happens early in the development process, your story loses precious flexibility. Elements of plot and character start to become nailed in to place, whilst others remain fluid, and when it comes to change you will find yourself reluctant —

perhaps even unconsciously unable — to mould or even remove those elements with which you have fallen in love. Even though these iconic moments, compelling characteristics, hilarious interplays — whatever it might be — are no longer right for this story, it is so much more difficult for you to persuade yourself to chisel them out. Now your story will become bent out of shape as you change it to accommodate these precious moments that you cannot bear to part with, but which, in the cold light of day, no longer sit comfortably in this story.

Of course, you want to act when you feel inspired and there is nothing more joyful than writing with that inspiration, so you need a technique for managing this problem. A scene has to go... but you *love* it. You simply cannot bring yourself to throw it away. Well, the good news is that you are not throwing it away. It *is* brilliant and you must keep it. It's just that it is not right at *this* point in *this* story, so it needs to be saved for later.

Initially, you simply pull the index card out and put it off to the side. You are parking it to see how life works without it and there is no risk attached. You can always simply pull it back in. Listen to your instincts. You will soon know if it should play a part or not.
You will never actually throw it away forever. If you have a nagging feeling it should be chucked out, you can tell yourself — quite honestly — it will be right one day, and when it is in the correct story, it will truly shine. Rather than forcing it into a story where it does not belong, you must give it special, precious status in a treasure trove of **Good Ideas Waiting for a Home**. Open yourself a file (I call mine the GitWah, obviously) and keep these ideas and moments safely there in your GitWah. You will never forget this inspired material. Make enough notes and gather enough information to bring it all back to you when the time comes

to allow this magic to fly. You never know, when you read it back later, it could inspire an entire new story.

This is another reason for putting lots and lots of material in the GitWah. At some later date, when you are not sure where to find inspiration, or especially if you are suffering the dreaded writer's block, having a read through the GitWah can seriously wake up your inspiration; partly because of the quality of the material you have placed in there, but also because it takes you back to a positive, inspired creative mindset.

These days, when I feel that niggly feeling that something has got to go, I sigh at having to take a step backwards, but do recognise more readily that it is facilitating two steps forwards. I make a new copy of my draft or step outline so I can always find my way back to this point if it turns out it was right all along (it never is...) and I get the dirty deed done. I actually feel really good chopping the deadwood out nowadays. It used to feel negative, but it is not. It is progress. I know it is right and the project is moving forwards.

2. **Postpone your pleasures**

As you gathered from the previous tip, falling in love with the detail *can* be problematic, so it is worth mentioning that the step outline also works like a sort of pressure cooker. With each scene, sequence, character, moment and event you bring to the step outline, you will find yourself champing at the bit to get on with it! You want to write the detail because it is burning inside you! With every story event that you add to the line of index cards, and with every inspired idea you have on how that event will unfold in the detail, you build that creative pressure. It's hard to resist just getting stuck in and writing the detailed scene or the chapter! It builds and it builds... but let it build. The more you resist the detail, the more you let it simmer and marinate in the pot and the more pressure you build, the more urgent and immersive and scintillating and authoritative your writing will be when you finally let it all out. More on 'letting it all out' shortly, but for the moment, note that there is a lot of value in spending as long as possible at the bullet-point and summary level that the step outline encourages. The payoff that comes later is extraordinary, so defer your pleasures.

What we are aiming for with the step outline in this card form (or a version of it) is WHAT HAPPENS on the front. HOW IT HAPPENS on the back, and a note of the knowledge gaps we can craft on the other side. (I know there's only two sides, but work with me here..! We need three elements.) And we keep working the big picture. Ultimately, we will have, say, 25 index cards. For example:

FRONT OF INDEX CARD: SARAH MURDERS BOB

BACK OF INDEX CARD: Sarah pulls the panel off the bath. She rigs up the metal plug to the overflow on the outside of the bath with a mains electric cable and replaces the panel so her handiwork cannot be seen. Sarah says her loving goodbyes to Bob and heads off to her Botany conference in Sweden.

KNOWLEDGE GAP: Audience knows bath is rigged. Bob does not.

That might be all for this index card. It has a nice intrigue right there with a lovely knowledge gap through the middle. I feel sure you can see that when you come to write the detail for this, the job is a creative, imaginative joy because each card works like writing a standalone short story. You do not need to care what happens elsewhere, you can zoom right down into the depths of the detail of these characters, their behaviours and interactions and simply immerse yourself and love every scintilla of it. Wonderful.

Do not forget that the step outline is a very personal tool. Nobody else will ever see it. It is going to serve a purpose as a development tool, and then it will disappear, so let it get messy or use colours or doodles or write in Chinese or do whatever you like that helps it to be what you need it to be. You are the God of your story world and you are the God of your development method. It's yours, and you are not going to show it to anyone.

Whatever your method, in the end, your index cards will represent your whole story in a series of bullet point events (front of the cards) and a sequence breakdown for how it happens (backs of the cards), along with a recognition that there is power in the event through the clear presence of at least one knowledge gap. Your process is:

1) Using your imagination, comb backwards and forwards through your story, from front to back (index card 1 to index card 30) and up and down through framing, characters and storifications.

   Some cards will stay as bullet points (what happens), some become more detailed (how it happens). Some will be face up, some will be face down. Keep adding new cards and taking old ones from the line as you feel it. Do not fear moving, changing, adding, removing or replacing cards. It's the tool for doing exactly that. You are not throwing things away; you are parking them for a while to get a feel for the story world without them or with an alternative.

2) Listen to your guts on this. Don't worry about wholesale and almost reckless changes, because it's no problem to simply put everything back! That is the glory of the step outline. Endless fluidity and flexibility. Changes to the final draft are

painful, time-taking and prone to errors from the ripple effect. Now is the time to try everything that your imagination throws at you. You might well end up with 50 index cards. 60. 100! It doesn't matter! Lots of meat from which to choose the best cuts. The bin is your friend.

3) You will get lots and lots of temptation to go into depth but resist it. Any depth you give in to at this stage punctures a hole in the creative pressure you are building up.

4) If an index card had three sides, the third one would be a quick note on the knowledge gaps that are in use. In my own version of the step outline I include a column for knowledge gap dynamics on the back too. Additionally, you might spot some of the other elements we discussed earlier:
    - A literal or metaphoric 'journey' for a character. What changes over time for a character?
    - The motivation and ambition for that character. What might fulfilment mean?
    - A clear conflict may offer itself, an aim for the character or a problem to solve.
    - A moral dilemma or argument.

    These things are important at the scene or sequence level as well as for the whole story, so make notes in these areas on the back of the card as each step brings you thoughts and inspiration.

5) In particular, look for storification dynamics. You need the storifications to know how the characters and framing need to be, so finding them is hugely beneficial. As and when you find the storification for the whole story, now you are getting into a very strong development position to define a good deal of how your story must go to build up to delivering that storification and what must happen in that

storification to make it work and what may happen as a result of it to derive the outcomes. Knowledge gaps and storification. That's what you are searching for. Now your story development will progress quickly and with good focus.

6) If you are experiencing frustration with the development process, or <gulp> the dreaded writers' block, there is a good chance that you are focussing too much on 'what happens'. You are trying so hard to think up clever and wonderful things that can happen that you are forgetting that the main driver for original story is character and character decisions. Reset your thinking to the more simple task of getting your characters to make choices. Introduce more characters. Find ways the new character can disagree with the existing characters, and suddenly you are away again. What the characters do is make choices under pressure of conflict and the choices they make drive the story forwards and become 'what happens'. Much more on this in the next section.

7) At some point you will be surprised to find that you suddenly have no more changes suggesting themselves. Every index card has a completed front that nails what happens and a completed back that details how it will be delivered. You understand the storification of your whole story and — you are done! The step outline is complete! You will sit back feeling vaguely stunned, because you will have been working at this level for quite a while, and now... oh, wow! Every card is doing its job, and not one of them makes you feel unsatisfied.

8) Some people add an optional stage here, one that is particularly useful if you do still have any doubts at all. They write a very quick and dirty 'novel' version of their story. Just bash it out in one go — a precise version of say 3000 to 5000

words, and/or a treatment of between around 10,000 words. Do not worry about editing or grammar — just write the whole story, in rough, in a few days. In the era of speech-to-text you could even speak your story out loud into a word processor in basically no time flat.

There is great value in doing this, because the step outline is still likely to change as you progress into the depth of the story. (This treatment may also become part of your sales and marketing pack at some point.) The main point is that it will give you several new insights you were not expecting. Use these to make final adjustments to your step outline (the job here is still to refine the step outline) or to learn more about your story if you still feel nagging doubts that you cannot properly identify. This rough 'novel' version will either consolidate your happiness with your story OR it will reveal the issues you are feeling and suggest the areas that need attention, and possibly the nature and form of the changes that you are searching for. Or you may not do it at all. It's optional.

It will also help you to truly understand the characters and the story world. This will, in turn, help you to refine the knowledge gaps. You can punch more holes in the narration; make the whole thing more metaphoric. Do not forget, you are not building a story here as much as building meaning in mind for your audience, so finding more and more ways to remove the supports and deliver that meaning in the gaps is hugely increasing the quality of your story. The more you understand it, the more you can confidently abstract away from it.

9) Another hugely positive piece of development work to do here is to tell your story out loud. Sit someone down and tell them your story. Look in their eyes, listen to your own telling. Note when you change things on the fly — this is the

natural storyteller in you cutting to the chase or reacting to your own sense of something being wrong. This is much more important than their feedback. What they have to say in response to receiving your story might ring a little bell, in which case, act on it, but for the most part, the reviews of people you know will not help you get the right story. Place much more emphasis on what you thought about the telling than their criticism.

10) Which brings us to the most exciting part of the story development process. Your step outline is now the most perfect imaginable template for you to use to guide you through your first full draft. You can drop into your story world safe in the knowledge that whilst you are deep down in the detail, the top level story is already taken care of. You can stay in the story world with your characters and live and move with them there. You can follow the step outline, from beginning to end without thinking about what is going on outside of the 'here and now' in your story world. You can 'go there'. It's magical. You simply drop yourself into your story world and walk and talk with your characters as they live their lives.

It is at this point that you can easily write way more than 2000 words in a day. The preparation is all done, and you can just go and live in that place. For me, this is the time to find somewhere else in the world to go and work. A writer's retreat works brilliantly at this point. An isolated cabin or holiday home with no disturbances. Remove all distractions and obligations so you can get up close and personal with your characters. So close you can smell them.

The reason for this advice is not only to get the job done but because it is the most extraordinary opportunity to go deeply and immersively into your story world. There, you will truly meet your characters. You will know them. You will feel their emotions and responses. Smell their gardens. Live their lives. It really is incredible. Because you are *there* and nowhere else, it all slows down. The detail of that story world fills in. I wrote my first book on my own in a flat, at night in the dark and I truly 'went' to that world and visited those places and lived those events. It was a very special experience, and it is only through all of the preparation discussed above that you can have the privilege of this experience.

Tucked away on your own and working from a solid step outline you might find yourself trucking along at the rate of ten pages of script or 5000-7000 words of novel per day. Do not worry about grammar or polish or editing or niceties — they are all potential distractions that will drag you out of the story world. They can all get sorted in a more pragmatic edit run in future. For the moment, just write. In this way, you may write an entire 2-hour movie or 90,000 word manuscript in a fortnight, all done whilst revelling in that fictional place. It feels like an out of body experience. You've isolated yourself, however, you are not on your own. You are with people you know and love. You are on a unique adventure with your beloved characters in the world you have created. I cannot tell you what a privilege and a wonderful experience this is. You will genuinely remember going there forever, a memory as powerful as any holiday you ever had in the real world, and you will crave getting to this stage again with your next story.

Back in reality, you are likely to discover yet more changes to the story as you create this first full draft. I recommend strongly that you now go back up a level and integrate those changes into your step outline. It is still your central management tool and it is entirely possible that you still have quite a way to go before the story is truly finished. It is surprising how many times you might think you are getting near the final version, and yet you might be much further away than you think. As you integrate the changes into the step outline, the overview that the step outline facilitates will help you to capture the ripple effect of changes you made. Quite often, a change that seems innocent enough will have unforeseen or far-reaching effects that will hit you the moment you bring the step outline up to date.

From here, I think it should be very much within your own ownership to take it to completion as you see fit. I would say two more things: firstly, <u>make sure</u> it is finished before you start sending it off to agents, producers, publishers and so on. The clue here is this: When you think it is finished... It is not finished. When you have just written THE END, that is not the end. It is still settling. You are hyped and excited and desperate to share it and send it off and move to the next stage... but guess what. When you read it back once you have had a little while to calm down, it is probably still a fair way from completion. A bad thing you might well do right now is send it off. You could blow your best three contacts by sending it now when really it is still months away from completion. My advice is, if you write THE END, or FADE TO BLACK but it is anything less than your third draft, it is absolutely, definitely not finished yet. I know you want it to be, but it is not. Set an expectation that you will write at least six drafts, probably ten, before it is genuinely approaching a finish. Give yourself time to be sure before you start sending it out.

As you may have gathered, I find the step outline to be the ideal, definitive, critical and central tool for the story development process. I have written a book on The Step Outline which does four rather wonderful things to add to what you have read here:

1. It talks you through the entire moment-by-moment development of a film story (*Bella – A Love Story*; Baboulene, 2020) from the first seed of an idea all the way to the silver screen.

2. It includes the entire complete step outline I used to develop the film story.

3. It updates the design of a step outline to include knowledge gap dynamics for every step.

4. You can watch the glorious final product; the short film that results from this story development process.

The book is called: *Working with a Contemporary Step Outline: the tool of choice for story development* (David Baboulene, 2020).

The book is available from all the usual outlets, and the film is accessible somewhere, probably best to start from my websites at www.dreamengine.co.uk or www.baboulene.com. I do hope you love it!

4.6 The Mystical Art of Crafting Characters

Whatever happens, it happens through characters. Whatever storification arises in the mind of the receiver, it got there through character behaviours and interactions. Whatever framing goes on it is there to orientate us to the situation in which the characters will do stuff.

Characters are central to story. There is no getting away from that, so as you build your step outline, you should also be building a good understanding of your characters and what makes them tick. When I talk about combing backwards and forwards to find ways to inspire and generate your story the chances are that the changes you make will be changes to (and/or outcomes of) a character's five core defining elements:

>Motivation (section 2.5.5.1)
>Meaningful conflict (section 2.4.10)

Decisions under pressure (also section 2.4.10)
A character arc (section 2.5.5.2)
A moral argument (section 3.4)

Remember from section 2.5 that plot and character are one and the same thing in that both are a function of character. The actions taken by a character define who they truly are and the actions taken by a character also define what happens.

In terms of the development phases of your story, that means you need to be conscious that plot events are a function of a character's motivation, driving them towards whatever fulfilment means to them. Or, to put it the other way around, if you come up with some event or action you would like in your story you will need a character with appropriate motivation to make that event happen through their drive towards fulfilment. If you have a character who wants to murder her husband, now you have certain actions and events that this motivation demands, so we analyse her motivation:

Facets of motivation
- What does she want?
- Why does she want it?
- What is she prepared to do to get it?
- Why now?
- What does fulfilment look like for this character?
- Why do we care?

Do the same thing for the husband. From detailing these driving forces, other aspects of character will come. Conflict, for example, can be a function of motivation. Using these facets renders conflict in a knowing and focussed way for the author. Knowledge gaps are screaming out to be opened up and held open. We see Rob have sex with a woman. Knowledge gap: we in the audience don't find out until he goes home that... this woman was not his wife. We now know that he has been unfaithful, but Sarah does not. Now she finds out. We know that, but Rob does not. She decides to kill him. We know that, and he does not. She plans his murder. A plan has three gaps (see section 2.4.7) — identify them and make sure they work. Ask: would that plan work better in revelation?

What about The Other Woman? Maybe Rob told her he wasn't married. She now stalks him on Facebook, finds where he lives and decides to go round and give him a sexy surprise… More knowledge gaps. More intrigue… Do a deep character exploration on her motivation, morals, arc and decisions as well. You just never know what she might bring to the situation…

All the time we are asking: How can we turn this into a storification? What growth and learning can go into these characters' journeys? How can we reflect some life truth here? Can we use events to force Sarah and/or Rob into a terrifyingly difficult choice? A choice that will reveal who they truly are and will have outcomes that will make us think? Is there some morality in play that we can use to create dilemma and an interesting argument to set up between the players and have them learn/teach us something?

The headline being this: If you know the <u>plot</u> event you want to deliver, explore the characters involved and their motivations in order to deliver it using knowledge gaps through character actions.

Alternatively, start with a character drive, and develop the story from there. Let's say we have a character. What aspect of their personality can we use to drive events? Let's say Sarah is the super jealous type. Now I can instantly see a situation where we create a character who has the moral high ground… but we really don't like her very much. Excellent. Let's make sure her husband is attractive and she cannot bear the idea that he might be unfaithful. So, Sarah has her motivation. What does she want? Control over Rob's actions. Why? To satisfy her jealousy. Why now? Because he just got an attractive young intern at work. He is with that girl all day every day. What does fulfilment look like for Sarah? Aha! What an interesting question! The story might lie right here, because fulfilment on the surface (outer arc) is to get rid of the other woman OR to gain control over Rob and his relationship with this woman... but genuine fulfilment lies in getting over her jealousy... and that would give us an inner arc (overcoming her jealousy) and an outer arc (acting on her jealousy).

NOW we can see a character arc taking Sarah from events driven by passionate jealousy — these could be pretty extreme — to a point where that jealousy impacts her life — either positively or negatively — and provides outcomes that show her — and us in the audience — that trust is essential in a relationship and that jealousy is a relationship killer. Now, this all started out from a premise that 'Sarah kills Rob'. I rather like the dynamic in this jealousy thread, so I will consider changing character actions and motivations to go along this 'jealousy' road for a while and see how things take shape. What I do like very much is the clear storification possibilities. That is what makes me feel there is a strong story down this path.

The headline being this: Let the character's motivation drive the action, let the action put the character into conflict, let the action therefore lead to choices under pressure, and ensure there are clear outcomes from the choices made. let it all be done in a context of knowledge gaps. Is there a difference between the internal drives (the character's inner arc and secret motive) and their outer arc (their behaviours on the surface that they have to act out if they are going to satisfy their inner desire)? This is the most wonderful form of creative play, and top story potential arrives from this kind of thinking.

The character development feeds the step outline, index card by index card. The step outline feeds back into the character definitions, so develop both at once. This is preparation. It is very important to allow your character to change according to the needs of your story just as readily as you might have your story change according to the actions your character would naturally take, given their underlying motives.

Of course, once you have settled on characteristics for a player, from that point onwards your characters have to be true to themselves. The actions they take must be credible given who they are and consistent with the personality you have given them throughout. Biff is always a bully every time he is on the screen. George McFly is always weak and unassertive every time he is on the screen. You may challenge that because both these characters have changed by the end of the story. This is not the case. They did not change their personality. They were put under pressure and through the decisions they made under pressure *their true character was forced to the fore* and they learned — and we in the audience learned — who they really are.

4.7   The Mystical Art of Crafting Sequences

By 'sequences' I mean any story event — a chapter or scene, act, subplot or whole story - whatever... The key point to remember is that every story event is a mini-story in itself, so the trick with crafting it is to ensure there are knowledge gaps. It does not matter which type of gap, it just has to have one to be assuredly compelling. So, when you have your step outline and you know what happens and you have a fair idea of how it will happen, now it is time to form that up using knowledge gaps.

Initially, I would suggest you simply write it as you feel it. Let yourself go and let your imagination fly and let your creative heart deliver it for you. You have decided that Sarah is going to kill Rob by rigging the bath plug to the mains. When he gets into the bath, as soon as the water level reaches up as far as the metal overflow — Zap! Fried Rob.

In which case, Sarah has a plan. We can use that. We can put her plan in revelation at first. She goes to the shop and buys jump leads. Eh?! What is she doing? She buys a big roll of aluminium foil and bypasses the fuse in the fuse box. She takes the side off the bath and gets busy with wires underneath it. What on Earth…? She books a plane ticket. Where is she going?! As she speaks on the phone, the camera pans across her handiwork and gradually we realise what her plan is. It moves into privilege, so we know her plan (but Rob does not). We watch her weave her web, we watch her begin to draw Rob into it…

She welcomes Rob back from the gym… "I'll run a bath for you, my gorgeous, wonderful husband."

we watch Rob get closer and closer to becoming ensnared… we watch the water level rise as he gets into the bath… will it fry him?! And so on. Yeah! Lovely. Tense. Good knowledge gaps. We know it will work.

I prefer it in privilege. We can know the plan. We get a nice key question dynamic from it (Will the plan work? Will Rob die? Will she get away with it?). However, we cannot simply allow her plan to go smoothly, can we?! We know the plan, so now let's have it go wrong. She rigs up the bath then goes to her conference safe in the knowledge that Rob has a bath after gym. However, he knows she is away at a conference, so he brings his lover back. And she wants a bath… Nice twist… and when Sarah returns to deal with Rob's dead body, and finds a woman there, now we have a realisation for her. Anagnorisis. Rob will have worked out that the shock was meant for him (and Sarah does not know that Rob knows…). OK, so what does that mean for Sarah? In the house on her own… and where is Rob? The possibility of a peripeteia? What will she do now?

How will you do it?! The possibilities are limitless. Simply keep on blocking your characters from achieving their desires and new possibilities will continue to offer themselves as they take action under the pressure of their situation. When you get an action, think about how it can be turned into a knowledge gap. A secret, a lie, a plan, a conflict, a subterfuge, a choice of evils, a moral dilemma, a cultural allusion — whatever. If there is a knowledge gap, there is story. Simple as that. Understand the gaps, hone them in order to deliver the scene through perfecting those gaps. You can be confident that if the gaps are there, your story cannot fail to entertain.

Section 5 - In a Nutshell

Stories are made from knowledge gaps. Subtext is the knowledge that goes into the gap. The finest authors are those who are best at creating the conditions for subtext.

In this final section, I want to focus on the main points that a writer should take from this book. There is a lot of material from all sorts of angles and coalescing it into a smaller number of keys to success is challenging but hopefully helpful. To round things up before we set you free to go forth and write scintillating stories, here are my top tips:

1) **Understand knowledge gaps and subtext**
   Obviously, you know by now that writers work with knowledge gaps in order that the receiver can work with subtext.

   Subtext is the knowledge that goes into the gaps.

   A knowledge gap is a difference in the knowledge held between participants in a story. Look at every event and find a way to introduce a difference in the knowledge held. That is the route to story power in your story idea.

   Your mission is to switch your mindset to stop thinking about structure and see, in everything you write, where gaps can be driven in, what those gaps are doing to the receiver's mind and how these gaps are driving the direction of your story.

   It can take a while to really change your mindset and lock on to this but I can assure you: Knowledge gaps are how your story is delivering and understanding and working with that is the secret to being a brilliant writer.

2) Understand storification

Over and above this knowledge gap context, it is storification that really brings home the bacon. Once your audience is providing subtext at a meta-level of lateral thinking between other elements they have already derived for themselves — then your story is hitting home in major ways, impacting personality, creating memories, teaching about life and how it should be lived.

Storification is the ultimate power in story.

As a writer, this is the key to making your audience feel engaged; have them take ownership of your story; *feel deeply* for your story. It is the process whereby they fill the gaps and thereby discover the *meaning* in your story.

When you leave a gap, think about the work the receiver is likely to do in providing the subtext that fills it. Work with them. Stimulate them. A receiver is not an absorber of text but a producer of story. Get it into their heads and get them working on it and they will love it. Of course they will. They have produced it for themselves!

3) Don't try to learn 'how to write'

No course or method or guru can tell you how to write. There's only one person who can tell your story your way, and that's YOU! Those who get somewhere as writers have confidence in themselves and their output. They write what THEY think is great. they write for themselves and they care not a jot what others think.

This is great news for you! It is so much easier for you to just pour your story out of your natural inspiration and imagination. If YOU think it is right, then guess what. It is right. You are the God of your story. Nobody else. Only you can tell your story your way, so just do it! Write with the aim of satisfying YOU. The practical work you do on your story is to refine the gaps. Make the story more and more abstract and it will become more and more appreciated. That's all. Advice should not change the story as much as polish the gaps.

4) Understand character

All the finest stories take us on a physical or metaphoric journey. On that journey a character will transform through the experiences of the story and climb up or fall down the ladder of life along the way. You will find that their change across the course of the journey is the true power of your story, and this is what resonates with your audience and elevates your story.

A character has motivation. This causes drive towards fulfilment. Achieving fulfilment is made difficult through conflict. Difficult choices and decisions must be made under pressure of conflict and dilemma. The outcomes of these decisions are what happens in your story. The outcomes complete a narrative which when formed up in the mind of the receiver carries meaning. For example, that these decisions under these circumstances lead to these outcomes. In the strongest stories, this meaning will make the receiver think about their own life.

In developing your story, understanding this final, ultimate meaning is the ideal starting point. Working back from here to create the characters and the situations that will pressure them through the storification is the easiest way to ensure a cohesive, unified, dimensional story.

The storification gap is the most important and powerful knowledge gap — the one that defines the greatness of your story. It lies between what the receiver knew at the beginning of your story and what they *have taught to themselves* by the end having built your complete story in their own working memory.

Coupled with this...

5) **Understand conflict**

...true character only emerges when you put your characters under pressure to make difficult decisions. Theoretically, stories can happen with little or no conflict, but it is very unusual and it is probably best to understand and embrace conflict, especially in your early career. Learn about the types of conflict — especially the immense power of internal conflict — and make sure the conflict is *meaningful*.

Pressure comes from dilemma. A choice of evils is more story-powerful than the most spectacular of intergalactic battles. Conflict is often found more in the moral stance and the fight for a moral position than from fielding a regiment of storm-troopers or unleashing a psychotic Dr Evil.

6) **Write every day**

Make it a priority, build it into your schedule and discipline yourself to it. I KNOW that is hard - believe me, I've been there - so set yourself a manageable word count and make sure you achieve that. I challenge writers to hit 500 words a day - that's a single side of A4. Could you manage that?

Of course you can. Guess what. That will get you 100,000 words in 7 months. And that's with Sundays off. Follow that up with five months of editing and polishing - that's a book or a feature script in a year, every year, no problem. Self-discipline, folks. Yes, being a writer is glamorous to talk about and a romantic place for dreamers, but the ones who make it tend to work very hard, are professional and productive. Don't wait for that mythical year off you have promised yourself. Don't wait for that writers' retreat or that day you call "One day..." Every successful writer gets their head down and writes every day.

I have worked in publishing, music and movies. I have met a huge number of exciting, talented artists with great merit, most of whom do not make it. The common denominator amongst those who succeed is that they work harder than everyone else. The ten percent that is golden turns into a career for those who work ten times harder. When you are on that same plateau as a million other brilliant people, this is the key differentiator.

7) **Do marketing. Do rejection.**
Be professional and unemotional in marketing your story. The vast majority of artists in the world, in any discipline, do not get very far because nobody ever finds out what they have done. The winners are the ones who embrace the idea that marketing yourself and your work is part of what you must do.

Unfortunately for those of us who like our own company and wish we did not have to meet other people or do any of that networking stuff, marketing is not simply having a website and a twitter account. You will do far, far better if you go along to industry fairs and conferences and festivals and meet actual, real people. I wish it was easier than that, and of course, we would all much rather spend a day doing art than going to such things but, it works. When you talk to artists and say 'you have to work harder than everyone else,' they can shrug and say: 'Well, I do my art every day. No problem.' That's not what is meant. **Selling yourself** is properly hard work. Successful people are the ones who put themselves out there.

As part of this, it is really important to learn to handle rejection (there WILL be rejection...). I know many, many writers who develop their stories... then develop and develop some more... and the real reason they never finish is because they are so scared of the Judgement Day that comes the moment they admit that the story is finished. There's no easy way. You have to grasp the nettle and get it out there.

Put your ego to one side, because the vast majority of rejections are nothing to do with your ability or the merit of your story. Dig deep, be strong, and put it out there.

When I asked John Sullivan for his advice for aspiring writers he gave me this series of steps that should define a writer's life:

A) Write the best stuff you can.
B) Send it off.
C) Go to A).

It ain't rocket science! But you do need to be brave, or you won't get anywhere. I have a huge folder of rejections. I know – unbelievable, isn't it?! We never like rejection, of course, and it will always bring pain and disappointment, but I promise, those rejections become a source of joy and a badge of honour once you hit home somewhere, so persevere. Send stuff out.

Once you have sent your material off, the worst thing you can do is sit wringing your hands by the letterbox, desperate for a response, because nine out of ten will be rejections. Let marketing yourself become part of your week. Make good, professional marketing material for you and your material. Send it off and move on with your work. Fire and forget! Get busy with the next one, and when rejection comes it won't bother you so much; you'll be deeply involved in the new stuff and that makes handling rejection OR success that much easier.

As soon as your material is good enough, you WILL get a deal. The commercial world is **desperate** for great stories. Think of all the channels to market there are these days with books and radio and films and television — all the new streaming services — you do not need to be a professional writer to see that there simply is not enough good stuff out there to fill demand!

Are you productive? Are you learning your craft? Are you sending stuff off? Are you networking with your industry? Do these things and you will give yourself the best chance of success.

Fade Out

And that is it! Thanks so much for reading my book. I hope it has inspired you and that it helps you to make the most of your ability, to get success (whatever that means for you!) and to absolutely love your writing career.

Now stop reading this and go write a classic. Take it to market, sell it, then find me at that same festival, shake me by the hand and commission me as your story consultant.

I look forward to seeing you there and hearing of your successes!

With all the best for your story future.

David
March 2020
Nerja, Andalusia, Spain

www.baboulene.com and www.dreamengine.co.uk
@StoryMeBad on Patreon, Twitter, Facebook.

Section 6 - Glossary of Terms

This glossary is not a set of dictionary definitions. It is intended to help with understanding in the context of writing and story theory.

Diegesis: The diegesis is the formally narrated component of the narration. The text itself, delivered via a form of narrator. Conceptually it is also used to refer to the period of immersion in the story world for the receiver. In this book it is what I have referred to as 'the text itself'.

Genre: Categories of story, grouped by common criteria.

Hermeneutics: The study of interpretation.

Hermeneutic Boundary: The point at which information in the outside world, through stimulating the human senses, converts into knowledge in mind.

Information: Stimulation to the human senses.

Knowledge: representations of information converted into human causal logic in mind.

Mimesis: The component of a narration in which the characters live out the real-time events in their story world.

Narrative: An event or series of events that involve change-over-time.

Narration: A real-time telling of a narrative. It is only meaningful if there is a human receiver to experience it.

Narrafication: The conversion of the information contained in a narration into a cause-effect chain that makes sense in mind.

Narrafication adds the diachronic dimension (change over time) to the principles of signs. (See also 'storification'.)

Paratext: All contributions to a narration that are not within the diegesis.

Phenomena: Structures of meaning in mind which comprise a system of signs, significations, narrafications and storifications. A mental representation of experience.

Phenomenology: The study of mentalised experience.

Plot: An arrangement of selected information for narration. The narration is the live, real-time delivery; the plot is what happens — the planned content for a narration.

Readerly: Barthes term for denoted material. 'Readerly work' links information in the narration to clear and unambiguous knowledge in mind. A shopping list, for example, is readerly, requiring no imagination in deriving the meaning. (See also 'writerly'.)

Receiver: The audience, spectator, viewer, reader; the person receiving the narration.

Scripts: memories in narrative form, laid down in long-term autobiographical memory and available to be used by the owner as mental maps for achieving a predictable outcome from working methodically through the steps that comprise the script.

Semiology: The study of signs and symbols.

Sign: The base unit of linguistics comprising a signifier/signified pair.

Signified: The meaning in mind inspired by receiving a signifier.

Signifier: the information component of a sign.

Signification: Signifier + a cultural overlaid meaning. The second-level meaning of a signifier when cultural significance is added (thus 'rose' means 'romance', not 'plant').

Storification = narrafication + cultural overlaid meaning. The addition of writerly work to a narrafication, creating a story that is unique to the receiver of the narrafication. (See also readerly and writerly.)

Story: A narrative in mind.
In communicating information, a story is any form of communication that has knowledge gaps in the telling.

Subtext: The knowledge delivered into the gaps in a story by the receiver of a narration. Subtext comes from the receiver's existing knowledge, cultural understanding, history and experience.

Text: The material that comprises the real-time delivery of the diegetic component of a narration. Although 'text' implies words on paper, it is a generic term. When you sit in a cinema and receive a film screening, you are receiving 'the text'.

Writerly: Barthes term referring to the work done by the receiver of a narration to complete the story. Writerly work requires the receiver to use their intelligence and imagination to project into gaps in the narration and complete the story production in mind using their own input. (See also 'readerly'.)

Section 7 - Bibliography and Further Reading

Aristotle, 1996 [~335BC] *Poetics*. Heath, M. E. (ed.) UK: Penguin Books.

Aristotle, Butcher, S. H. & Fergusson, F. 1961. *Aristotle's Poetics*. New York: Hill and Wang.

Askham, 2020 – *The Man from Del Monte*. Unpublished at the time of writing.

Baboulene, D. 2010. *The Story Book.* London: Dreamengine Media Ltd.

Back to the Future (1985) [film]. Director: Robert Zemeckis. Universal. USA.

Bardon, A. 2005. *The Philosophy of Humor in Comedy*. In: Charney, M. (ed.) *Comedy: A Geographic and Historical Guide.* Connecticut, USA: Greenwood Press.

Barthes, R. 1978. *A Lover's Discourse*. New York: Hill and Wang.

Barthes, R. 2007. *Mythologies*. Paris, France: Edition de Seuil.

Barthes, R. & Balzac, H. 1990. *S/Z*. Oxford, UK. Blackwell.

Barthes, R. 1968. *The Death of the Author* in: Johnson, P. (Ed.) *Aspen* Magazine; vol.5.

BFI. *Sight and Sound Magazine.* September 2012 Edition. (Decennial poll of critics and directors for the greatest films of all time). London. BFI.

Bordwell, D. 1985b. *Narration in the Fiction Film*. Wisconsin, USA: University of Wisconsin Press.

Bordwell, D. 1989 *Making Meaning: Inference and Rhetoric in the Interpretation of Cinema*. Cambridge, MA: Harvard University Press.

Bordwell, D. 2006. *The Way Hollywood Tells it - Story and Style in Modern Movies*. California, USA: University of California Press.

Bordwell, D., Staiger, J. & Thompson, C. 1985a. *The Classical Hollywood Style. Film Style and Mode of Production to 1960*. London, UK: Routledge.

Branigan, E. 1992. *Narrative Comprehension and Film*. London: Routledge.

Carver, R. 2003. *What We Talk About When We Talk About Love*. London. Vintage.

Chandler, R. 1939. *The Big Sleep*. USA Penguin.

Chatman, S. 1978. *Story and Discourse: Narrative Structure in Fiction and Film*. Ithaca: Cornell University Press.

Cook, P. E. (ed.) *The Cinema Book*. London, UK: BFI.

Damasio, A. 2010. *Self Comes to Mind: Constructing the Conscious Brain*. Random House. Kindle Edition.

Dyer, R. 2004. *Heavenly Bodies: Film Stars and Society* (2nd Edition). London: Routledge.

Dyer, R. 1998. *Stars*. London: BFI/ Palgrave MAcMillan.

Eagleton, T. 2008. *Literary Theory: an Introduction*. London: John Wiley and Sons.

Ebert, R. 1997. *The Big Sleep*. USA: Chicago Sun Tribune.

Ebert, R. 2012. *27 Movies From the Dark Side*. Kansas, USA; Andrews McMeel Publishing.

Field, S. 1979 [1985 revised edition]. *Screenplay: the Foundations of Screenwriting*. New York: Random House.

Genette, G. 1980. *Narrative Discourse - an Essay in Method*. New York: Cornell University Press.

Gombrich, E. 1994. *The Sense of Order: A Study in the Psychology of Decorative Art*. London: Phaidon.

Gray, J. 2010. *Show Sold Separately: Promos, Spoilers, and Other Media Paratexts*. New York: New York University Press.

Gruner, C. 1997. *The Game of Humor: A Comprehensive Theory of Why We Laugh*. New Jersey: Transaction Publishers.

It's a Wonderful Life (1946) [Film]. Directed by Frank Capra. RKO Radio Pictures, USA.

Johnny B Goode (1958) [Song] Chuck Berry, Chess Records, USA.

Macherey, P. 1966 [1978]. *A Theory of Literary Production*. London, UK. Routledge & Kegan Paul.

Modern Times (1936) [film]. Director: Charlie Chaplin. United Artists. USA.

Mulvey, L. 1975. *Visual Pleasure and Narrative Cinema*. In: *Screen* 16.3. UK: Oxford Journals.

Neale, S. 1980. *Genre*. London: BFI.

Neale, S. & Krutnik, F. 1990. *Popular Film and Television Comedy*. Oxford, UK: Routledge.

Orwell, G. 1945 [2003]. *Animal Farm*. London, UK. Penguin.

Parkinson, D. 1995. *The History of Film*. London, UK: Thames and Hudson Ltd.

Propp, V. 1928. *Morphology of the Folktale*. USA: The American Folklore Society.

Rumsfeld, D. 2002. *Rum remark wins Rumsfeld an award*. [Web page] Viewed at http://news.bbc.co.uk/1/hi/3254852.stm. Accessed 21 Dec 2016.

Saussure, F. 1916 [1983] *Course in General Linguistics.* Bally, C., Sechehaye, A., Riedlinger, A. (Eds.) & Harris, R. (Translator). Chicago, USA: Open Court.

Schank, R. 1991. *The Connoisseur's Guide to the Mind: How we think, How we learn, and what it means to be intelligent.* USA. Summit Books.

Schatz, T. 1981. *Hollywood Genres: Formulas, Filmmaking, and The Studio System.* USA: McGraw Hill.

Some Like it Hot (1959) [film]. Director: Billy Wilder. United Artists. USA.

Stanislavski, C. (1936) [2015]. *An Actor Prepares.* Aristophanes Press. USA.

The Big Sleep (1946) [film]. Director: Howard Hawks. Warner Bros. USA.

Thomson, D. 1997. *The Big Sleep.* London: BFI.

Tudor, A. 1974. *Theories of Film.* London: Secker and Warburg/BFI.

Whipps, H. 2008. *How the Hyoid Bone Changed History.* Live Science Magazine. [Web Page] http://www.livescience.com/7468-hyoid-bone-changed-history.html. View date: 15/05/2017.

Zaltman, G. 2003. How Customers Think: Essential Insights Into the Mind of the Market. Boston, Mass. Harvard Business Press.

---

[i] In all seriousness, the use of language is also a function of our huge brains, processing power and pattern-matching capability. This is why, even though parrots can talk and whales have more vocabulary in their language than we do, neither can develop civilisation. It could be argued, however, that language also has a 'return feed' back into the brain and has played a large part in developing the capabilities of the human mind.

[ii] In this book the term 'language' refers to any semiotic system of communicating meaning, including linguistic, visual, audio, gestural and spatial systems.

[iii] Saviours have included children who have watched, for example *Spongebob Squarepants*: http://time.com/4103402/teen-who-saved-choking-classmate-says-spongebob-taught-him-heimlich-maneuver/

And Disney's *A.N.T. Farm:*
http://abcnews.go.com/blogs/headlines/2012/05/6-year-old-saves-best-friends-life-with-heimlich-maneuver/

And this one – a seven-year-old girl saves her mother having seen the film *Mrs Doubtfire* (1993, director Chris Columbus): http://newsfeed.time.com/2013/11/18/mrs-doubtfire-is-not-only-the-most-brilliant-film-of-our-time-it-also-saved-a-womans-life/

These links may not work at the time you read this, however, an internet search will return you many examples.

[iv] There is a space-time logic that contends Doc does not have a bullet-proof vest on in the first hail of gunfire. However, from the audience viewpoint in terms of knowledge gaps and story he does!

[v] This is a weird one for me. I think I invented this quote, but I have a sneaking suspicion I might have stolen it. It doesn't come up as anyone else's on a search, but if you came up with this first, do let me know. I do not wish to claim something that is not mine. It's really good though. I do hope it was me.

Section 8 - About the Author

David Baboulene is a published author, filmmaker, story consultant, film producer and Ph.D. academic of narrative theory, speaking internationally on his subject to both academic and commercial audiences. His research has provably shifted the cutting edge of narrative theory from a focus on structuralism to an approach based on evolutionary psychology and factors such as knowledge gaps and subtext that cause stories to exist and to have such power.

David Baboulene 'A Story Ninja' (Nick Wild, Director)

David is one of the first highly qualified story consultants to also have published works of fiction and film deals in his own right. He has studied stories back to pre-biblical and Greek times, classical literature as well as talking to big names in contemporary storytelling, including:

> **Lee Child** (20 million Jack Reacher novels sold);
> **John Sullivan** (*Only Fools and Horses; Just Good Friends; Citizen Smith...*);
> **Willy Russell** (*Educating Rita, Blood Brothers, Shirley Valentine...*);

Mark Williams (The Harry Potter films; *101 Dalmatians; Shakespeare in Love*...)
Bob Gale (*Back to the Future* trilogy);

and many others. Conversations with these fine people feature in *The Story Book* (2010).

In addition to dozens of story consultancy credits, David has written six books on the subject of story theory: *The Story Book* (2010); *Story Theory* (2014); *Story in Mind: A Constructivist Narratology* (2019); *Narrative and Metaphor in Education* (2018); *Working with a Contemporary Step Outline,* (2020); and *The Primary Colours of Story* (2020).

David lives in Brighton, UK. He has four children and an irrational and slightly obsessive love of football.

Connect with David:

www.baboulene.com
Social Media: @StoryMeBad
Find my seminars: www.dreamengine.co.uk
Twitter: http://www.twitter.com/StoryMeBad
Facebook: http://www.facebook.com/StoryMeBad
IMDB: David Baboulene

The question is: Can a story consultant write a good story? Find out for yourself with David's books, comprising stories from his time travelling the world and working on ships.

FURTHER READING...

"Interesting, raucous and very, very funny to the point that some bits will make your eyes water.

The story on Barbados is one of the funniest I've ever read."
                                    TALKSPORT

"This truly absorbing and at times astonishing tale will have you laughing out loud... Baboulene has an engaging, informative and gripping style... a real page-turner."

In Touch Magazine

www.ingramcontent.com/pod-product-compliance
Lightning Source LLC
Chambersburg PA
CBHW070137100426
42743CB00013B/2736